Pacific Northwest
Gardener's
Almanac

The Complete How-to Book for the Vegetable Grower

by **Mary Kenady**

Master Gardener

Alaska Northwest Publishing Company
Edmonds, Washington

Library of Congress Cataloging in Publication Data
Kenady, Mary, 1930-
    Pacific Northwest gardener's almanac.

    Bibliography: p.
    Includes index.
    1. Vegetable gardening—Northwest, Pacific—Handbooks, manuals, etc.
I. Title.
SB321.K43 1988   635′.09795   87-33323
ISBN 0-0-88240-327-3

Alaska Northwest Publishing Company
130 Second Ave. S.
Edmonds, Washington 98020

Printed in U.S.A.

Table of Contents

Acknowledgments

When I go over the long list of contributors and resources for this book, I begin to wonder just where I come in. So many people have so very generously given their help and knowledge in its creation that I must call it almost a group project.

Thanks to my friends who gave me encouragement and information, lent me books, magazines and files, recommended gardeners and gardens, put me up when I came through their towns, traveled with me and helped read the maps, and generally stimulated my endeavors with their enthusiasm:

Dorothy Allen, Alsie Campbell, Mike and Vicki Elledge, Diana Field, Barbara Kenady-Fish, June Skidmore, and Helene Steinhardt.

Thanks to Nancy Wendel, who befriended me on a Missoula street corner and steered me in the right direction.

Thanks to the cooperative extension agents and government horticultural experts, who by phone and letter supplied me with names of gardners and local gardening information:

Tonie Fitzgerald, Spokane County, WA
Dr. Walt Gary's office, Walla Walla Co., WA
Charlie McKinney, Kittitas County, WA
Ray McNeilan, Multnomah County, OR
Brent Nixon, Moscow, ID, planner
John Parsons, Regional Vegetable Specialist, Oliver, B.C.
Rick Reisinger, Snohomish County, WA
Kerry Retzel, Chelan/Douglas Counties, WA
Rosemary Saul, Master Composter, Seattle
Marcy Williams, Lincoln County, MT

Special thanks to Beth Burrows, Maurice Mitchell, and Stan Gessel for supplying extra photos.

And not least of all, thanks to my husband Reid, for patiently working around all the stack of papers and books in the office for so many months.

CHAPTER 1

Groundwork

Soil properties, sources of organic matter, soil pH,
other amendments and fertilizers

"Il faut cultiver notre jardin." — Voltaire

Properties of Your Soil

Your particular garden soil has a name and belongs to one of several thousand identified and mapped soil types of the Pacific Northwest. Fortunately for you it is not necessary to know its name, but it is necessary to know its general properties because successful gardening begins with understanding your soil and what you can do to improve it.

A good way to do a little home investigating of your garden soil is to take a sample down through the first eight or ten inches. A thin slice with a shovel will do; if you feel you may have quite a mix of soil types in your proposed garden, take only a tablespoon or two at a number of different levels and locations in the garden. If, as some of us do, you find a great many rocks in your soil sample, leave them out for now but keep in mind that your sample is not going to be totally representative and that those very large particles will need some consideration. Place the sample in a large glass jar, add water nearly to the top, give the jar a very thorough shaking to mix the ingredients well, and let sit undisturbed for several hours (or days, if necessary). If your soil is dry and does not mix easily, you can add a bit of dishwashing detergent. When the concoction is settled you will have a representative picture of your soil's texture.

A mineral soil (with no organic matter) will be made up of sand, silt and clay particles, which determine the texture. The sand (and stones) will naturally settle first at the bottom. Later, a silt layer will form. Last of all, if ever, the clay particles will settle. The longer the water stays murky, the finer the clay particles. If you have predominantly clay soil you may find your patience runs out before all the particles have settled.

Use Figure 1 (on page 2) to determine what kind of soil you have, estimating the percentages of each type of soil that shows up on the side of your jar.

Sand, along with stones and gravel, constitutes the coarsest part of your soil. This part has a very grainy feel with no plasticity or capability of being molded into a lump. Pore sizes in sandy soils are large, so the water-holding and nutrient-retaining capacity is very low. There is excellent drainage and movement of air in sandy soil, however.

Silt particles are diverse in shape, rather like very tiny sand particles, still slightly grainy to the touch but with some adhering qualities, so pressed together when damp they will form a lump. Like sand, silt is primarily composed of quartz. With its smaller pore spaces, silt holds water much better than sand does.

Clay has more surface area per unit, which means that the capacity of clay for adsorption of water and for plasticity and cohesion is much higher than for silt or sand. When clay is wet it is sticky and makes streaks on your hands if you rub it, and when it is dry it is rock hard. Clay holds nutrients and water well, but its nature precludes good soil aeration and easy cultivation.

The answer to good soil is none of the above alone, but all of the above in the right proportions, plus organic matter.

The right proportions are thought to lie in the vicinity of sandy loam (see the pyramid diagram). Since good soil is only about half solid particles and the rest water and air, you need a mix of all three types. Sand gives your soil porosity and drainage, while silt and clay give it the ability to hang onto nutrients and retain water through capillary action.

Another good test for your garden is a perc or drainage test: dig a hole or two in your garden about two feet deep and fill with water. The amount of time it takes for the water to percolate through tells a lot about your soil. If it drains in only a few

minutes, your soil is far too sandy and porous. If it takes three or four hours or a day, it is far too dense — or you may have an impermeable layer below the surface that refuses to allow drainage, even in good soil. An hour, or two at the most, is about right.

An observant gardener looking at an untilled piece of land for a possible garden can tell a lot by what is growing naturally on it, if it hasn't been recently disturbed. A field of shallow-rooted annuals may indicate hardpan or impermeable soil just below the surface. Reeds, rushes, *Vaccinium* species and hardhack

Figure 1: *Successful gardening begins with understanding your soil. This soil-texture triangle shows the relative percentages of sand, silt and clay in each soil class.*
(U.S. Department of Agriculture)

(Spiraea) grow in high-acid, boggy soils. Mosses, fungi and liverworts indicate high surface moisture and low light. No greenery at all is indeed a bad sign. Generally, a diversified and healthy stand of native vegetation will inhabit the best soils and the good prospective gardener will take the hint.

ORGANIC MATTER

If your soil isn't sandy loam, do you throw up your hands in despair? If your garden fails the perc test, do you have to move?

Nothing quite so drastic. There is one general answer to the whole problem: add organic matter. And more organic matter. And then again more organic matter. At least a third of your soil should be organic matter, if possible. If you have a hard layer of compacted material (hardpan or plow sole) under a thin layer of soil, your garden may never pass the perc test and you will have to use raised beds with underlying drainage tiles (which is easy to say, but a lot of work to do). Even so, don't forget the organic matter.

Sources of Organic Matter:
1. Compost (which may contain any or all of the following)
2. Garden, kitchen waste
3. Animal manures
4. Sawdust, wood chips, bark
5. Green manures
6. Peat
7. Hardwood leaves and conifer needles
8. Newspapers/cardboard
9. Hay
10. Seaweed

This list is not complete. You may have a local source of organic matter that is quite unavailable to others. In southern Oregon it is possible to get rice hulls in sufficient quantity to use as a soil improver (although not necessarily desirable—they may sprout).

The advisor-gardeners who have lent their expertise to this book have nearly all relied heavily on annual additions of organic matter. For those who had no soil to start with, it was necessary to bring in topsoil from elsewhere, then add other materials when needed. Only a few—those with a rich accumulation of valley-bottom loam—have not applied regular doses of organic matter. But it is good to be aware that even with the best of soils (a rarity in the Northwest), you are systematically depleting it—mining it, actually—when you do not add organic matter. Much more commercial fertilizer must be used if you garden year by year on the same raw material.

Compost

Composting is an art. The very idea of turning the unattractive detritus of kitchen and yard into the finest growing material available is a lesson in grace.

Most expert home gardeners have compost piles. For some it makes the difference between gardening and not gardening. For others it is a way of keeping up the quality of their soil and produce.

Proper composting is not only a boon to your garden, it is a necessity in urban areas where garbage disposal problems are becoming acute. In Seattle, a program of home composting has been promoted by the Seattle Engineering Department and the Tilth Society, a nonprofit organization which maintained a demonstration garden in the Wallingford area. During 1986-87 a full range of composting options for the home gardener was on display there, and Master Composters were available for consultation.

In general, a home compost pile of diverse materials will contain about 2 to 3 percent nitrogen, 1 to 2 percent phosphorus and potash, and trace elements.

Handy materials for composting

Anything from your yard except diseased plant parts and what has been sprayed with a pesticide. Sod, grass clippings and leaves are choice ingredients. Large items such as tree branches will not break down easily unless they are chopped small or ground. A power mower will chop some coarse refuse into compostable size.

Composting can be done in specially constructed bins, barrels, even plastic bags or directly on or in the ground. It turns the detritus from kitchen and garden into the finest growing material available.

There are compost grinders available if you wish to get fancy.

Anything from the kitchen except meat, bones, fatty substances or oils, which are harmful and attract unwanted animals; and clam and oyster shells, which are not in the least harmful but which take eons to decompose.

Newspaper—the black and white kind, cardboard boxes, paper sacks—best when shredded or torn into pieces. (Newspaper and other household paper products have recently been found to contain dioxin, a cancer-causing substance. Perhaps until this problem has been resolved, paper mulching in the garden should be resisted.)

Sawdust, hay or straw, bark. These and the paper products are primarily composed of cellulose and will need nitrogen added to help break them down. Sawdust, for example, has 500 times as much carbon as nitrogen, whereas a good ratio for composting is 30 parts carbon to 1 part nitrogen. Grass clippings, manures, commercial nitrogen or compost starter should be added.

Wood ashes lighten heavy soil and add a small amount of potash and an even smaller amount of phosphorus.

Methods of composting

Compost can be made in bins especially constructed for it, in barrels, in plastic bags, or directly in or on the ground. The simplest method is to dig a trench eight inches to a foot deep in your garden and add waste, covering it up as you go. When you have reached the edge of the garden, start a new trench next to it. This may be the fastest and best way to return residue to your soil, according to Cornell agricultural scientists, and it does

circumvent all the fussiness involved in composting separately.

Wire fencing can be fastened around metal fenceposts for an easy, airy container. Some gardeners build wooden bins to hold their compost. A favorite method is a two- or three-bin succession. As the material composts into finer and less recognizable pieces, it is moved to the next bin.

In any composting it is important to turn and mix the pile, to be sure there is enough nitrogen to break down the cellulose components and to keep it moist. For quickest compost, keep your pile small and turn it at least once a week. A large pile, four to five feet high, should take no more than about three months to finish.

Heat in a hard-working compost pile will reach 140 degrees Fahrenheit or more. Such heat can be utilized. A large pile can supply heat to a greenhouse. A small pile of grass clippings in the bottom of a planting hole, covered with a bit of soil, can deliver temporary warmth to the roots of a young plant.

In very cold areas, the compost pile will cease working for the winter. To get it going in the spring you may want to buy a starter or make one of your own as follows:

    2 parts dolomitic limestone
    2 parts superphosphate
    4 parts sulfate of ammonia
    1 part muriate of potash

Spread about a quart over a three by five pile and mix in. Or throw on a shovelful of manure.

Problems of composting

There is sometimes a problem trying to maintain a compost pile, especially in a city. Rats and other rodents take up residence, dogs and cats investigate it regularly, neighbors complain about the smell. Generally, these problems can be surmounted.

A bad smell can be counteracted by keeping the pile systematically turned, as it usually needs more air. If the smell is ammonialike you are losing your nitrogen, so get some more carbon into it in the form of wood chips, hay, shredded newspaper and the like. There are also compost deodorizers for the hard

Composting in urban areas helps to solve the mounting problem of garbage disposal. A full range of composting options is displayed at the Tilth Society's demonstration garden in Seattle's Wallingford district.

cases. Simply throwing a layer of garden soil onto the pile will allay temporary difficulties.

Slow composting can be remedied by more frequent turning and watering when it starts to dry out, or adding nitrogen if it won't heat up sufficiently. You want your compost hot; it is a sign that all those microbes have begun to decompose the material. If the temperature of the pile is where it should be, most (but not all) of the weed seeds and grass roots will be cooked so they won't show up later as an unplanned crop.

In densely populated areas it may be necessary to buy one of the rather expensive but pest-proof composters now being manufactured. Metal drums that can be rotated by turning a handle at the side are good for small amounts of compost. Metal bins with lids are also available from some suppliers. Although requiring more capital outlay to start, these metal compostmakers are likely to outlast most everything else that can be built for the purpose.

Red earthworms can be bought from growers in some areas. The service of these worms is valuable in working the compost and adding their own castings. If you can get some, they may be well worth your while. Be sure to find out from the grower what care must be given to assure their continued existence.

Animal Manures

Northwest gardeners use animal manures if they can get them. Even city gardeners can get sterilized and bagged steer manure. In Seattle, residents can buy Zoo-Doo, a well-rotted mix of bedding and very exotic manures, from the Woodland Park Zoo by calling in and getting on their customer list. Discovery Park Police Stables make a fresh horse manure mix available to Seattle residents.

Portland's Zoo-Doo is pure elephant manure, higher in nitrogen than steer manure. It should be composted or laid on the garden over winter. Although the zoo's elephants produce 2,000 pounds a day of this material, in springtime it is in high demand and may not always be available. Call the zoo before you show up with your pickup and shovel.

Rotted manures are often available from soil and sawdust supply houses. Country gardeners have an easier time of it, often having neighbors who are glad to give the by-product of farm animals to anyone who comes after it.

Many gardeners prefer to keep a separate pile of manure, covered with plastic to keep the nutrients from leaching out, and add a shovelful or two to the compost pile when they think of it for a boost to the microorganisms working away inside.

If fresh manure is used, it must be used carefully. Like any hot fertilizer, it will burn the plants. A favorite way is to spread it over the garden area in the fall after the harvest, sheet composting it and cooling it over the winter. In the spring it is incorporated into the soil by digging or tilling, and after a short resting period it is ready to go into use.

Manure can be used as a side dressing as well. After plants are well established a strip of manure may be laid down along the rows, away from the leaves and stems, or circled around individual young squash or melon plants, which are heavy feeders and

appreciate the added nutrients. By the time the vines are creeping over the circle, the manure has cooled.

Manure may be soaked in water in a barrel or bucket, giving a mild manure tea with which to water young plants or those in containers. Exact measurements are not important so long as the volume of water is considerably greater than the solid content of the tea—estimate about two or three trowels of fresh manure to a five-gallon bucket. Packaged manure may also be used. You can tie up the manure in an old dish towel and suspend it in the bucket of water.

If you become fond of this method, you might want to get a 50-gallon drum with a cover, put in two or three shovelfuls of manure, and fill it with water. If it sits outside in the summer it will heat up most satisfyingly and you will avoid shocking your plants with cold tap water when you dip it out to water them. For a very small garden this is an ideal way to water if care is taken to get adequate amounts of moisture to the plant roots.

Another way to use manure tea is to pierce large cans or plastic containers several places around their circumference and sink them into the ground. When placed among several zucchinis or cantaloupes, for instance, and filled with the tea, they will gradually release the fertilized water to the plant roots. But don't expect the liquid to go far. It is a good idea to experiment with this method before relying on it.

Contents of manures vary according to what the animals are eating. Table 1-1. gives approximate values of fresh manure.

Table 1-1. Nutrient percentage of animal manures

Type	Water	N	P	K
Chicken	75	1.5	1.0	.50
Cow	86	0.60	0.15	0.45
Horse	78	0.70	0.25	0.55
Sheep	68	0.95	0.35	.40

Pig manure may carry roundworm eggs, which can be transmitted to human beings. If you know your pigs are parasite-free, the manure is safe and useful. Dog, cat and human feces are not recommended, even when composted.

One more thing about manures: they may contain salts which build up in the soil. It is possible to create a toxic condition in your soil with too much manure, even when it is well composted. A high salt content in the garden soil will cause your plants to wilt easily. Salt build-up is more likely in areas with low rainfall. As with everything in nature, diversity is the key—a variety of soil additives will keep this condition from occurring.

Sawdust, Wood Chips, and Bark

Most Northwest gardeners have some kind of forest tree product or residue readily available. Most likely it will be sawdust from a nearby mill. Any native tree except the western red cedar, which seems to contain somewhat toxic oils, can supply

beneficial additives to the soil. The process of breaking this material down, however, requires nitrogen.

For example, a hundred pounds of fresh sawdust has a nitrogen content of about .2 percent. For microorganisms to decompose the sawdust, they must have six times that amount of nitrogen,

Earl Chambers of Penticton squeezed his compost pile between his garage and the edge of his lot, and encourages neighbors to add their leaves and grass clippings. "It makes up into humus fast," he says.

or 1.2 percent. If microorganisms and plants are competing for the same supply of nitrogen, it is likely the microorganisms will win.

The moral is that you must supply the extra nitrogen with the sawdust unless you are fortunate enough to get it very well aged. For every 10 cubic feet of sawdust add 4 pounds of blood meal, or 5 pounds of 10-10-10 mix. Eventually, of course, even your fresh sawdust gets decomposed, the microorganisms die, and most of the nitrogen they tied up is released. But on the time scale of the seasonal vegetable garden, that is not very helpful.

Green Manure

Green manures are simply cover crops that add something to your soil as they grow or when they are dug in. They may have deep roots and bring nutrients from far below the usual rooting depth of most vegetables. They can be seeded in early fall for a winter crop or in beds that are idle to prevent weeds from taking over. The pea-family plants such as clover, alfalfa and fava beans add nitrogen to the soil. They are also important for the large amounts of organic matter they produce with little effort on your part.

It may be easier to mow and remove the green manure crop and compost it separately if you wish to use your garden bed immediately. Soil that has had green manure plowed or tilled into it must be left unplanted for at least a couple of weeks while the organic material decomposes.

Alfalfa and red clover are used on large fields where commercial crops of vegetables are grown. They require deep cultivation to turn them under permanently, and are not recommended for small gardens. They replenish soil and bring up micronutrients from the soil depths.

Fava beans are cold-hardy and grow in wet soils. This means they can be used as a winter cover crop in some parts of the Northwest. The added benefit of this crop is the harvest of beans before they are turned under in early spring. Takes about 2 lbs. seed per 1,000 sq. ft.

Rye is an annual grass that can be used to improve the soil. Its contribution to soil fertility is not notable, but it will crowd out weeds. Only ½ lb. seed per 1,000 sq. ft.

Buckwheat is a fast-grower with abundant organic matter to add to the soil, and will easily reseed itself if it isn't plowed under before its flowers begin to set. Like rye, it is not high in nutrients. 1½ lbs. per 1,000 sq. ft.

Seeds for these and other green manure plants can usually be obtained at feed stores, or ordered from some seed companies.

Peat

Peat is formed when many generations of dead plants collect under water, where oxygen is excluded. Water and compaction keep the material from complete decomposition. Once it is exposed to air, decomposition processes set in.

Peat is usually thought of as being acidic. If you live in a peat bog, the probability is that your soil pH is down around 4. But it depends upon the formation of the peat deposit, where it is, what vegetable matter went into it. In northeastern Washington, for instance, Master Gardeners are experimenting with the use of local sources of a peat that has a very respectable pH range.

Peat moss of the sphagnum variety is thought to be best in soil or soilless mixes. Some of the sedge peats can be saline and unusable, and in any case, it is best to know the quality and analysis of the peat you are using.

On the whole, peat—unlike sawdust—contains enough nitrogen to take care of its own decompositon. Although it is difficult, unless treated, to get wetted down the first time, it is an excellent retainer of water. It has a tendency to compact into a cold, sodden mass and is best mixed with other materials.

Hardwood Leaves, Conifer Needles

Most of us have seen the big plastic bags full of the fall leaves at the curb waiting for the garbage pick-up. There goes one of the best materials for mulch and soil improvement you can get, right out to the landfill. Do yourself and your neighbors a favor and get harvest rights to the local leaf fall for your compost.

It is possible, however, that your community has made arrangements for a town leaf dump. Eugene, Oregon, residents effect a sort of leaf exchange: those who don't want them bring them in to find new homes with those who do. Eugene has gone a step further and is now using the leaves to make a compost for sale.

Hardwood leaves are more useful if they are shredded with the lawn mower or chipper, because they tend to mat together. Matted or shredded leaves can use some nitrogen at about two-thirds cup per 100 square feet to break them down, since their principal offering is carbon. They have a tendency toward acidity, so lime may be needed to correct the pH.

Conifer needles are seldom considered a major component in the organic matter of the garden, but in the ponderosa pine country, such as in Regions III and IV and parts of most other regions except the coastal areas, enough may be gathered to make a significant addition to the garden. They are very slow to decompose, however, and are more often used as a mulch along paths than as a direct soil additive. They are, like broad leaves, in need of lime to balance their acidity, although in gardens that tend toward a high pH this would not be necessary.

Newspaper and Cardboard

Gardeners have learned that mats of newspaper or plain cardboard make good walkways between rows of vegetables. The material eventually rots so it can be incorporated into the soil, adding organic matter.

This material is high in carbon and will need added nitrogen for good decomposition. Any paper product that is not printed with colored inks is a good candidate for the compost, but large amounts tend to mat and prevent proper aeration and water saturation. (See note under Newspaper, page 3, for caution about dioxin in household paper products.)

Hay, Straw

Barn sweepings can often yield rotted hay and straw, good additions to the garden either directly or through composting. The method of choice is composting, since there is often a plethora of weed seed in hay.

Again the biggest benefit to the soil will come from the cellulose. If the hay is rotted it will need little or no nitrogen, but fresh hay may need a small addition of manure or a high-nitrogen fertilizer.

Seaweed

Washed seaweed contributes a fair amount of nitrogen and carbon as well as phosphorus to the soil, but its greatest virtue is its 3 or 4 percent potash content. Seaweed also is high in trace elements such as iodine, which is good for root crops.

There are various commercial seaweed fertilizers, both liquid and dry, but gardeners who have access to fresh seaweed can collect it and put it right onto the garden in the fall. Winter rains will wash out the salinity. Indeed, a small amount of salinity is recommended for some plants. Asparagus and the Brassicas will do especially well with additions of fresh seaweed. (See Part II, Region I, for Dick Berry's method of utilizing seaweed that washes up to his front yard.)

Wood Ashes

There was a time when wood ashes were in short supply, but in recent years Northwesterners have been filling the air with wood smoke and carrying out the ashes—to do what with them? If they aren't going in the garden or around the roses, it is too bad.

Wood ash in the garden lightens a heavy soil, contains calcium, potash (6 percent), magnesium and a little phosphorus. The ash of hardwoods has more mineral content than that of softwoods.

Around five pounds per hundred square feet of garden is plenty, and it may be mixed into the compost. Do not use on acid-loving plants. Coal ash, which really is scarce these days, is a low-nutrient material which will lighten soil too, but potatoes do not do well in it the first year.

Soil pH

The pH of your soil means the p(arts) (H)ydrogen, or the measure of hydrogen and hydroxyl ions present in the soil solution. More hydrogen ions mean the soil is acid. More hydroxyl ions mean it is alkaline. Neutrality, at pH 7, is achieved when there is a balance between the two. Each point up (more alkaline) or down (more acid) means ten times more or ten times fewer hydrogen ions. Soil pH may influence the growth of plants by a direct effect of hydrogen ions and by an indirect effect which influences nutrient availability. Gardeners need to consider the latter effect.

Nitrogen (N) is most readily available to plants within a central range, from pH 6 to 8. Phosphorus has a smaller ideal range, from about 6.5 to 7.5. Potassium is most accessible at a pH from 6 all the way to 9.

Of other desirable minerals, iron, manganese, boron, copper and zinc are most readily available at a pH between 5 and 7.

The important thing to remember is that below about 5.5 and above 7, few minerals necessary to good plant growth will be accessible to the plants, due to chemical reactions which bind them in insoluble compounds. Expert gardeners generally aim for a 6 to 6.5 reading.

How do they get this reading? Some don't bother about it. If vegetables grow, the pH must be all right, they say. If there is a steady application of organic materials going into the garden, the pH is likely to be satisfactory. Those who do want to know send their soil samples to government soils labs or to private testing services for detailed analysis. There are also soil testing kits available at garden stores and supply houses if you want to do it yourself.

If your soil is likely to be acidic—which probably means you live in western B.C., Washington or Oregon, or in any area with plenty of precipitation—you want to watch your spinach, beets, asparagus, and the Brassicas. Cabbages will become leggy; beets will show zoning lines if they aren't getting enough lime in the soil.

On the other hand, if your potatoes, eggplant, rhubarb, endive or watermelon aren't doing well, you may have a soil that is too alkaline.

But if the beans and tomatoes, the potatoes and spinach are all thriving on the soils of your garden, you need not worry about pH. There are undoubtedly other concerns, and excessive lime or sulfur can cause as much trouble as not enough.

Correcting Acid Soils

In rainy areas the soil carbonates are dissolved and the hydrogen ions from the water replace alkaline components, which means the soil acidity is high or the pH is low. To correct this, the commonest soil amendment is limestone. To raise the

pH one unit, you need to add 5 to 7 pounds of ground limestone to each 100 square feet of garden, although in very sandy, porous soils it will take less.

Ground limestone on acidic soil not only helps to make minerals available to the plants, it aids the soil microorganisms as they decompose organic matter, releasing nutrients. What's more, limestone improves soil texture, helping clay particles form aggregates that allow air and water to pass through the soil, and in sandy soils it acts as a cohesive force to make the soil more loamy.

Lime is not a fertilizer, it is a conditioner. It should not be applied with fertilizers because it may slow down the action of fertilizer components. Apply it early in the year if it is needed. Dolomite lime contains a little magnesium and is preferred to calcitic lime. The finer the grind, the sooner it gets to work in the garden.

Correcting Alkaline Soils

Sulfur in some form is usually applied to an alkaline soil to bring it into a proper state of production. Finely ground ferrous sulfate should be added at the rate of 1 pound per 100 square feet to lower the pH by a point or more. Powdered garden sulfur can be used at a rate of ½ pound per 100 square feet.

The same effect can be gained a bit faster with the use of iron or aluminum sulfate, which are quicker to act but require twice as large a dose and do not stay around as long. Any of these soil amendments should be applied in the fall or very early spring, allowing them time to take effect before fertilizers are added.

A common indication of high alkalinity is chlorosis of plant leaves. They turn pale yellow from lack of iron, which is unavailable to plants when soil pH is above 7.

Many inland Northwest areas have alkaline soils, some testing well over pH 7, but better ask around or test your soil before jumping to any conclusions.

Gypsum

A word about gypsum, which contains a balance of calcium and sulfur and may be added to clay soils to improve their consistency without changing the pH. A large amount of gypsum must be applied over several years before any improvement can be seen, but in clay soils that is true of just about any amendment.

FERTILIZERS

Macronutrients essential to plant growth:
   *carbon, hydrogen and oxygen—obtained mostly from air and from water
   *nitrogen, phosphorus, potassium, calcium, magnesium and sulfur—obtained from soil

Micronutrients essential to plant growth:
   *iron, manganese, boron, molybdenum, copper, zinc, chlorine and cobalt—obtained from soil

From 94 to 99.5 percent of fresh plant tissue is made up of carbon, hydrogen and oxygen, all supplied by the atmosphere

By liberal use of compost and space-saving strategies, Earl Chambers grows both vegetables and flowers on his city lot in Penticton, where the soil was sand and silt with a high pH.

and the water the plant gets. Your concern is the 6 to .5 percent of the plant that is made up of other elements.

Primary fertilizer elements are nitrogen, phosphorus and potassium, the familiar N, P and K of commercial fertilizer sacks. In some inland areas, sulfur is listed with N, P and K as a primary fertilizer. Calcium, magnesium and sulfur are secondary fertilizer elements (Ca, Mg, and S). Calcium and magnesium are lime elements and sulfur is an acid element.

Micronutrients are those needed in only small amounts, so small that only a trace of them is needed—so they are sometimes called trace elements. In some cases only a few ounces per acre are necessary to improve crops. On the whole people who are using proper applications of organic matter do not need to add trace elements.

Nitrogen is right up there with organic matter as a prime garden-soil ingredient and in fact is most likely to be richest in soil with high organic matter, and is most likely to be leached out of the soil, oxidized, or used up by the vegetation. Therefore it merits your close attention.

Nitrogen is the ingredient that encourages fast growth and dark green leaves, because chlorophyll is a nitrogenous compound. Nitrogen in natural form comes from dead plant and animal material passed through the systems of microorganisms which convert it to ammonia, which is then changed to nitrites by more microorganisms, and on to nitrates which are then assimilated by the plant. Nitrogen is a gas; it will enter the soil in small amounts in rain, and is released by lightning.

It is important to build up vegetable plants in their most rapid stages of growth with proper nitrogen applications, although it is possible to overdo it and get more leaves than you want. Nitrogen can be lethal to plants as well, as they are easily burned by an overabundance.

Phosphorus in liberal doses is a necessity for all crops, and an all-around vegetable fertilizer will usually be highest in this element. Phosphorus is necessary for strong, sturdy plants, for flowers and for roots. A lack of this element may prevent the up-

take of other nutrients. It is especially necessary to nitrogen-fixing plants such as peas and beans. It is somewhat less available to plants than nitrogen, being less water soluble, but a beneficial effect of this attribute is that plants are not harmed by overdoses. It is better to supply small amounts of it as side-dressing than to rely on one yearly application.

Potassium is particularly beneficial to root crops. It is necessary for good plant vigor and resistance to diseases, and it counteracts overfertilization with nitrogen. It also seems to give plants a certain cold-hardiness. In the Northwest it is the least likely macronutrient to be in short supply unless the soils have been seriously depleted, but sandy soils may need additions of potassium. It is not harmful to plants in large quantities.

Sulfur is rarely lacking in coastal soils but may be added to fertilizers used by some inland gardeners. **Magnesium** may be low in heavy-rainfall areas, but is easily restored by applications of dolomitic limestone or epsom salts of the drugstore variety. **Iron** is tied up when the soil is excessively alkaline, as discussed before, and should be released when the soil pH is brought into a proper range.

The **micronutrients** are all required in very small amounts. Only .5 percent of the dry weight of plants is composed of these "other" elements. Generally, soils do not lack in micronutrients except where they have been heavily cropped. Some fertilizers come fully equipped with micronutrients, but again the organic matter in the compost is the best supplier of these elements.

Sources of Nutrients

Gardeners who try to follow the pure and straight organic line will use only what are generally called organic fertilizers, not the commerically produced chemical kinds. Organic fertilizers are often slower to act than chemical fertilizers, but at the same time can be considerably longer lasting. They work less well on cold soils in spring, and for that reason it is sensible to apply some chemical fertilizer to get the garden started—especially phosphorus—even though you may have plenty of organic matter and fertilizers already in the soil.

Organic fertilizers are usually required in much greater amounts. Five pounds of a balanced chemical fertilizer can supply the nutrients of many pounds of blood or bone meal and many shovelfuls of manure. Superphosphate analysis reads 11-48-0, having 11 percent nitrogen, 48 percent phosphate, and no potassium, while chicken manure has 1.5 percent nitrogen, 1 percent phosphorus and .5 percent potassium. Nevertheless, the chicken manure is 100 percent organic matter, whereas the useful contents of superphosphate add up to only 59 percent of the total and do not contribute organic matter.

Another way to put it: one pound of nitrogen may be had from any of the following: 3 pounds of ammonium nitrate, 5 pounds of ammonium sulfate, 2 pounds of urea, 16 pounds of milorganite (sludge), or 16 pounds of cottonseed meal.

Soil chemists generally agree that when fertilizer has dissolved into the soil and is in a form which plants can use, there is no difference between organic and inorganic forms of the nutrient.

Table 1-2. Nutrient Content of Some Commercial Organic Fertilizers

Fertilizer	%N	%P	%K
Blood meal	12	1	1
Bone meal (steamed)	2	20	0
Cottonseed meal	6	2	2
Fish emulsion	5	6	2
Granite dust	0	5	0
Greensand	0	1.5	6
Kelp meal	1.5	.6	5
Phosphate rock (ground)	0	30	0
Sludge	6	4	0
Soybean meal	7	0	0
Steer manure	2	.5	2

Table 1-3. Nutrient Content of Some Commercial Inorganic Fertilizers

Fertilizer	%N	%P	%K
Ammonium phosphate	12	48	0
Ammonium sulfate	21	0	0
Muriate of potash	0	0	48
Sodium nitrate	16	0	0
Sulfate of potash	0	0	48
Superphosphate	11	48	0
Urea	45	0	0

If you are using a mixed vegetable fertilizer, pay attention to the nitrogen content, as that is the important ingredient. For a 5-10-10 fertilizer, apply 3.5 pounds per 100 square feet. Triple 16 fertilizer will take only 1 pound for the same area.

Dry fertilizer is best added to the soil by broadcast before the final tilling, side-banding after the plants are growing, or digging in along each furrow.

There's no use getting in a tangle over fertilizer analysis. Most of the Northwest gardeners interviewed for this book take the subject quite casually. A layer of manure, some handfuls of bone meal, and for some the ashes out of the fireplace, in a soil high in organic matter, is more than sufficient for any of their needs. Making sure there is plenty of phosphorus available for new plants is a good idea. Giving an extra shot of nitrogen to corn and leafy vegetables as they gain in stature is another good idea.

CHAPTER II

Conditioning

Cultivation, weeding, mulching, irrigation and tools

"I never saw any point in perfectionism for its own sake, such as carving the eyelashes of angels on top of church towers a hundred feet in the air . . . (but) a certain amount of digging is absolutely necessary." —Henry Mitchell, *On Gardening*

As Henry Mitchell also says, "some work has to be done." It is unavoidable, no matter how many books come out with no-weed, no-dig, no-water, no-labor attached to their titles. Too often the subtitles should include "no-vegetables." At the same time, there is no use in setting up routines only a determined masochist would follow.

Conditioning is the name of this chapter because conditioning is what your body gets when you work on your garden and, with luck, that is what your garden gets as well.

CULTIVATION

Before Planting

The first-time gardener wishing to turn a sodded backyard into a bed for vegetable raising will probably wonder how it is possible to get rid of this compacted, resistant nuisance. The gardener with a piece of uncultivated native vegetation will have an even more difficult job. But it is possible.

Northwest soil that has never known the plow or shovel will wear a covering of ancient stumps, blackberries, huckleberries and quack grass with associated species, or the generic group known as sage brush, bunch grasses, and endless deep-seated arid-type species of the drier areas. A person with one of these types of vegetation will either undertake many weekends of strong-arm labor, or hire a bulldozer or plow or large rototiller, preferably with operator, to make the first inroads. Even if mass herbicide is contemplated, somebody will have to dig into the soil.

It is advisable to outline the proposed garden section with string and stakes. Keep in mind that small is beautiful. Most gardeners complain that they started with too much space. It is easy to add a bit more next year if you think you didn't have enough this year to keep you busy.

Those with sod can slice out sections of the erstwhile lawn with a sharp shovel, or rent a sod cutter for an afternoon if there is a well-equipped tool-rental place in the vicinity. Sod makes excellent compost and, unless there is a place to replant the strips that come up, you can cut them into pieces, stack them upside down and cover them with black plastic until the grass dies.

There's another way to denude your new garden plot, if you have the time. In the spring, or sometime during the growing season, take a roll of black plastic and cover the section you wish to cultivate, leaving no cracks or openings for weeds and grass to push through. Peg it down with pieces of bent wire or weight it down with lumber or rocks. Wait about a month (time will depend on the season — the hotter it is, the less time it takes) and check it to see what is still alive. When all unwanted vegetation seems defunct, you should be able to remove the black plastic and simply rototill the area. There may still be viable roots and seeds lurking in there, however, so you will have to get them out as soon as they appear. Several tillings or diggings may be necessary for difficult places.

Last of all, you can use a herbicide like Roundup during the time of year when the vegetation is putting on most vigorous growth. In three weeks or so you should have the same sort of weed graveyard you would get with the black plastic. There are other types of herbicides also; some are of the pre-emergent kind that kill seeds as they germinate, but do not use any of them lightly and do not use them at all if you won't follow the directions on the label absolutely without deviation.

From this point you can take up spade, hand cultivator, rototiller or tractor — depending upon the size of your garden, your purse, and the time you have to spend. It is entirely possible to keep up a good-sized garden with only a shovel or spade, a rake, a trowel and something to water with. All other tools can be acquired as specialization sets in.

For small gardens and raised beds, hand-digging is the only way to go. But large gardens, dug in sections as needed over several months' time, can benefit from hand-digging as well. Mechanical digging fluffs up the top layer and breaks down its structure, while hand-digging is less radical.

The point in spring cultivation is to incorporate organic matter that has been put on during the months since the last growing season (or that you have just put on the garden), get the weeds up so you can collect them and run them through the compost, and loosen soil that has been compacted by winter snows and rains. Walking and driving on it compacts it again, so it is best to stay off as much as you can. If you are hand-digging, stand on the undug side.

This is the time to dig in the (aged) manure or general garden fertilizer and the compost pile ingredients. Double digging, which means trenching along the width of the garden at twice the depth of your spade, loosening the lower layer and adding manure or fertilizer, then moving the top layer from the last trench to fill in the one before, is highly regarded by many gardeners and garden writers — often in theory more than in practice. It is particularly beneficial in an area devoted to root crops.

Tilling in the fall is most popular in the colder areas of the Northwest, where all crops will probably be out by about the end of October. Leaving a rough surface may hasten snow melt in the spring.

In milder regions, many people will carry winter crops all the way through until early spring, with perhaps only a short resting time for the soil before more crops go in. In this case, tilling is done in that interim period.

Hand-digging is best done in heavy soils with a fork and in lighter soils with a spade. Hold the tool upright and sink the full depth of the digging end into the soil. Apply a little leverage to get the clod of soil out, turn it over as you put it down, and give it a few jabs if it does not break up as you move it. It is hard work, but it is not work that has to be done all at once. A few yards a day is not only possible for most nonhandicapped people, it is positively beneficial exercise.

After digging, you will want to rake out the beds, getting rid of any coarse material and rocks that will interrupt the planting rows or patterns.

Ward Briggs, Region 1, recommends placing black plastic on the prepared bed about a month ahead of planting in early spring to germinate weed seeds in the top half-inch of soil, creating a weed-free bed especially good for slow-sprouting vegetables such as carrots.

Cultivation After Planting

Especially in new gardens, or those that have not been tended very carefully, there will be uncountable weed seeds lurking in

Narrow beds with permanent walkways between them help to prevent compaction of the soil by foot traffic. Walkways can be attractive, too.

the depths of the soil waiting for enough heat or light to germinate. Once you have smoothed over and planted the garden it is wise not to disturb the soil any more than necessary. Don't hoe more than an inch or so down at the most when you are going after the weeds. Cut them off at soil level. This not only keeps from giving weed seeds an opportunity to germinate, it saves your developing vegetable plant roots as well, as the fine root hairs are growing out into the uncrowded areas to find more nutrients and water.

Another result of too-vigorous hoeing is that the organic matter you have gone to so much trouble to get into the soil decomposes faster on the surface, where there is more light and heat. Thus, the more you bring it up to the top, the faster you lose it.

But many experienced gardeners like to do their weeding by hand. It is another chance to see what is going on down at the soil level, they say. Pulling out weeds gives you a feel for what is happening with the vegetables. If the roots of the weeds are damp and have clumps of soil clinging to them, then your vegetables will have the same. If the weeds are nearly impossible to pull, perhaps the soil is too compacted from the traffic up and down the rows: although you will not want to disturb the plants now, you may want to think of new ways of planting to keep you, the children and dogs and cats out of the rows. Permanent walks and narrow beds which can be reached across may be the answer.

A neat gardener usually carries a bucket along and puts the weeds in it as they are pulled. The weeds go in the compost and come out as unrecognizable organic matter for future use. Other

gardeners will pile the weeds along the rows to use as a mulch. If the weeds are infected with bugs, that is not a good idea, but a modest amount of clean young weeds causes no problem. If you can't keep up with all of them at once, at least keep them from flowering, as that means they will be setting more seed to start the next cycle.

MULCHING

Organic mulches such as sawdust, grass, leaves, hay or straw can be put around the plants once the soil is sufficiently warm. In some areas, a drawback to mulching is that slugs take up residence in the mulch. Hay and straw are particularly to their liking. Of course, high-carbon mulch material will take nitrogen to break it down, and you will have to take that into consideration. Newspapers, flattened cardboard cartons and old carpet strips are also used for mulching by Northwest gardeners.

Black plastic is also a favorite all-around mulch here. It helps to warm the soil, keeps weeds down, keeps moisture in. A complete plot can be covered with black plastic, slit later to accommodate whatever transplants or row vegetables the gardener wants to put in. Slug bait can be used underneath it, if necessary, with little danger that animals will get into it. Various kinds of mulching paper and rolls of mulching materials can be obtained at some garden supply houses.

IRRIGATION

Very few places in the Northwest get enough rainfall during the prime growing season to keep the ground sufficiently moist for vegetables. All gardeners need an auxiliary system of irrigation.

Usually it is a hose attached to the house, at least to start with. Small gardens are easily watered by hand — or by sprinkler, if standing around with the hose is too time-consuming. But at some point the certified hard-core garden tinkerer will get together a warmed, automatic underground drip system with liquid fertilizing alternatives, if circumstances allow it.

Watering necessities are determined by the kind of soil you have. Clay soils can retain moisture far longer than sandy soils, but if they dry out they will take up to four times more water to wet them thoroughly again. Organic matter contributes moisture-holding qualities.

The best watering systems will get the water down where it is needed, at the roots. Hand-watering allows you to see what you are doing. Soaker hoses are useful for this kind of watering, too, and to be most efficient can be run down double rows of plantings.

It is possible to overwater vegetables in the garden. Tomato blossoms will drop off if either over- or under-watered, and carrots become stumpy and misshapen. Overwatering is a danger in heavy soil only, when flooded soil pores cannot retain oxygen needed by the plant roots.

Underwatering, which is a far more common problem than overwatering, can cause plants to flower early in an effort to produce a "stress crop." Early, stunted corn can be a result of improper watering. Yet for some herbs and for tomatoes, a judicious withholding of water is a method for hurrying production of seeds and fruits.

The principal ingredient in a vegetable's makeup is overwhelmingly water — as much as 96 percent. Vegetables subjected to water stress will not completely recover, no matter what you do. It is therefore of utmost importance to see that your garden is thoroughly and regularly watered. The best production can be obtained with a steady, slow supply. Considerable observation will be necessary to find out the best watering regime for your garden. Dig down after you have watered to see how far the irrigation reached. It should go well below the rooting zones of your plants — otherwise they form shallow root balls, and are thus subjected to faster dry-out between waterings.

Gardeners in this book have a good idea of how much watering is needed in their own particular gardens, and how often they should water to get that amount. Usually they water deeply once a week. If the temperatures are very high and the wind is blowing, they water more often. Those who mulch extensively have the least onerous watering duties.

Favorite watering times vary, but on the whole morning or evening is preferred. If your environment is on the dampish side and your garden is subject to mildew or fungal diseases, water early and let the sun dry out the plants during the day. If you have hot winds and a lot of sun, water in the evening so you don't lose a lot to evaporation during the day. In a few places, on a few days of the year, watering during the day can burn the leaves of your vegetables, due to magnification of sun's rays by the water drops.

Your garden will appreciate warmed water if you can get it. Leaving a long hose out in the sun will give you a small supply of hot water which peppers, cucumbers and other heat-loving plants will be delighted to get. A trickle irrigation system can be devised with a large drum of water set up on a platform above the garden level. The drum is filled from the hose, the sun warms the water (painting the drum black will help), and the water runs through an outlet set in the bottom of the drum into the hoses laid in the garden (see Region IV, Earl Chambers). If water is in short supply and your garden is placed near the house, you might even fill the drum with water led in from the downspout (assuming it will rain enough to fill it).

TOOLS

The best advice about tools is to find what fits you. If you are five feet tall you will not use the same long-handled hoe with ease that a six-footer uses. Most of us have picked up a garden tool that feels just right, and we will go back to it again and again for various jobs.

There is a burgeoning business in garden supply equipment and it is impossible to cover all the tools available. A few basics will have to suffice, and you may take it from there by looking through the catalogs and garden stores. There is even a catalog for tool sources, put out by Rodale Press (*Tools for Homesteaders, Gardeners and Small-Scale Farmers, 1978*).

Quality is important, since you don't want your hoe handle splintering in the midst of a heavy weeding job or your regular hose turning unannounced into a soaker hose. A few good basic

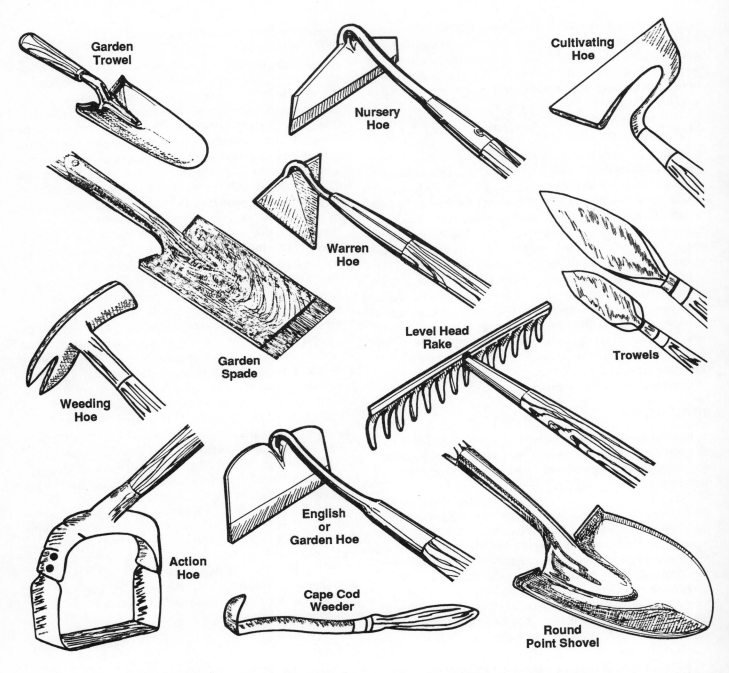

Garden
Trowel

Nursery
Hoe

Cultivating
Hoe

Warren
Hoe

Trowels

Garden
Spade

Level Head
Rake

Weeding
Hoe

Action
Hoe

English
or
Garden Hoe

Cape Cod
Weeder

Round
Point Shovel

implements will surpass a whole truckload of cheaply made specialty items. Look carefully at construction, at the way the handles of different-quality tools are made, at how the tool is wedded to the handle. Examine the grain and smoothness of the wooden handle too, to make sure you are getting a good hardwood.

Hoes and Weeders

Hoeing is another word for weeding. Hoes are for cutting and chopping weeds, except for the Warren style which is a good furrow-maker. They come swan-necked and flat, with wide or with narrow blades. Small hoes are for small places. Because they are for chopping weeds, the blades should be kept sharp.

Weeders and cultivators have prongs to scratch out weeds, or blades to cut and dig at the same time.

Diggers

Digging tools come in fork, spade, shovel or trowel style. It is important to check the set and angle of the handle on a digger, because you must exert more muscle when the proper angle is not built in. Straight up and down handles require more work.

Rakes

Rakes are necessary for cleaning and smoothing the soil in the garden, for gathering leaves and other materials for the compost, and for leveling out raised beds.

12

CHAPTER III

Planting

Planning what, where, when and how to plant

"A garden managed with ease will be of such size that its cultivation will not unduly interfere with relaxing activities of a sort other than gardening."

—Angelo Pellegrini, *The Food Lover's Garden*

"In autumn, when the leaves are brown,
Take pen and ink and write it down."

—Lewis Carroll, *Humpty Dumpty*

Planning your garden is a good fall or winter activity. All the problems fade and the possibilities bloom as you sit by the fireside looking over the new seed catalogs. The vision of order and plenty rises anew, obscuring the remembrances of last year's failures and disappointments. A gardener is a dreamer and an optimist, not a scoffer and a pessimist.

PLANNING WHAT TO PLANT

You will need to know first what you and your family will eat and how much you will want of each crop. It is common to overplant — especially squash. Especially zucchini squash. ("One is not enough and two are too many," says one Northwest gardener.) Vegetables that are hard to get in their freshest state, vegetables that are expensive, vegetables that you use the most, gourmet vegetables — these are the kinds that you should consider planting. The list might include:

Sweet corn
Tomatoes
Lettuce
Peas — pod, snow and sugar snap
Green beans
Asparagus
Yellow or Finnish potatoes

Cucumbers
Endive
Anything you want small and young, such as carrots and green onions

Of course there are many, many more candidates for the list. Choose yours according to your taste and the capabilities of your climate.

The varieties of vegetables you choose are important. If you know your growing season averages 100 days, do not plant 120-day corn. Many new varieties are developed each year for specific areas. It really does make a difference to choose the right variety for you. Suggestions and recommendations for varieties in each region of the Northwest are given in Appendix B, as well as sources of seed.

PLANNING WHERE TO PLANT: RAISED BEDS

For the new gardener, planning where the garden will go is the first consideration. It would be nice, if impractical, to spend a year observing Nature on your property. You would find where the sun shines the most hours of the day during summer, what parts of the yard are well drained, where rainwater puddles, where tree roots take up all the moisture, which spot would be easiest and most convenient without being in the way of flower beds and possible play yards and patios.

It has been said, but I'll say it again: a new gardener should keep a first vegetable garden small, and small is no more than about 20 by 25 feet or the equivalent, and can be considerably less. If you are making raised beds, that would be about four 4-foot wide beds each 25 feet long and space between for paths. This size garden should produce plenty of vegetables for the prover-

bial family of four. If you are looking for enough food to freeze, can and otherwise store for winter, you may wish to increase the size of your garden, but do consider the time you have available for all this increased labor, both in the garden and in the kitchen.

If I were starting over in a new place, I would begin with raised beds. These are some good reasons:

- Raised beds heat up faster in the spring.
- There is no more work to making raised beds than there is to fixing up a square patch of soil for rows. Well, maybe a little more shovel work.
- You don't have to have sides on raised beds, you can just pile the best soil up into the shape you want and leave the paths between for the poor soil or rocks.
- You will never have to walk on the beds if you keep them narrow enough for you to reach to the center easily.
- All the manure and fertilizer you put on the beds will go for vegetable production and not for unproductive foot traffic.
- You can grow compatible plants together and separate others.
- You can keep track of your rotation needs.
- You can retire one bed for a season, plant rye grass on it and let the others produce until their turns come to rest.
- You can use one bed as a nursery for late crops.
- You can create a cloche of the same proportions as one of the beds and extend your growing season.
- You don't have to stoop over so far.
- If your soil is poor you can create a totally different growing medium above the surface.
- You can grow flowers in one and herbs in another, if you like to keep them segregated.

I can think of one serious drawback: in very hot-summer areas they dry out too fast. But even there, with lots of organic matter, mulch and high rims so the water doesn't run out, they ought to work.

In fact, come to think of it, even if I weren't starting a new garden I would make raised beds (and I have). Any conventional garden lends itself well to raised-bed restructuring. Just because you've done something for ten or twenty years doesn't mean it has to go on that way. Of course, some crops lend themselves to raised beds better than others. Even some avid raised-bedders still grow corn in rows in flat sections preserved for such things.

To construct a raised bed on an established garden plot, turn over the soil in the bed area, remove rocks and debris, and add the best topsoil from the sides and ends, making a path about a foot and a half wide around the bed. Amend the fluffed-up soil in the bed with steer manure, compost, fertilizer, perhaps some bone meal. Mix thoroughly and rake into a tidy rectangle a little wider at the path level than at the top. If you slant the sides enough, you won't need rocks or boards for side support. (They make good hiding places for slugs and other pests.) If you make a ridge all around the surface of the bed, rather like a pie crust, irrigation water won't run onto the path.

The lesson to be learned from raised beds is that you can have vegetables growing in nearly any environment where you can get water, and six or more hours of sun a day, if you tend to your

Raised beds vary with the space and the gardener's preference. They may be mounds of soil with or without side support, or, as in this Okanagon garden, containers in or on the surface.

soil properly. Raised beds can be seen as simply large containers set in the vegetable garden. Those containers can be enclosed, reduced in size, set on the patio or deck, and you can still have lovely crops of vegetables.

Of course there are many gardeners who like the orderliness of rows stretching the length of the garden, and are uneasy with methods that have not been used before in the history of the family. And for those who grow truly prodigious amounts of vegetables, either for sale or for supplying relatives and neighbors, rows are possibly more practical, especially if a tractor or mechanical tiller is used on the fields in the spring. Further, anyone with a particular passion for a rototiller is not likely to look with approval on raised beds.

There are modifications. Some gardeners use raised beds but create them fresh each year after spring plowing. Some gardeners keep one or two raised beds for special plants and put the rest out in flat rows. Some gardeners plant in flat rows, but divide the total garden into small sections with permanent paths between for better handling.

Orient your beds of your garden to maximize the sun you get, especially if you live in an area that tends to be cloudy or cool

With raised beds you don't have to stoop so far. Here, Beth Burrows seeds a bed in the Marysville Demonstration Garden, where beds are narrow enough to be reached across.

during the growing months. A slight slope to the south increases the amount of radiation you get, whereas a north slope will be more difficult for gardening. The reasons for orienting beds or rows north and south — less shading by plants at the south end of plants at the north end during the brightest hours of the day — can be circumvented by planting the tallest crops at the back. But if you live in Walla Walla, you may be glad to have some shade for such things as lettuce and broccoli plants during July and August.

Possibly you will not have one particular spot devoted to vegetable gardening. Tomatoes can be grown at the back of a bed of marigolds; cabbages and chard can add spectacle to the petunias; cucumbers can be trained along a fence, and lettuce can fill in the spring bulb bed.

Planning Aids and Schedules

Many experienced gardeners do not use a written plan each year because they have developed a routine that is almost second-nature to them. It is wise, however, for the less experienced gardener to keep notes, draw plans, make schedules and record results. Memory is not always reliable and most of us have a selective way of recalling things ("Did it really rain all spring, or did it just seem like it?")

Graph, gridded or lined paper is useful for drawing out a simple plan. It is also helpful to have a seed catalog or two at hand, or the seed packets themselves, to tell you something about space required for the plants you want to put in your garden. Most catalogs are very helpful with general planting directions and spacing. (It is also possible to buy garden planning kits which come with plant cutouts, but they are rather expensive and not likely to do any better than you can with paper and pencil.) Here is how to make your own planning kit for garden designing. Equipment needed:

- 8½ x 11″ paper, blank, or ½″ gridded or lined
- sharp pencil
- ruler
- triangle or T-square (if you draw your own lines)
- circles — use a circle template, available at art stores, or

copy the patterns shown below and cut out, retrace on heavy paper and cut out again
- seed catalogs or packets, for planting distances

On an 8½x11″ sheet of paper, you can draw out a garden of 16x20 feet, at the maximum, if ½″ equals 1 foot. If you have a larger garden than that, you will have to get larger paper, use a smaller scale (¼-inch) grid, or divide the garden into sections, with one section to a sheet.

Using the gridded paper and the circle patterns, draw in the appropriate size of circles for each type of vegetable that you wish to grow. For the smallest vegetables, such as radishes and green onions, you can put in 4-6 dots per lineal foot, or 16 per square foot (square half-inch on the chart). The sample garden plots shown here would be 16x18′ in real life, 8x9″ on the paper, divided into half-inch squares, each foot represented by one square.

Table 3-1. Approximate Space Needed For Selected Garden Vegetables, in Ground and on Planning Chart.

Vegetable	space on the ground	space on the chart
Tomato, squash, pumpkin, sunflower, rhubarb	3 feet	1½ inches
Potato, pepper, Brussels sprouts, cantaloupe, eggplant	2 feet	1.0 inch
Broccoli, cabbage, cauliflower, kale	18 inches	¾ inch
Corn, cucumber, head lettuce	12 inches	½ inch
Asparagus, bean, celery, kohlrabi, leaf lettuce, spinach	6-8 inches	¼ inch
Beet, carrot, onion, spinach, salsify, pea, radish, turnip, green onion	2-3 inches	⅛ inch (4-6 per ft.)

Now, how many of these vegetables can you grow in a 16x18 foot plot? Sounds like a story question in arithmetic class. The answer is, it depends.

Plan 1 — Row Garden:
We will arbitrarily choose 14 kinds of vegetables that we want

Plan 1

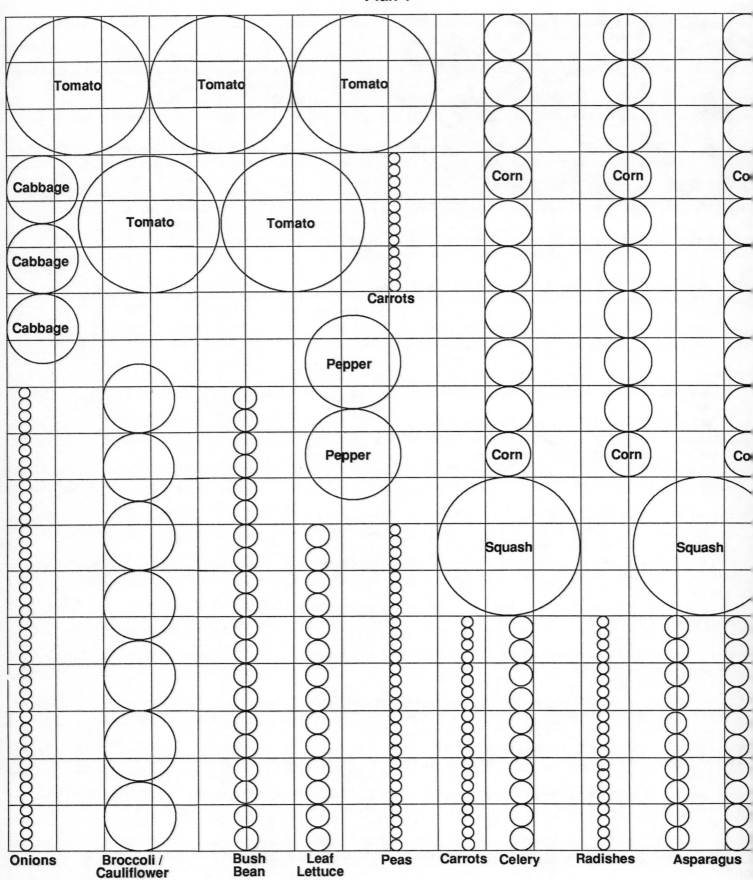

Plan 2

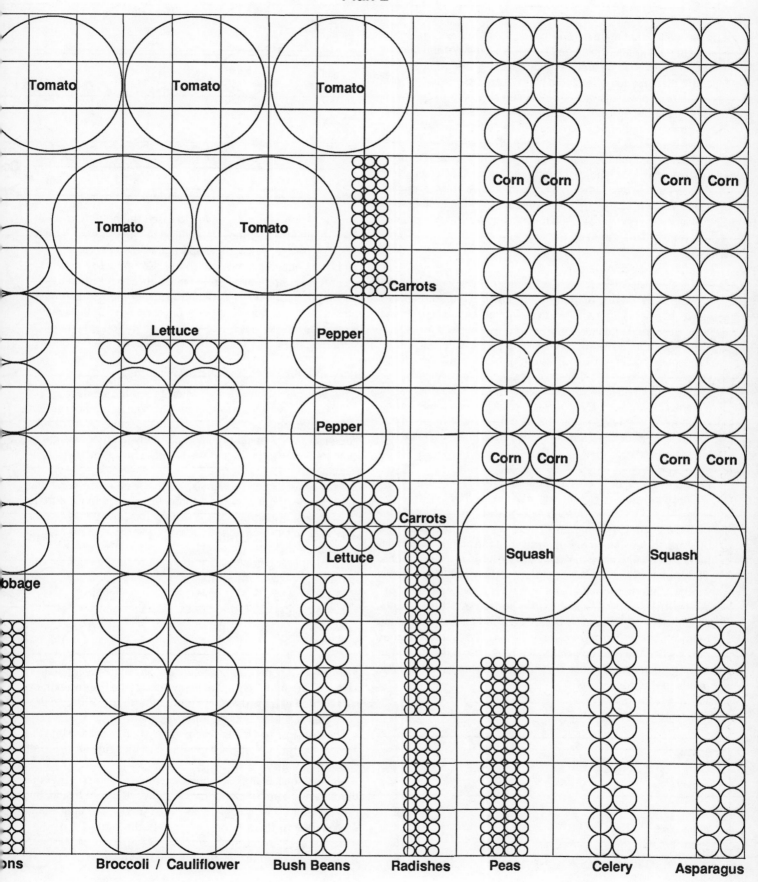

to plant and plant them in three types of gardens. The first is the straight row garden, shown on page 16. Keeping in mind that we have decided that five tomato plants are the minimum for our family, that we need at least thirty corn plants to provide us with a good taste of fresh sweet corn this summer, and that none of us is exceptionally fond of squash so two plants will be enough, let's draw those in first. Then we will see what is left. We need to leave a foot or foot and a half for path space between rows. Besides corn, tomatoes and squash, we want peppers, carrots, cabbages, broccoli and/or cauliflower, asparagus, celery, leaf lettuce, bush beans, radishes, peas and onions. I have arranged them as shown, although there are undoubtedly many other ways to fit all these vegetables in. You might try your hand at it for practice, remembering to keep the vegetables in rows.

Plan 2 — Wide-row Garden:

This time we will redesign the garden to incorporate the idea of wide rows — two or more rows side-by-side, and spaces between (page 17). When I put in the tomatoes and squash and get to the corn, I find I have more room so I can plant 40 instead of 30 — another couple of meals of corn for us, with luck. I leave the pepper plants at two, but the numbers for the rest of the varieties increase — in some cases, quite dramatically. For instance, I will have 48 carrots instead of 12 if I use this type of planting. Obviously, the vegetables that take the smallest growing space are the ones that can be increased most in numbers. Tomatoes cannot be adapted to wide rows; they are a wide row all by themselves.

Plan 3 — Block or Intensive Garden:

Here's where your creativity can take off. This time the vegetables are planted in solid blocks, with just enough space for us to get in between them. These may be in raised beds. If they are, they will be more uniform than the plan I have drawn here. This is only one of the many ways to arrange the vegetables. The point is to see how we can increase the yield. This time we can have another tomato plant — always a welcome addition. We get the same number of corn, squash and bean plants, actually reduce the number of cabbages and onions (we had too many onions in Plan 2 for our needs, and late cabbages can be put in when the peas come out), but otherwise raise the output of the garden considerably. Let's compare numbers of vegetable plants in the three plans:

Vegetable	Plan 1	Plan 2	Plan 3
Tomatoes	5	5	6
Corn	30	40	40
Peppers	2	2	3
Squash	2	2	2
Asparagus	20	20	36
Cabbages	3	5	3
Broccoli/Cauliflower	7	14	16
Celery	10	20	36

Vegetable	Plan 1	Plan 2	Plan 3
Leaf lettuce	14	18	36
Bush beans	20	24	24
Radishes	20	36	72
Peas	28	64	96
Carrots	12	48	96
Onions	40	80	72
Totals:	213	378	538

In simple numbers, we have increased the holding capacity of the garden by 2.5 times by planting in blocks rather than in rows. For people with limited space, the lesson is clear.

It is not quite that simple, of course. Cropping so intensively requires close attention to proper moisture and nutrition needs. I might have done better to plant in smaller blocks in an interspersed pattern to foil insect pests. But there are definite benefits besides increased yield. In this type of garden, plants often overlap, shading out weed growth and retaining soil moisture.

PLANNING WHEN TO PLANT

You will next want to know when to put the seeds in.

There is no use trying to start seed in cold ground because it will not come up. You may want to take the temperature of your garden soil at various times and find out when it does begin to show some warming. To start seeds earlier, plant them inside in containers.

Many experienced gardeners start at least some vegetable plants inside, but it may not be something you will want to do if you are just beginning. Flats of healthy transplants may be purchased at reliable nurseries. Growing your own from seed is explored in the next chapter.

Here is a list of varieties that many Northwest gardeners will start inside early in the spring:

Tomato	Pepper	Eggplant
Brassicas (broccoli, cauliflower, cabbage, etc.)		
Lettuce	Cucumber	Melon
Squash	Beans	Peas
Corn	Celery	

Tomatoes, peppers and eggplant are grown inside for at least a couple of months because in many areas of the Northwest there isn't a shred of hope that they would grow to maturity and produce fruit if started outside from seed.

The Brassicas and lettuce can perfectly well be seeded into the garden, but many Northwest growers start them inside, to go out as soon as the soil is ready.

Melons, squash and cucumbers need warm germinating conditions and there is better survival if they're begun inside, but they are difficult to transplant and need special handling. Many gardeners start them from seed right in the garden, too.

Beans, peas and corn are sometimes started, or at least germinated, inside to make sure the seed is viable.

Plan 3

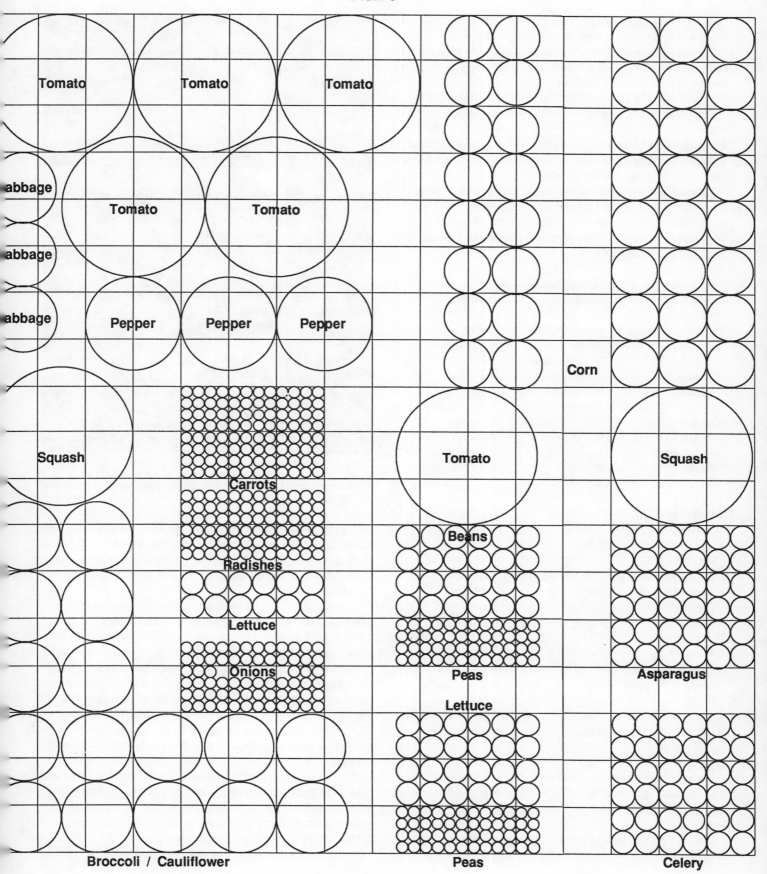

Celery is started inside because it needs a controlled environment and it doesn't do well in cold temperatures.

Of course, the more you start inside the more trouble it is, but if you have a warm place in the house, a greenhouse or greenhouse window, a coldframe, or a sunny windowsill, you have the essentials for getting your garden started early.

Except for lettuce, vegetable seed germination requires warmth rather than light. Use the top of a hot water heater, the top of a refrigerator, the back of a gas stove with the pilot light going, a place on the furnace, a radiator cover — any already warm place that can encourage seeds to sprout.

As soon as they are sprouted they must be moved to light — the sunny windowsill, the grow light, the greenhouse or the coldframe. They must be watered carefully, not be allowed to dry out, be moved to larger pots when they have gone beyond the seedling stage, and fertilized.

In general, plant the following seeds early:

broccoli	cauliflower	cabbage
endive	kohlrabi	kale
lettuce	onion (sets)	parsley
spinach	turnip	radishes
peas	Brussels sprouts	salsify
rutabaga	rhubarb	asparagus
garlic	horseradish	leek

Mid-spring seeds:

beets	carrots	parsnips
rutabagas	chard	onion (seed)
leeks	potato	mustard greens
endive	collards	

Late-spring seeds:

beans	corn	squash
cucumbers	melon	tomato

If you buy or raise transplants, put these out earliest:

broccoli	cauliflower	cabbage
lettuce	kohlrabi	kale
endive	parsley	spinach
peas		

Put these transplants or seeds out when the soil is warm — above 50 degrees F:

bean	corn	squash
cucumber	melon	eggplant
tomato	pepper	celery
lima bean	sweet potato	

If you order or buy your seed all at once it is very helpful to sort it according to what should be first planting, middle planting, and last planting; or what is started inside and what is started outside.

Once all of the above, or that part you have chosen to plant, is in the garden, you may not sit back and rest. In June you will

One strategy in intensive gardening is to plant late crops, such as cabbage, where early crops have been harvested, as Earl Chambers does in Penticton. Marigolds repel some insects and add color.

need to get another crop of lettuce in, and perhaps some late carrots and potatoes. Another row of beans may be useful now. Many gardeners like to make a last planting of corn at this time, as they can harvest from August up to frost-time by staggering the maturity dates.

In midsummer it is time to plant late cabbage, more lettuce, bok choy, fall cauliflower, Brussels sprouts, Chinese broccoli.

Some vegetables, like carrots and beets, are easy to harvest over a long period of time. You can thin as they grow and eat the tender thinnings. Lettuce, chard, spinach, kale, Chinese cabbage and other greens can be picked a leaf or two at a time. Broccoli produces one large head early and many small lateral clusters of buds for a long time after that, if it is not allowed to flower.

Other vegetables (corn, peas, beans) produce all at once, or for only a couple of weeks. Stretch the harvest time for these by planting one variety over several plantings, or by planting different varieties or cultivars which have "early," "mid-season," and "late" attached to their names or descriptions. For instance, there is 90-day early corn and there is 120-day late corn. You can plant both and have corn for a month from the 90-day variety and another month from the 120-day variety.

Planting the same variety of vegetable in several seedings is

not always successful, for the weather may sabotage your efforts. Cold temperatures may hold back the first crop and warm up just about the time you get your next one in. As a result they will mature at about the same time.

These are general hints only. In some of the Northwest regions where it is cold until late and warms up swiftly, it is hard to get such things as spinach to do well in the quick spring. Better plant in the fall, in a place set aside for it. If it gains a height of 3-4 inches by hard frost, and is well mulched, it should winter over and come up first thing after spring thaw.

HOW TO PLANT
Intensive planting
Companion planting
Succession planting
Rotation

Do not plant if the soil is soggy or too cold. If you are impatient, use black plastic mulch, transparent polypropylene (which heats the soil even better but also encourages weed seeds to grow under it), or make raised beds.

Seed packets and catalogs have the planting information you need. Follow the directions. In general, plant four times the diameter of the seed. Lettuce and carrots do better with a light soil and little covering.

Some Northwest gardeners with heavy or coarse native soil make a furrow in the soil and sift a layer of very fine compost or peat along the row. The seed is sown in the fine planting medium, which gives it a more luxurious start in life, and by the time the seedlings get to the regular stuff they will be vigorous enough to handle it.

Some advisors will have it that you slow down germination of larger seeds by putting the wrong end up. Should beans, for example, be planted with the little "eye" up or down? It should be easy enough to figure out that Nature has not usually arranged for seeds to fall from plants with the same side always up. Nor have seed scientists developed cultivars with seeds that have a strong urge to be planted one way. We have enough things to think about without arranging each tiny seed head-up in its row, even if it had a head.

While we are debunking, we may as well look at the old advice about soaking seed. It has long been thought possible to hurry up beans, corn and peas, in particular, by soaking them over-night or for a day before planting, so they are full of water for their early germination. Lately, scientists have found that this may weaken the embryo and promote fungal growth.

But people always knew that. Here is an old English saying:
This rule in gardening ne'er forget,
   To sow dry and set wet.''

Let us suppose that "dry" here may be a relative, not absolute, term. Considering English weather we can be quite sure of it. Seeds will do better in a very lightly damp soil than in a soggy one. "Set wet" refers to transplants, which have not grown their roots well into the soil yet and need plenty of water.

So. The soil is warm, slightly moist, thoroughly mixed with whatever organic matter and soil amendments you put in it many weeks ago and possibly with a general vegetable fertilizer, and smoothed out with no large lumps in the way. If you have chosen to plant in rows it is pleasant to have them straight and an even distance apart at head and foot. Score the handle of your rake or hoe in one-foot increments, so you can lay it down and measure both ends of each row from the row before.

Or make a row measure or planting board from some light-

Squash, cabbage, potato, broccoli and beet leaves overlap in the raised beds of the Marysville Demonstration Garden. Such dense cover gives weeds little chance to grow.

weight lumber. Or put small stakes at each end and run string down the length of the row to keep it straight.

Check your seed packets to find out how deep the furrow should be and run your hoe — regular or Warren-style — down the length of the string to that depth. Don't plant deeper than suggested, but in heavy soils plant a little less deep. If you have put black plastic out, make holes or slits where necessary and proceed in the regular manner. Drop your seeds in carefully at the recommended spacing — here again you could use your homemade planting measure if you have added small dents to show the inches. Cover gently and push down firmly with your hand or the back of the hoe. Very fine seeds can benefit from a sifting of pure, fine peat or compost over them.

If you are planting wide rows or intensively, you can use a stick or dibble and make small holes where each seed should go, or you can scatter-sow fine seed, as with carrots, broadcasting the seed over the entire area designated "carrots" on your plan with no attempt to follow a pattern. Pat the soil down and make a firm bed before sowing, and reserve fine soil or compost to cover the seed lightly, again patting down. The carrots (or lettuce or whatever) will need to be thinned after a time, so be prepared for that (it isn't always easy, you know, rooting out tender little seedlings).

Intensive Planting

We have talked about the intensive, raised-bed method of gardening, but let's give it a little more attention. You are planting seeds or transplants closer together than is normally recommended. For this to work, you must have very well fertilized soil to start with and plan to feed the plants as they grow, because they cannot reach out in the rooting zone without running into a neighbor. Watch the irrigation needs carefully too until the plants have reached full size. At that point they shade out weeds and sun that would dry the soil, and may take a good deal less watering than if they were planted in rows.

Intensive planting lets you grow more in less space because you have supplied plenty of water and extra-rich soil, and you are not walking around the plants, stomping down the earth over the roots.

Companion Planting

Planting things together that are supposed to be friendly is called companion planting, but we can also call it planting for the best use of space, or *interplanting*.

A good example of a type of companion planting that has been practiced for many years (attributed to the American Indian) is putting beans with corn. The beans supply the corn with nitrogen and the corn stalks supply the beans with support. There is a clear advantage to this association if the corn does not shade out the beans or the beans do not choke the corn.

Another useful twosome is lettuce tucked in between tomato plants, because lettuce grows well in cool, semi-shady spots. There is no benefit to the tomatoes from this association, but no harm either, and you get two vegetables for the space of one.

Squash in corn will work well if the squash is given room at the edges to twine about and collect sunshine.

Onions, garlic, chives and the like are said to be repellent to insects in general, and small sections of these planted throughout the garden benefit those varieties subject to insect infestation.

Marigolds repel some insects and can be used to edge the garden or to interplant. You have the added color and can use the cut flowers. Nasturtiums tend to attract aphids, and some people grow them amongst the vegetables, but do you want aphid-infested flowers? And don't the aphids just breed more with such encouragement?

Sunflowers can be grown against a wall or a fence; they can use some support as they get large, and cucumbers can be planted between them to twine up both fence and stalks. Neither actually benefits the other, but they are compatible, and you get the cucumbers up out of the way.

To get a late-season crop of Chinese cabbages, beets or lettuce in a very hot region, start them in midsummer between already growing rows or beds of early bush beans, where they will be well shaded during early growth. Once the beans are finished producing and you have pulled them out, the other vegetables are ready to bounce up.

Radish seeds may be planted with any slow-germinating crop (carrots, for instance — which are not only slow, their tiny filiform foliage can hardly be seen for the first days) to mark the place

Wide-row planting, a space-saving technique, works well with cabbages and onions in the Marysville Demonstration Garden.

of the slow-grower, so it doesn't get hoed up with the weeds.

It is notable that not one of the Northwest gardeners interviewed for this book had any strong feelings about some vegetable's particular affinity for any other. Although they all admitted a readiness to keep an open mind, they had not noticed much neighborhood bickering amongst their vegetables.

Other examples of companion planting or interplanting are: deep-rooted with shallow-rooted varieties, heavy feeders with soil builders *(Leguminosae)*, long growing-season varieties with short, wide with narrow plants.

Succession Planting

Keeping your beds producing at their top capacity will require succession or relay planting, but this is not always possible. Short-season gardeners in particular are limited in their use of this method.

Succession planting is keeping something in every space of your garden for the whole growing season. Once the first planting of lettuce is out, something in the nursery bed or greenhouse is ready to replace it, like Brussels sprouts. You may even have set the Brussels sprouts transplants out before the lettuce was finished, to give them an extra few days — and since Brussels sprouts don't mind a little shade they will do well.

Between the old crop and the new one you need a short session in reconstituting the soil, cleaning away old debris and fertilizing again. If you've put the successional crop in before the earlier one was finished, it is particularly useful to have manure tea or liquid fish fertilizer handy to keep the later plants moving along strongly.

Bill Stevens of Baker, Oregon, visits neighbor Opal White's garden. Bill keeps his own planting beds small and scattered for easier wheelchair access.
(Maurice Mitchell, OSU Extension Service)

Rotation

Although in very small gardens it is of doubtful use, in most medium and large gardens it is beneficial to rotate or change the places you put your kinds of vegetables from year to year.

For the purpose of rotation, it helps to know what family your vegetables belong in. Appendix B groups vegetables by family, giving Latin names and origin. *Brassica* is a large family of northern Europe, for instance, to which cabbages, cauliflowers, broccolis, kohlrabis and Brussels sprouts belong. It will do no good to go from cabbages to cauliflower, therefore, because they are closely related plants, subject to the same difficulties. Try carrots or beets instead.

Another thing to consider is that root crops take heavy doses of potassium from the soil and leaf crops take the nitrogen.

Remember too that the *Leguminosae*, or pea family members, have a beneficial association with a genus of bacteria known as *Rhizobium*. These bacteria convert atmospheric nitrogen to a more useful form for plants when they are associated with the roots of these pea family members. Together, the pea (or bean) plant and the nitrogen-fixing bacteria create nitrogen in the soil — a very helpful activity. It would follow, then, that growing corn in a place recently vacated by peas or beans would be logical, since corn needs a lot of nitrogen.

Potatoes will not do well in soils with a high pH. Beets, carrots, celery, leeks, spinach, lettuce, onions, cauliflower, endive, cantaloupe, parsnips and salsify will not do well in soils with a low pH. If your garden soil has a tendency to be acid and you add lime occasionally, it would make sense to do this in sections, one section each year, growing the potatoes in an unlimed section, the above-named vegetables in the most recently limed section, and the rest somewhere in between. In an alkaline soil, where you are adding sulfur, reverse the procedure.

There are many things to consider in rotation, yet few gardeners spend a lot of time worrying about it. If the garden is well fertilized and composted over the winter, you will easily smooth out the highs and lows of acidity and nutrients that have developed over a season of growing. Another thing, gardeners are always trying to improve things. They aren't likely to keep planting the same things in the same places each year for no good reason.

Last, I have met several excellent gardeners who have built permanent structures for such crops as peas, beans and tomatoes. Year after year the same thing goes in the same place, yet the yield does not suffer. And all perennial inhabitants of the garden, such as asparagus and rhubarb, stay right where they are.

Table 3-1. Distances to Thin Between Plants

Vegetable	Distance Between Plants	Vegetable	Distance Between Plants
Beans	4-5"	Lettuce	12"
Beets	3"	Onions	3"
Broccoli	16"	Parsnips	3"
Cabbage	16"	Radishes	3"
Carrots	2"	Spinach	7"
Corn	8-12"	Turnips	3"
Kohlrabi	8"		

Table 3-2. Approximate high, low and optimum temperatures for germination of vegetables:

Vegetable	Low	Optimum	High
Asparagus	50	75	95
Beans	60	85	95
Beets	45	85	95
Broccoli, Brussels Sprouts, Cabbage	50	80	90
Carrots	45	80	95
Cauliflower	50	85	90
Celery	50	70	75
Chard	45	75	85
Chinese cabbage	45	75	95
Corn	55	85	95
Cucumber	65	85	95
Eggplant	65	85	95
Endive	45	75	80
Kale	50	85	90
Lettuce	45	75	80
Muskmelon (cantaloupe)	65	95	100
Onion	45	85	95
Parsley	45	85	90
Parsnip	50	70	85
Pea	45	75	85
Pepper	65	85	95
Pumpkin, squash	60	90	95
Radish	50	85	95
Spinach	45	75	80
Tomato	60	85	90
Turnip	45	85	95
Watermelon	75	90	105

CHAPTER IV

Climate Modification

Extending the growing season from winter to winter;
starting your own seeds; greenhouses and coldframes;
cloches, tunnels and plastic mulches; special methods

"Difficulties are things that show what men are." —Epictetus

"When you get down to it, as sooner or later you must, gardening is a long-drawn-out war of attrition against the elements. . ."
—Alan Melville

WINTER TO WINTER

Some folks like to take the winter off. Winter gardening is not for them.

Others see that new methods of growing and new varieties of vegetables make it possible to have year-around home-grown produce, one way or another.

It is getting easier and easier to do something besides talk about the weather. New products and new methods for early starting and late harvesting pop up regularly. Horticultural scientists are breeding so many new varieties to suit cold climates, it is hard to keep up with them.

Even without a lot of paraphernalia and manipulation, it is quite possible for some enterprising Northwest gardeners to harvest new greens by February or early March, and other greens and root crops well into December. That's gardening from the end of one winter to the beginning of the next. For those who live in the maritime or coastal parts of the Northwest, there is year-around gardening, as Binda Colebrook[1] and others have demonstrated.

If you are not a winter gardener at heart, please excuse us. The enthusiasm some of us have for season-lengthening strategies is not to be construed as a criticism.

But if you are the type who would get a kick out of producing

[1]*Winter Gardening*

vegetables long before and after your neighbors do, or you simply see the practicality of getting at least some produce from your garden all year around, there are many methods, small and large, for achieving that aim.

First, though, it would be a good idea to determine what kind of weather you want to change. Appendix A, page 139, gives you some climatological statistics for your general area. As you well know, climates differ from valley to valley, block to block, yard to yard, and you can learn a lot by keeping your own records over a period of time. One year will not give you a representative sample, but if you are committed to this gardening habit for an indefinite stretch of the future, a couple or three years can be enough to indicate what your own weather might do.

An idea that comes from North Carolina might be useful, especially if you belong to a gardening group. Organize a group of volunteers to keep a year's weather records around your area. Each observer needs a calibrated maximum/minimum thermometer, a V-type plastic rain gauge, data sheets, a notebook or journal to keep records in, and a central data-gathering point. Each observer reports daily max/min air temperatures, precipitation, general conditions (e.g., sun, wind, type of clouds) at time of observation. A soil thermometer for observing soil temperatures is also a good idea. A newsletter provides each one in the group with current detailed weather information for the area. This might be coordinated through the county extension or local government agency, but the work should be done by trained volunteers.

When you know your weather conditions, you can decide what to do about them. Even in very cold winter spots it is possible to grow a basic variety of vegetables. Many of the oriental vegetables grow in chilly temperatures. Cabbages, kohlrabi, kale,

A greenhouse may be a simple walk-in box with a plastic cover, a glass house with heating and cooling systems, or anything between. Any greenhouse needs vents to let out excess heat on hot days.

collards — lots of fresh greens can be grown in the open or with a simple cover. Root crops can be held in the ground for months if a thick mulch is put on to discourage deep freezing.

Winds can be ameliorated, sun's rays can be enhanced, soil can be warmed under plastic and snow and rain can be kept off with covers.

STARTING YOUR OWN SEEDS

Taking charge of your plants from seed onward gives you the flexibility of having your transplants for the garden when you want them, not when the nurseries begin to get them out on the sales rack. Growing your own transplants can lengthen your growing season by one or two months at the least. You can also choose the kind of seed you want.

Be practical, though. If you have no facilities other than a sunny windowsill for your nursery, you must not attempt to plant numerous large flats of seed, for where will they all go? Usually you will start the seed in something small and once they get going, "prick them out" as the English garden writers say, and

transplant them to something larger where they can maintain healthy growth until the time comes to get them outside.

There are suggestions from invidual gardeners in Section II of this book about when and how to start seed. Here we will keep the discussion general.

Getting Organized

If you have to wait for the grocery stores and nurseries, you may not get the kind of plant you want when you want it. A few nurseries are now beginning to recognize the need for late plants to put in autumn gardens. Large garden stores in high population regions, or where there are enough sophisticated gardeners to create a demand, will have off-season transplants.

If you order seed, wait until all of it has arrived—or if you buy locally, gather the whole stack together at the same time. Sort them out. What will be started inside? Anything that will not mature from outside planting (tomatoes, peppers, celery, eggplant, for example). Anything that needs special attention to germination (cucumbers, ultra-sweet corn). Anything you want very early (lettuce, cabbage).

Now you have a stack of seed packages for inside starting and one for starting in the garden. Divide them for time you want them to be growing inside. Few plants do well through months of inside growing. The young and vigorous *Brassicas* of March will be the discouraged and bedraggled *Brassicas* of May if left in flats that long. On the other hand, tomatoes enjoy a long, warm stay inside, and benefit from repotting.

Your packets are now divided as to inside and outside starting, and arranged—perhaps marked with pencil—according to when they are to be planted. After you have used from the leaf lettuce packet for one sowing of early seed in a pot, put it into your outside seeding pile for later, and still later, if there is any left, for a second outside planting. Certain other vegetables can be treated the same: carrots, radishes and beets, for instance. The special varieties you have chosen for late planting, however, may be different from the earlier varieties of the same vegetable. Cabbages can be early or late, and have certain properties that make them desirable for use in one season but not the other.

Your seed packet piles have now been subdivided into early inside, mid-inside, late inside; early outside, mid-outside, late outside; and fall and winter seeds.

To use your sorted seed file effectively, you must determine your last spring frost date and your first fall frost date. This can be done approximately from the chart in Appendix A, or for more precise information, contact your county extension agent or weather service. Remember that whatever dates you are given, they are not guaranteed — they may be a couple of weeks off either way in any particular year. Figure out from your seed package how long you will want your young starts inside. If your last average frost date is April 15, you wish to grow cauliflower and want it inside no more than six weeks, start March 1. But tomatoes, which can be started at the same time or even earlier, do not go out until the ground is warmed up—so they will need a place inside until sometime in May in most places.

Just about the time you set the last eggplant out and put in the

last late corn seed, and think the planting chores are over, you will remember that you want some late kohlrabi, kale and Chinese broccoli. Start your seed inside again if you wish, but it is easier to put it in the garden in a special nursery area, preferably in a shaded spot so July heat doesn't discourage these cool-weather plants. After they are up and going, carefully transplant them to a spot where you will leave them for fall and winter harvest. This is a good time to practice interplanting, setting them in the burgeoning pea patch, for instance, where they will be shaded for their young life and given space when the pea plants come out.

Where to get seed

Choose your varieties carefully, very consciously. Not all seed is the same. Take the time to read the seed packets in the store or in the catalog, if you are not familiar with the available stock.

There are seed racks in nearly every kind of store in town during the spring months. The seed packets should be marked as to the year for which the seeds were produced. Some seeds last for years but others don't, and it is best to get them fresh if you aren't sure. The companies are reputable, the seed is usually viable and there is no reason not to buy it where you find what you want.

The drawback to the grocery store seed racks is that you will not find a very large selection. The next step is to find a garden store that takes its seed selection very seriously. Most likely it will have an extensive display of many brands and varieties. Not every town in the Northwest has such a source of seed, however.

If you like a large selection of seed and the ease of ordering at home, there are the seed catalogs. I put it in the plural because one will not be enough. Each seed company features special varieties often not available from others. Some specialize in flowers, some in vegetables. Some specialize in Northwest varieties — an advantage to you because you will have fewer unsuitable choices, which in all reason should result in fewer failures. In Appendix C is a list of the seed companies recommended by our gardeners, with addresses. Request that your name be put on the catalog list and you will receive one — usually without charge — in plenty of time to make selections for the new season.

Some long-time gardeners have saved seed from such plants as tomatoes or beans. These strains have often been in the family for years, some of each summer's seed saved for the next. Generally they have no name and are not recognized as a variety by horticulturists, although lately a few companies are taking it upon themselves to collect and save some "heirloom" seeds that have had value to generations of gardeners. Where vegetable gardeners get together, there is often a chance to obtain someone's special, noncommercial seed. It may be just the thing for an area with particularly bad soil or difficult climate, but often is grown more for curiosity or sentiment than better productivity.

Seeding

Plant seeds are living organisms within a protective shell. The embryo is the actual plant in miniature and is supplied with enough nutrients to start it growing in the right conditions.

To start seed without soil — especially the larger seed such as squash, cucumber, bean, pea and corn — use plastic food containers or bags with wet paper towels. For smaller seed it is more convenient to plant in the medium it will grow in through the seedling stage. The best of these are actually soilless mixtures of sand, vermiculite and/or perlite, peat or sphagnum moss, and perhaps sterilized compost. Obtain commercial mixes at a nursery or garden store, or make your own. If you use your own garden soil, it should be sifted to a fine consistency and sterilized. Pour boiling water through it several times, or bake or fumigate it. Also sterilize the pots, if they have been used before.

Germination is dependent on other environmental factors, too: moisture, temperature, oxygen, and in some cases light.

Moisture: for most species, too much water in the germination stage is harmful — celery is the only vegetable that can tolerate wet soil. Tomatoes, on the other hand, can germinate in nearly dry soil. Very wet soil promotes fungal growth and damping off, especially in cool temperatures. Most seed does well in a lightly damp planting medium.

Temperature: optimum germination temperatures for garden vegetables were suggested in the last chapter. In general, better and faster germination can be obtained at the higher temperature ranges, although some of the cool-weather vegetables will eventually germinate even in quite low temperatures. Since you are trying to get a good start on the season, it is best to supply heat: around 75-80 degrees Fahrenheit if you can. Because heat is more important than light for most seed germination, gardeners are often quite inventive, using the hot spots in their homes (water heaters, furnaces, gas stoves).

Oxygen: a light planting medium with a good mix of inert material (e.g., sand, perlite or vermiculite, peat) and not too much water will insure proper oxygen.

Light: most vegetables will germinate in dark places. After all, they are planted underground. Lettuce seed needs a small amount of light and should not be planted deep. A wafer-thin layer of soil gently sifted over the seeds and patted down will be sufficient.

Damping Off: a generic name for several fungi which attack germinating seed. The seedling may not show up at all, or it becomes black around the stem and falls over. The best prevention is rapid growth of the seedling, promoted by light, proper heat, not too much moisture and good soil. The fungicide benomyl may be used at ½ tablespoon per gallon of water to soak your potting soil ahead of planting.

Seedling Growth

After germination, you need to get the seedlings into light if they aren't already. A windowsill with sun at least six hours a day is the minimum requirement. For the cloudier areas of the Northwest, where sun cannot be expected to shine in even the lightest of windows for most of the winter, artificial light is required in the form of fluorescent lights. These should be about 6 inches above the seedlings and left on at least 12 hours a day, preferably as much as 16 hours, but no more. Reflective material can be put

around the seedlings to enhance the amount of light available. Aluminum foil used under and behind the planters is one obvious aid.

Try to keep your plants at about 70 degrees during the day and 55-60 at night. This isn't always possible and in fact some gardeners don't mind offering a little less, even for tomatoes, as the practice turns out very sturdy and vigorous — if slightly slower-growing — transplants. But if the heat is reduced, guard against overwatering. Also, remember that too low a temperature will cause plants to stop growing entirely, and that is nothing short of disastrous.

What to Plant In

Start seedlings in quart milk cartons sliced in half lengthwise, or half-gallon cartons cut off short, cottage cheese cartons, frozen-food containers, sawed-off plastic fruit juice jugs, or any other throwaway container you find around the house. Punch holes in the bottom so water can drain out.

There is an array of commercial seedling pots available in the stores, too. Cucumbers, melons and squashes do not like transplanting and are best started in peat or pulp pots that can be put right into the soil without disturbing the roots. Tomatoes, peppers, eggplants, or any other plants which grow out from lateral and top branches — as opposed to those which grow from the base like cabbages — do well if moved from a flat to a larger pot, and even again before going into the garden. Each time they should be set in a trifle lower in the soil.

No plants like to be roughly handled. The nourishing root hairs, nearly invisible to you, are the active ingredients in the root balls, and can be easily damaged. For *Brassicas,* take the seedlings right after they have grown their first set of true leaves (not the first embryo leaves) and replant into larger containers where the roots can expand rapidly. Before they have filled the containers and stopped growing, they should be put out into the garden. Once they have stopped growing because they lack space and nutrients, you will have a hard time getting them going again and they likely will never be truly fine specimens.

This means that you will have to calculate when you want to get the plants into the garden so you can count back to the time for starting. It isn't necessarily true that the longer you grow some plants inside, the better. The cold-resistant ones need to be outside. Tomatoes, peppers and eggplants can stay in as long as you can give them enough soil and light. Unlike seeds, transplants appreciate a lot of water to start out, and some people like to give them a weak transplanting fertilizer to get them started. A very light solution with some phosphorus in it can be used for watering in the transplants. Handle transplants with care, holding them by their leaves, not their stems, fluffing out the roots, and firming the earth around them so there are no air pockets.

Fertilizing

Commercial nurseries often use a weak fertilizer solution for regular watering. You can do the same with a commercial liquid such as Grow or a fish emulsion, or you can provide a slow-release

Bushmans' Famous Homemade Potting Soil (see page 65 for ingredients) *is one key to Charles Bushman's spectacular success as an urban gardener in Portland.*

dry fertilizer in the soil. The main thing to avoid is too much nitrogen, as it will burn the seedlings. Some commercial seed-starting soils have no nutrients in them and must be amended just as soon as the plants are up and growing if you plan to leave them there.

Other commercial mixes have enough nutrients to get the plants started, but will not provide sufficient fertilizer for full transplant growth. Be sure to read the label if you buy one of these.

Ideally, your potting mix should be composed of non-soil ingredients like perlite, sand, peat moss, sphagnum moss, vermiculite, sterilized compost or commercial manure. You can get a commercial mix, as discussed above.

Watering: Seedlings must be kept lightly but thoroughly moist. Do not drench. They must be started and grown in material that drains well — poor drainage causes most seedling failure. Top watering is likely to beat them down no matter how careful you are. One way to avoid this is by setting the containers in shallow trays which will hold water. Plastic meat containers, if cleaned, are good for this job. Keep a close eye on the pots to make sure enough water is being drawn up into the soil to keep the root zones damp but not soggy.

Other ways of keeping your seedlings moist: use a wick, obtainable at garden stores, one end threaded through the bottom hole of the pot and into the soil, the other end in a pot of water; set pots in larger pots with peat, vermiculite or other absorbent material surrounding the inner pot.

Hardening Off: Before setting out the transplants, give them a few days of hardening off. This means getting them used to outside conditions. Set them in a shaded, protected place, let them dry out slightly, be sure they are brought in if it looks like frost, and in a few days you should have hardy transplants that can take all the sun, wind, rain and temperature changes the real world has to offer them.

GREENHOUSES

Greenhouses work by admitting the short-wave or ultraviolet rays of the sun, absorbing these in the soil and other surfaces as heat, and radiating back long-wave infrared (or heat) rays which do not get through the plastic, fiberglass or glass so easily.

We won't take up greenhouse construction here. Eventually you may want a greenhouse, and that is the time to investigate plans and ready-made greenhouses.

A greenhouse may be the simplest polyethylene-covered walk-in box, or an automatically cooled and warmed glass house ordered from and installed by a manufacturer.

There are some things to think about, though. A greenhouse attached to the house can often give two-way benefits: the house will be warmed by the air from a greenhouse attached to a south wall, and the greenhouse will need less insulation and heating when backed up against an insulated house.

Most people need only very small greenhouses. Many transplants can be raised in something no larger than 6x8 feet or even less. Those gardeners who plan to grow tomatoes, cucumbers, melons and peppers inside the greenhouse will want a larger space. Even so, staking and training the vining plants up along the walls will allow maximum use of a small area.

A "pit" greenhouse can be built which gives good protection and insulation by being set in the ground. A hole as deep as 4 feet and 6 or 8 feet long by 1.5 to 2 feet wide can be dug and lined with cement. The north wall should be solid and well insulated, with a heat-absorbing material or a reflective surface — depending upon whether heat or light is more important to you. The double plastic, fiberglass or glass south-sloping roof (about a 45-degree angle) will sit only about two feet above ground at the highest point, so the entire structure is well protected from the weather. Vents have to be constructed in the side walls to allow for heat escape during hot days, and access is through one side.

In any greenhouse it is important to keep heating costs to a minimum. There is little reason at this latitude to have a greenhouse with a transparent north wall or roof. It's more important to use the area for insulation and heat retention or reflection. A single-wall construction can be made double with one of the insulation materials available from seed companies and nursery supply houses. A bubble-textured material can be attached to the inside of the roof and walls to help prevent heat loss. The good ones will cut heat loss by as much as 50 percent, and light loss by only 10 or 15 percent.

Plants do very well, it has recently been learned, in a greenhouse kept to 60 degrees F. until late evening (11 p.m.), then dropped to 45 degrees until just before sunrise, when the temperature is again raised. This is not only healthful for plants, it has a noticeable effect on the heating bill, but unless you plan to be in the greenhouse regularly at 11 p.m. and just before dawn, it would be wise to get a timer for your heater.

There are several methods of passive heating for a greenhouse: a rock wall at the back, large containers painted a dark color and filled with water, a mud pit in the floor, dark materials on the floor (old carpet for example), are common passive heating devices. There comes a point, however, where the heat collecting units take up so much space there isn't room for the plants they are supposed to heat. Some kind of balance has to be reached.

COLDFRAMES AND HOTBEDS

Coldframes

Coldframe is an inexact name for a small outdoor structure which can be used as a warm seed-starting spot in the spring and for growing cool-weather crops in the summer, especially in very hot areas where it is difficult to get late-season crops started in July. A plastic, fiberglass or glass cover is usually used, and for summer a screen can be installed.

Usually a coldframe is heated only by the sun. The cover keeps some of the heat from escaping at night. Black plastic can help absorb some heat during the day. Reflectors at the back can increase the light received. Black containers of water, or rocks or bricks, can help retain the heat.

The frame of the coldframe is usually wood, treated with a copper naphthenate solution. A coldframe will typically have a high north side, slanting east and west sides and a short front. The closer to the ground, the less heat will be lost. Piling soil up at the back or north side will protect and insulate it. Those partially below ground surface will be more efficient. They can be insulated around the walls and in the floor. Some coldframes are so large they might be called greenhouses; others are so small they are used for only a few plants at a time. They should be set in a sheltered sunny spot close enough to the house that you can keep an eye on them.

If a heavy frost threatens, it is well to have a thermal blanket, insulation or mulch to throw over the top of the coldframe. During warm, sunny days, open the cover to allow ventilation. It is easy to cook your plants in such a small area where there is no circulation of air. A thermometer (especially a maximum/minimum type) inside will help you monitor interior temperatures.

Hotbeds

A hotbed is a coldframe with heat. An elaborate hotbed can be built with a soil heating cable and automatic venting mechanisms, but for this you will need to have a source of electricity. A heating cable, which should have a thermostat for regulation, is placed beneath the bottom surface of the bed, or hot water can be piped through copper tubing laid along the floor. The heating source is usually placed beneath a protective layer of sand, which retains the heat well and keeps the bottoms of the pots away from the heating source. A layer of hardware cloth or mesh can be used with sand or growing medium shoveled in on top, so plants can be grown right in the soil rather than in containers set inside the hotbed.

Plain light bulbs within the frame can give enough heat to stave off temporary cold spells. In any hotbed where electricity is used, the wiring must be done properly and maintained regularly to avoid a short.

A temporary and rather easy way to heat a hotbed is to layer

Black plastic mulch warms the soil and retains heat in this Montana garden, thus extending a short growing season. Clear plastic is better for warming soil, but it lets in light that germinates weed seed.

fresh manure in the bottom a foot or more thick, then cover with regular soil to insulate. This hot manure will keep on composting and giving off heat for a spring and early summer start, but it doesn't come with built-in thermostat and it will need to be manually regulated and vented.

CLOCHES, TUNNELS AND PLASTIC MULCHES

A cloche (French for bell, for the glass bell jars that were used by French market gardeners to cover their plants) and a tunnel are just about the same thing. Anything portable that can go over a plant or several plants or a whole row is a cloche or a tunnel. A hot cap, plastic bottle with the bottom cut out, or any of the various homemade protectors used to keep out cold or augment natural heat, is a cloche or a tunnel. In some parts of the Northwest it is common to grow at least some tomatoes, pepper and such under or within a protective cover all summer.

Expert gardeners often use tunnels and various devices in their gardens, and you will find ideas that may be adapted to your own garden in Part II. A simple way to build a tunnel is to cut five-foot lengths of #9 wire and use these as hoops along a row of vegetables, stuck in at intervals of four feet or so. Two-mil polyethylene five feet wide can then be stretched along the row of hoops and held down with rocks, pieces of bent wire, or mounds of dirt.

Black plastic may be used directly on the ground as a mulch under the row cover to help warm the ground. Be sure to give your plants plenty of stem room if they are in black plastic — the sharp edges where it is cut can ruin a plant if there is any rubbing or friction on the stem.

For comparison, clear plastic will raise soil temperatures about 10 percent. Black plastic raises soil heat about 6 percent. Both mulches help retain heat during cool nights. Another benefit: they keep melons, squash and cucumbers up off the ground so they won't rot.

Black plastic mulch when used with a row cover has been found to increase yields of muskmelon in Alabama 61 to 72 percent. The melons also ripened two to three weeks earlier than those grown on bare soil. Needless to point out, this is very significant, even if you don't live in Alabama.

In Texas, tomatoes increased in stem diameter and numbers of fruit produced (not in weight of fruit, however) when grown with black plastic and a slitted plastic row cover.

On the other hand, black plastic mulch covering a cool soil and itself covered with sawdust, leaves or other insulating mulch, will keep the ground cool. This is good for cool-weather vegetables (lettuce, cabbage, etc.) in very hot climates.

Since the row cover is in place to ward off the extremes of cold it will not be suitable for very hot weather. You must be there to roll back the plastic or remove the cloche if the sun comes out strongly. Plastic may be slitted to allow air circulation, but you will lose some of the cold-air protection at the same time. Many plants cannot withstand temperatures over 100 degrees, and any of them will burn if crowded so the leaves or flowers touch the plastic. Cucumbers and squash, if covered, cannot bear fruit unless you uncover them or go to the trouble of pollinating them yourself.

A more rigid and permanent material for tunnels is the clear corrugated fiberglass material obtainable at lumber and building supply stores. See Ward Briggs's suggestions in Region 1, Part II.

New spun-bonded materials are available for row covers as well. Reemay, which is the name of a Dupont Company product, has been chosen as the generic term for spun-bonded coverings, but there are other names for similar products: Agryl and Agronet are two. These materials cut out more light than clear plastic, and are well suited to starting and growing leafy and cole crops, both because they can stand less light and because the fibrous material prevents invasion by the cabbage butterfly, the root maggot fly, and other pests. The covers are more expensive than plastic, of course.

The spun-bonded material allows good circulation of air and moisture and is very lightweight — all definite assets to consider. It also seems to offer marked protection from cold, frosty nights to plants growing beneath.

CONTAINER GARDENING

If you have a solarium, sun room, warm, sunny deck, or other protected spot, or live in the city with a lot of radiated heat around your doorstep, you may want to try year-around gardening in containers.

On the whole, the principle is the same and the varieties will be the same, although there are a few special varieties developed for container gardening, often called "baby" or miniature vegetables. You need to know what every gardener needs to know, but you will have less room for error. A necessity is a good, lightweight soil mix. You also need roomy containers, a way to keep the pots watered when you are away, and a place to put them

when the weather gets so bad (extremes of hot and cold) even your protected spot isn't protected enough.

Your soil mix will benefit from additions of compost, if you can find a place to make some. Otherwise, you will probably want to buy the ingredients: peat, vermiculite, perlite, sterilized steer manure and bone meal. If you want to grow tomatoes on your roof or a balcony or in window boxes, be sure the structure can hold the weight and use the lightest mix you can find.

Potted plants need more fertilizer than those in the garden, and a good all-around liquid fertilizer or manure tea should be applied every couple of weeks at least. In fact, if you keep the solution weak, you can give your plants a feeding every time you water them. If you don't like watching your liquid fertilizer running out the bottoms of the containers, you might try the slow-release

Earl Chambers uses an old lawn mower to wheel salad greens from one sunny spot to the next. Only a dedicated stay-at-home gardener could borrow this idea!

pellets, which are especially good for this kind of gardening. This kind of fertilizer costs more than most other kinds, but as the name implies, the benefits are long-lasting.

In general, conditions for potted vegetable plants are going to be more severe, and you will need to keep a wary eye out for problems. On the other hand, having such a limited space for a garden will encourage your close attention to details, and you'll notice quickly when something goes wrong.

If you construct your own planting boxes, they should be made of copper naphthenate-treated wood (most other wood preservatives are toxic to plants). You can buy this under the brand name of Cupranol at a hardware or lumber supply store. The boxes need not be larger than 8 or 10 inches deep if you aren't planning to put in parsnips or other long-rooted vegetables. Holes should be drilled in the bottom or along the bottom edges of the sides for adequate drainage.

Watering during hot summer months can be a severe problem for container gardeners. Even a large pot can dry out very quickly when many healthy, growing plants are drawing on the moisture

supply. Dig down beneath the surface of the soil to make sure your plants' roots are getting plenty of water — just because the top looks wet doesn't necessarily mean the root zone is. This is another reason to use a very light soil mix and avoid compaction.

SPECIAL METHODS AND SUGGESTIONS

- New super-hardy varieties of greens are being developed which can be cooked or eaten raw. Some of them will withstand very low temperatures.
- Make a protective wall around your tender plants by putting a black plastic backdrop on the north side, suspended between two poles.
- For starting cool-loving plants in summer, mulch the ground to keep it cool with newspaper (not with colored ink, however), brown cardboard, aluminum foil. Foil also increases amounts of light available to the leaves.
- A shelter for new transplants put out in summer can be made from small-mesh plastic hardware cloth or shade screen rolled into a cone and stapled to a wooden stake to stick into the ground.
- Make a compost ring by taking a five-foot section of chicken wire, or other kind of fencing, stake it in place, fill with good composting materials in layers with bone meal, manure, super-phosphate, and other good ingredients. When this is working, plant tomatoes around the outside of the wire, close enough to tie up the plants to the wire. The compost will give off heat early as it decomposes, and supply the plants with plenty of nutrients as they grow. This is also a good idea for gardeners with limited space.
- A strategy for tomatoes: large, flowering tomato plants grown in gallon containers are transplanted to a hole with a composting material underneath them. Dig the hole 14-16 inches deep, pack 6 inches of fresh grass clipping or hot manure into the bottom, put in a layer of soil and lay the tomato plant in with roots stretched out horizontally, the stem trimmed of its lower leaves and bent gently upwards, cushioned on a lip of soil so it doesn't break, and fill the hole with rich soil or compost. A mulch should be laid over the top to retain the heat. Surround the plant with plastic sheeting if you wish.
- Plants mulched in the fall to prevent freezing should have their mulch removed in the spring, as the mulch may prevent the soil from warming up.
- Check into the Walls-o-Water product of TerraCopia, Inc., Salt Lake City, available in many garden supply stores or through local gardening groups. According to the gardeners interviewed for this book, this is a truly revolutionary gadget for getting tomatoes, melons, cucumbers, peppers to produce in cold-night areas. (See photos on pages 32 and 123.)
- Cut off the blooming shoots of your tomatoes early in August if you expect frosts in early September. Small green tomatoes that will go nowhere take the plant's energies that should be devoted to producing the big red tomatoes set earlier.
- Seaweed or seaweed products are thought to encourage cold-hardiness in plants, besides supplying beneficial nutrients.
- In windy areas, make a temporary windbreak by stringing a

Walls-o-Water is an innovative way to extend the growing season in cold-night areas for sensitive plants such as melon and tomato. The water absorbs heat during the day and retains much of it through the night.

line between poles and clothespinning on a plastic sheet. Hold it down with rocks or a ridge of soil. Perforate or slit heavy plastic for this purpose, to let some air flow through.

- When planting a fall garden, put the transplants in a little deeper than you would in spring, to protect more of the plant from early frosts.
- Some varieties of vegetables respond quickly to pruning of blossoms and shoots by setting fruit faster, because you have convinced them that they may not get many chances to produce if they don't get busy.
- Corn in particular responds very well to added light which you can supply with reflective material on the ground, or to the north side of the rows.
- Raised beds warm faster in the spring (but might freeze faster in fall if not protected).
- If you garden on a slope, you might want to try building terraces — each level except the top one will have a protective and sun-catching step behind it (of soil, rocks, or whatever you choose), assuming the slope is toward and not away from the sun.

- Keep winter greens picked clean. Do not let lower leaves rot.
- Good vegetables for fall and winter gardens: kale, leeks, Jerusalem artichokes, salsify, corn salad, collards, horseradish, chives, onions and garlic, spinach, parsnips, Swiss chard, turnips, broccoli, cabbage, Chinese greens, beets, endive, cress, oriental radish; various herbs such as fennel, coriander, parsley.

Hydroponics

Hydroponics, or growing plants without soil, has certain benefits such as an absolutely controlled growing medium, but the hazards are considerable too. It is advertised as the way to avoid weeding, cultivating, watering or fertilizing. Weeding and cultivating should indeed be eliminated, but the water and fertilizer become a major concern for study. Not only are the ordinary fertilizers needed in precise quantities, all trace elements must be supplied as well, as there is no rich compost or organic soil to furnish them.

A grow medium is needed for the plant roots in any case; this will be sand, gravel, plastic particles, water, or even air. You supply the plant's nutritive needs with a solution flushed or circulated through the medium at regulated periods of time.

In general, a hydroponics grower will need a grow bed, a grow medium, a nutrient reservoir, a pump, a drain system and a timer. Commercial hydroponic fertilizer mixes can be purchased, complete with the essential 13 trace elements needed for plant growth. In addition you may want a microbe inoculant to control plant pathogens that tend to build up. All this should go in a permanent, well-lighted and protected place. Warmed water is beneficial to hydroponically grown plants and controlled air temperature is desirable. Night temperatures should be 10-20 degrees F. lower than day. If this sounds like the description of a greenhouse to you, you are probably right, although a fairly simple hydroponics system could be fitted into a coldframe.

If you decide to try hydroponics, there are several good books devoted to the subject which should be available from your library, and suppliers advertise in gardening magazines. So far, the practice of growing vegetables hydroponically is not common with Northwest home gardeners. None of our experts uses the method, perhaps because of the fussiness of detail and because traditional methods produce very acceptable results. Also, vegetables grown this way are certain to cost more.

CHAPTER V

Pests and Problems

Insects, diseases and cultural problems voted by our experts most likely to plague the Northwest gardener

"If there is a plant to grow, there is a bug to eat it."
— Elaine Porter

"Long live the weeds that overwhelm
My narrow vegetable realm;
The bitter rock, the barren soil
That force the son of man to toil; . . .
. . . With these I match my little wit
And earn the right to stand or sit." — Theodore Roethke

For all the scare literature on bugs and diseases, the truth is that most problems in the garden are caused by poor cultural practices and can be cured by the adoption of good cultural practices.

Another fact to cheer you on: ninety percent of the insects in your garden are either of no concern because they aren't around long enough to cause problems, are controlled by other environmental factors, or are beneficial. That leaves only ten percent for you to sit up nights worrying over.

Some insects are positively saintly: lacewings, with the pretty see-through green wings, eat aphids. The syrphid fly (a fly that colors itself like a bee) has larvae that eat aphids. Ground beetles eat any number of soil insects. We all know about the bee, the ladybug and the praying mantis, and whether we like them or not, spiders also help us out. If you have toads about, the best thing to do is encourage them by providing them with cool, damp hiding places — overturned clay pots and a little water might do — because they eat literally thousands of insects over the summer. The same can be said for snakes. And they eat slugs as well.

Nevertheless, there are still at least fifty major insect pests in Northwest gardens, and that is no small matter.

The easiest way to cut down on garden pests and problems is to provide a sunny spot with good soil and drainage and plenty of nutrients, keep the garden clean, leave space for air circulation, water plant roots deeply, and observe growth patterns carefully so you spot problems early before they have a chance to spread. Pull out and throw away (not on the compost pile) any clearly diseased plant.

Like people, plants generally succumb to an attack of a virus, bug or bacteria when they are weakest. Vigorous, healthy plants can easily ward off most of these sneaky attempts on their lives.

Since plant scientists have spent a lot of time and energy developing disease-resistant varieties for your area, you may as well take advantage of them. Catalogs give information on this aspect of their vegetables, and if you or a neighbor or friend are having a problem with a certain type of vegetable, it is well worth changing varieties to see what benefits ensue.

A few words about pesticides: all of them are toxic, even the so-called organic ones such as rotenone, which is a substance produced in the roots of certain tropical legumes. Insecticidal soaps, while on the whole one of the safest of substances, still will damage young plants on occasion, and kill beneficial insects along with the harmful ones. All pesticides must always be used with extreme caution, and on only the particular plants they are meant for, in the amounts recommended by the manufacturer. Most expert gardeners prefer *not* to use them, but when they are up against the wall, so to speak, they are happy to have something to help them out.

One bright spot on the pesticide horizon is a concentration of bacterial spores called *Bacillus thuringiensis* or Bt. Commercially it is sold under such names as Dipel, Biotrol, Thuricide, and others. It attacks moth and butterfly larvae, such as the cabbage

moth, and the potato beetle. It seems to have no effect whatsoever on mammals, birds, fish, reptiles, amphibians, or earthworms.

Growing marigolds, onions, garlic and pyrethrum daisies, or interplanting vegetables to confuse pests, the use of diatomaceous earth, cayenne pepper, ginger or mint leaves, wood ashes, paper or cardboard collars around transplants, a judicious use of row covers, sucking up insects from plant leaves with a small battery-operated vacuum cleaner — these are a few other harmless and often effective strategies for discouraging insects. It has even been suggested that a plastic mulch of sky-blue will confuse insects, possibly causing them to think they are headed for the sky instead of the ground. The reflected light from aluminum foil mulch sends aphids and flea beetles into confusion, and is also said to discourage squash bugs.

A small population of unwelcome guests in the garden does not spell disaster. If your tomatoes aren't quite perfect and an earwig ate off a few kernels of corn, don't despair.

Most gardeners learn early to put up with these nuisances. We have become so accustomed to having picture-perfect produce at the supermarket, we have put out of our minds just how it got that way. Often the varieties are not the tastiest, but are grown because they are the prettiest. There are no blemishes on them because they have been thoroughly and regularly dosed with pesticides — some of which undoubtedly get through to us when we eat them. This is one of the prime reasons why people decide to grow their own — so they can have blemished, chewed and misshapen but blessedly unpoisoned food.

INSECTS

Insects can be divided into those that attack leaves, stems and fruits, and those that attack roots; pesticides include rotenone, diazinon, malathion, Sevin, *Bacillus thuringiensis*, methoxychlor, endosolfan, chlorpyrifos and dicofol.

Bees, so important to the pollenation of many flowers, must be protected from insecticides. Sevin, diazinon, malathion, and Chlorban (chlorpyrifos) should not be applied on blooming plants. Endosulfan and methoxychlor can be applied when bees are not out, in late evening or early morning, if plants are blooming. Kelthane (dicofol), rotenone, and Bt can be applied any time.

Root Insects

Garden Symphylan: an arthropod of the same general family as the centipede and the sowbug, about ¼ " long, white, with 6-12 pairs of legs depending upon maturity, usually found in the warmest part of the soil, the first 6-8 inches. Do not like light. Feed on root hairs and cause stunting, wilting and death to plants. Look for small holes in below-ground plant parts. Thrive in moist, rich humus areas in cultivated fields, hatch in spring and greatly increase in numbers during the summer. The most troublesome spots in the Northwest are the Willamette Valley, around Portland, Oregon, and Vancouver, Washington, and in Lewis County, Washington, but they can be found in sufficient quantities to be troublesome in many other places. They are also easily transferred from one place to another in soil or manures. They can

"If there's a plant to grow, there's a bug to eat it." In fact, only ten percent of insect species in Northwest gardens are pests, but that includes fifty major species.

be controlled with insecticide such as diazinon, but will move down through the root zone to avoid applications.

Nematode: a very tiny worm found in most Northwest soils. Usually concentrated in one spot. If you have a vegetable doing well in one part of the garden and not in another, you may have nematodes. Avoid carrying soil from the infected spot to others. Marigolds may discourage but won't eliminate them.

Cutworm: (both under and above ground) grayish, curled-up worm a little less than an inch long, eats leaf vegetables, especially at night. Stays below soil surface during day, crawls up the plant to feed or attack underground parts. Handpick at night, with flashlight, or use Sevin.

Root maggot: less than ¼-inch white oval-shaped fly larvae, attacks roots of cabbage, broccoli, cauliflower, kohlrabi, radishes, rutabagas, turnips, and others. If a whole line of newly transplanted cabbages or their relatives promptly folds up, it is probably being attacked underground by the cabbage root maggot. Diazinon in the root zone when transplanting should stop them. *Bacillus thuringiensis* or a prepared parasitic culture available commercially are possible treatments of choice for organic gardeners. Where this is a real problem, the best solution is to use Reemay row covers at least until the plants have reached considerable growth. For winter gardeners, plant in the fall in coldframe, then set out in the garden in spring after they have reached a quite large size.

Onion maggot: attacks onions, garlic, leeks and shallots; larvae bore into the bulb and besides eating the bulb will cause rotting. Similar to its relative, the root maggot.

Onion thrip: larvae are pale green and wingless, attack leaves of onions, leaving them silver-striped; use diazinon, malathion.

Carrot rust fly maggot: threadlike, about ½ inch, attacks carrots, celery, parsnips. May be especially bad in winter crops of carrots. Wood ashes may help a little. Growing carrots under Reemay or netting will not be of much use in coastal areas as the material cuts out too much light. For those with more and

brighter sun, starting the carrots this way may be successful in keeping out the rust fly. Otherwise, use diazinon.

Sucking insects:

Aphid: comes in greens, grays, browns or blacks, tiny soft-bodied creature that likes the newest growth of plants. Aphids like many vegetables, including beans and broccoli, and will cause stunting and curling of the new growth. Carry viral diseases. Spray with a forceful stream of water from the hose, use insecticidal soap, malathion, diazinon, or endosulfan. They are also said to be attracted to the color yellow and a yellow bowl or pan filled with water can collect and drown them.

Mite: tiny but not quite invisible relative of spiders, which attacks peppers, tomatoes, eggplants in particular, during hot weather. Use dicofol (Kelthane) or better yet, catch early and spray them hard with the hose.

Leafhopper: wedge-shaped green and white insect that sucks the plant juices, and can carry viruses; especially likes beets, spinach, potatoes; can be attracted to red or orange-painted boards coated with a sticky substance such as Tanglefoot.

Squash bug: attacks squash plants; a rather large, darkish bug with an orange border, sucks sap from plant; can be handpicked from the plants rather easily after a rain, or after watering. Said to be repelled by horseradish or radish plants, and can be controlled with the use of Sevin.

Chewing insects:

Flea Beetle: little black jumpers hopping from leaf to leaf of potatoes, tomatoes, usually in early summer. Eggs hatch into larvae which make little tunnels in the skin of potatoes as they feed. Like leafhoppers, they can be caught on sticky orange or red boards set in the garden.

Potato beetle: black and yellow, red larvae; attack potatoes and tomatoes; remove by hand, destroy egg cases.

Blister beetle: large, soft-gray or black, found in beans and potatoes.

Corn earworm: moth larvae that eat into your corn, ruin young developing ears and chew away portions of mature ears. Mineral oil on the silks after they have turned brown may help; or try Sevin, diazinon or malathion.

Earwig: distinctive reddish-brown, shiny shell with pincers at the rear; feeds on various plants, may be found in corn; control with diazinon or Sevin.

Tomato hornworm: a large garden pest, strikingly marked, related to the corn earworm, is the larva of the large hummingbird or hawk moth; will attack tomatoes and eggplants voraciously; usually not numerous enough to get out the pesticide for — handpick or use Bt.

Wireworm: hard-shelled brownish larvae 1 inch, gets into potatoes, cabbages, etc. May be discouraged by use of marigolds (especially *Tagetes minuta*).

Weevil: Foliage and fruit attackers, cause holes, wilting, misshapen growth, can carry diseases.

Cabbage looper: pale yellowish green larva of a moth, "loops" itself along plant stalks, eats leaves, pea pods, etc. Use Bt or Sevin.

The tomato hornworm (above), *the larva of the hawk moth, is a voracious eater but big and easy to recognize, and it can be picked off by hand.*

Row covers keep out flying insects, as in the Marysville Demonstration Garden (below), but not all flying insects are pests. Bees, for one, are important pollinators.

Cucumber beetle: various types, yellow-striped or spotted, get on vine crops; often attack young shoots just out of the ground; later, wilting plant indicates that a bacterium has been introduced by the bug and it is too late to do anything about it. The beetle is attracted by the *cucurbitacin* content of the plant, hides out in old logs, vegetation until squash, cucumbers begin to emerge; use row cover, dust new plants with rotenone, or remove the bug by hand.

Cabbage worm: from white cabbage butterfly, green, matching the broccoli it likes to hide in; white eggs can be found on underside of leaves and picked off; will eat leaves of cabbage plant family members; pick off eggs and worms, use Bt.

Slug: not an insect, but has devastating effect on such vegetables as lettuce and tender young greens — voracious chewer, unmistakable in shape and size and slimy aspect. Eggs whitish or transparent small round balls in clusters. Raccoons,

Soil itself can be toxic, as in the "black alkalai" spots around Walla Walla where all soil is alkaline. The black, heavy in magnesium, looks rusty on the surface.

ducks, snakes, frogs and toads eat slugs; birds may eat the eggs. Dishes of beer sunk in the ground attract them, but make a mess; a plank or overturned melon or grapefruit rinds will attract them too, if you want them gathered for easy capture. Rough surfaces deter them from slithering across. See Pat Patterson in Region II for her remedy. Slug bait can be used if in covered or protected spots where birds and animals are not apt to taste it. Poisoning in early fall will get young slugs before they lay over-wintering eggs. Or you might take Alan Melville's advice in *Gnomes and Gardens* on how to get rid of snails and slugs: "Pick them up and throw them over the wall into the next garden."

Grasshopper: a real pest in a bad year, will work through a section of garden very quickly and move to the next; use commercial grasshopper bait, rotenone, Sevin, or diazinon; keep edges of garden weed-free.

Mexican bean beetle: found in some areas of the Northwest, very damaging yellowish beetle with black spots, lays eggs in June, produces small, soft yellow larvae with black hairs or spines; eats the leaf tissue and leaves the veins, or will attack stems and beans; use Sevin, malathion.

Leafminer: especially hard on spinach, chard and beets; the larva of a small gray fly; feeds on leaf tissue and makes winding, maplike paths over the leaves; control with diazinon if very serious.

Pea leaf weevil: usually attacks the young pea plants, causes notches in the leaves; not usually serious enough to spray on rapidly growing, healthy plants; can spray with methoxychlor or Sevin.

Pea weevil: attacks the pod itself, larvae hatch from eggs laid on the pea pods, burrow in and eat the peas; can dust with methoxychlor, Sevin, rotenone.

White fly: like bits of dandruff on leaves; the larvae chew at the leaves, leave a honeydew which encourages the growth of mold on the plant; especially in tomatoes, peppers and vines such as melons and cucumbers.

DISEASES

Diseases in plants may be caused by a fungus, a virus, or a bacterium (any or all). They generally show up as spots on leaves, discolorations, rotting, cankers or blisters, and misshapen plant parts. Diseases are usually encouraged by warm, humid weather, overwatering, bad air circulation and heavy soils. Besides correcting what you can of these conditions, your best bet for avoiding disease is rotation of crops to prevent a buildup of problems from one year to the next.

Fungicides such as benomyl, captan, or zineb can slow or stop a fungal attack, but there is very little to be done about bacterial and viral infections. If you suspect you have plants infected by one or the other, destroy them, and don't handle your healthy plants until you have washed your hands.

Viral diseases cause dwarfing, spots and streaks in the foliage, or unusual patterns, leaf curl and blistering.

Mildew: a powdery mold over leaves or on onion bulbs. Avoid watering plants late in the day, and do not work in the garden right after a rain.

Leaf spot: especially affects cucumbers, beets and tomatoes.

Rust: brown or orange spores, especially on asparagus.

Smut: black spores on leaves and stems of corn, onions.

Damping off: blackening and rotting around stems of new plants, causing death.

Black rot: in cabbages and cauliflowers, causes blackening of stems and leaf-veins.

Ring rot: spongy potatoes and yellowing leaves.

Root rot: especially in peas, vines are stunted, may dry up; roots are very small or nonexistent; avoid soggy spots in garden.

Club root: swollen roots on cabbages and other *Brassicas;* this is difficult to eradicate and may require that you do not grow these crops in infected areas for four or five years. Liming soil may help.

Potato blight: dry brown spots on leaves and stems of potatoes.

Bacterial blight: affects beans, peas, celery; causes brown spots, loss of leaves.

Verticillium, Fusarium wilts: especially on tomatoes and potatoes. Virus stays in soil and is not easily eradicated.

Plenty of ventilation, encouragement to fast growth, resistant varieties, and good luck in the weather are best prevention. Squash and melons also susceptible.

Pea wilt, Pea root rot: caused by *Fusarium,* a fungus of various forms which causes peas to wilt, become stunted and yellow. The vine with root rot has little root system and what is there is rotted and black. Rotation, well-drained soil, fast germination of seed and growing of the plant, and the swift destruction of all infected vines are the only measures possible. Some people have given up growing peas because of this problem. If you try various areas of the garden and still have it, you might consider a special pea-growing area with sterilized soil or compost and commercial soil

mix. Also, use the resistant varieties: Alaska, Perfection, Little Marvel with the letters WR (wilt resistant) attached, or Sounder, Grant, Conway, New Era, New Season.

Mosaic virus: affects cucumbers and other vine crops, beans, peppers. Yellowish patterns on leaves. Destroy affected plants immediately. Rotate.

Tobacco mosaic: infects tomatoes and potatoes; and can be carried into the garden in tobacco smoke or on the hands of a smoker.

NUTRITIONAL AND ENVIRONMENTAL PROBLEMS

Nutritional deficiencies: lack of nitrogen causes pale leaves, yellowing of leaves near bottom of plant, small foliage, stunted plant growth; lack of phosphorus causes slender, woody stems,

Deer have an appetite for cultivated growth that even animal lovers deplore. One sure way to keep deer out of the garden is to build a very tall fence.

stunted roots, purplish leaves or veins with yellowish mottled tissue and leaf margins, poor fruit or seed set; lack of potassium causes lower leaves to turn brown or rusty colored, stems are weak and base leaves are stunted or develop dead areas.

Other Nutritional Problems:

Retarded growth, growing tips die or dwindle, leaves may be distorted, root system stunted: possible lack of calcium.

Older leaves turn yellow or red between the veins, margins curl up, turn crisp, only newest leaves are left on plant: possible lack of magnesium.

Root crops are poorly developed and hollow, above-ground growth is stunted: possible lack of boron.

Black leaf margins, small new leaves, older leaves poor color: possible lack of sulfur.

Yellow leaves, possibly with green veins, stunted new growth: possible lack of iron.

Small, mottled new growth of leaves, weak growth: possible lack of zinc.

Environmental Problems

Leaf discoloration (yellow or purple) not caused by nutrient deficiencies: low temperature, too much lime, excessive watering, root diseases, insects or injuries.

Potato scab: encouraged by a high pH or excessive organic matter. Usually the youngest tubers are affected. Also found on beets, radishes and rutabagas. For prevention, a slightly acid soil is recommended, along with rotation and use of scab-resistant varieties such as: Nooksack, Russet Burbank, Netted Gem, Norgold and Red Norland.

Cold soil: no germination, transplants turn purplish and won't grow. Wait for ground to warm up; use black plastic to hurry it.

Bolting: especially in spinach, is caused by temperature ups and downs; pick out a slow-bolting variety.

Split cabbage heads: too much rain or watering, especially after a dry spell; or the heads are overmature.

Blossom-end rot, tomatoes: dark, rotted area at blossom end of tomato, caused by irregular watering or moisture stress; cause *may* be calcium deficiency in soil; spray with calcium chloride.

Cucumber bitterness: no one cultural practice can be found to produce this effect, although cool weather is thought to bring it about to some extent. The best way to avoid it is to use a variety which has been tested and found to produce no bitter fruit: Eversweet, Ashley, Sunnybrook, Saticoy Hybrid, or Lemon. Plenty of sun and water may also help to prevent this condition.

Fertilizer burn: leaves, plant parts turn brown, plant may die; too much nitrogen. Nothing to be done after damage shows up. Next time, follow directions more closely.

Overwatering: causes root rots, stunting of plants, mildews on leaves; soil is probably too heavy. Add organic matter, reduce watering regime if it isn't coming down from the sky.

Underwatering: causes stunting, early blossoming, wilting; if you have chrysanthemums in your garden they will act as indicators of underwatering by wilting before other plants show signs of distress. Be sure you are getting water deep into the roots of the plants.

Watery, low-sugar tomatoes: too much nitrogen.

Weeds

Weeds are garden pests because they compete with your vegetables for the nutrients and water available. They can also harbor insects and disease. How weed-free a garden is depends a lot upon the character and personality of the gardener. Many are content to keep the weeds out of the rows, without eradicating everything in sight. Weeds that are pulled out of the garden can add organic matter to the compost pile, and the deep-rooting kind bring up deep-buried nutrients. Some are even good to eat.

Weed seeds often last for many years. Every time you cultivate the soil you bring more seeds up within sprouting range. There have been many strategies for obtaining weed-free gardens, usually using thick layers of mulch, but you want to make sure your mulch is weed-free too. Some hays bring in more weeds than they eliminate. The same is true of manures. Sheep manure is said to be the only manure free from weed seeds because sheep digest their food more thoroughly.

Some weeds are annuals and seem to sprout everywhere at once. Others are perennials and creep gradually around the garden with underground runners. Dandelions are perhaps the most successful weed of all, having very deep roots for perennial success, even if two-thirds of the plant is hacked out, and producing a myriad of proliferating seeds over a long blooming season. (Nevertheless, remember that you can actually buy horticultural dandelion seed to raise as a green, and a very nutritious vegetable it is.)

A soil fumigant such as Vapam may be applied to the garden before planting and will destroy weed seeds and roots, but it will also kill earthworms and beneficial bacteria in the soil, so carefully weigh the advantages of such an approach to weeds.

Spray herbicides which are drawn into the vascular system of the plant through the leaves, such as Roundup, are popular and are reputed to have no long-lasting effect.

A way of sterilizing your soil before planting is solarization — a method for those with hot summer sun and a lot of time to fool around. By laying clear plastic over the garden area during the hottest weather, you may be able to raise the soil temperatures so high that over a six-week period all the weed seeds and pathogens will be cooked out.

Other

Moles: moles make rounded holes and eat grubs, worms and insects. The main runs are well below the surface, not the side branches you see in the yard or garden. Mice are often the real problem, not moles, because they use the runs and do feed on vegetables.

Gophers: make irregular mounds of soil at the side of the tunnel; have to be caught in gopher traps, not mole traps, as the gopher's way of digging is apt to spring a mole trap before it catches the gopher.

Mice: use the runways of gophers and moles and are often the culprits eating the roots of your vegetables.

Deer: noise, bags of blood meal, human hair, net bags with Irish Spring deodorant soap, wide plantings of marigolds, bands of chicken wire laid on the ground — all these and more have been used to keep the deer out of the vegetables. Some work better than others, but perhaps the surest way to eliminate the difficulty is to build a very tall fence and a stout gate with a good latch on it. The problem is worst for those who live near national forest land or woods and wildlands, and generally gives rise to ambivalent attitudes. The gardeners claim to be animal lovers. It is their eating habits which cause distress.

Rabbits, raccoons, opossum, birds: may help themselves to your choice fruits and vegetables. You might try encouraging golden eagles if you have a rabbit problem. Opossums and raccoons may do as much good as harm if they are eating slugs and slug eggs in the garden; otherwise you must trap. There are a few commercial products that drive away birds; cut out or buy a silhouette of a goshawk to perch on the fence or a nearby tree limb; use netting.

Conversion Table for Pesticides:

1 pint to 100 gallons = 1 teaspoon to 1 gallon

1 pound dry or wettable powder to 100 gallons = about 1 tablespoon to 1 gallon

800 parts per million = 1 teaspoon to 1 gallon

Pacific
Ocean

Vancouver

Strait of Georgia

MT. BAKER

Bellingham

Victoria

Skagit River

REGION I

Arlington

Marysville

Edmonds

Seattle

Puget Sound

Tacoma

Olympia

Cascade Range

Yelm

MT. RAINIER

MT. ST. HELENS

MT. ADAMS

OLYMPIC MTNS.

Penticton

Osoyoos

Oroville

Okanogan

REGION IV

Okanogan River

OKANOGAN
HIGHLANDS

Roosevelt Lake

Columbia River

Wenatchee
Dryden

Ephrata

Moses Lake

Ellensburg

Yakima

Yakima River

Washington

Spokane River

Spokane

REGION V

Snake River

REGION VI

Walla Walla

Umatilla

PURCELL MTNS.

REGION IX

Lake Pend
Oreille

Troy

Libby

CABINET MTNS.

Hayden

Coeur d'Alene

Coeur d'Alene
Lake

REGION IX

Kootenai River

Flathead Lake

Clark Fork River

Montana

Missoula

REGION IX

Lewiston

BITTERROOT MTNS.

Coast Range

Portland

MT. HOOD

REGION II

Corvallis

Willamette River

Florence

Eugene

Coos Bay

MT. JEFFERSON

THREE SISTERS

Redmond

Bend

Columbia River

Hermiston

Pendleton

Deschutes River

John Day River

OCHOCO MTNS.

BLUE MTNS.

WALLOWA MTNS.

Oregon

Burns

Malheur Lake

Salmon River

Snake River

Baker

REGION VII

Idaho

Boise

Nampa

SISKIYOU MTNS.

REGION III

Rogue River

Crater Lake

Upper Klamath
Lake

REGION VIII

HART MOUNTAIN

STEENS MOUNTAIN

Gold Beach

Medford

Ashland

Lakeview

THE EXPERTS

INTRODUCTION

You and I and just about everyone else know you don't plant radish seeds on a cement sidewalk or grow squashes in the forest. Tomatoes don't go under the cedar tree and corn doesn't like it in a swamp.

But from that point, many of us aren't so sure. Just where do radishes grow best? What edibles could you possibly plant in a forest, if that is where you live? If you want tomatoes in your front yard, how would you go about it?

Deciding to grow vegetables is something like taking home one of those cute puppies that somebody's appealing youngster is handing out at the door of a supermarket. The idea seems irresistible, but the responsibilities turn out to be overwhelming.

So you get a book and read about growing vegetables. But in vegetables, a little learning can be a dangerous thing. If the benefits of a tablespoon of nitrogen on a plant are unquestionable, what about putting on a cupful? If pruning tomatoes makes bigger fruit, what about pruning the peppers? If local gardeners usually keep a garden growing for four months, why not try for five or six? What about a greenhouse? And an underground automatic drip irrigation system with the water warmed to 75 degrees F? If digging the soil to a foot in depth is good, why not three feet? Or how about no soil at all?

It is after all another matter for common sense. Good gardeners seem to apply that ingredient in larger doses than any other one thing. If something doesn't work, try something else, they say. If you don't have the time to handpick the aphids from the broccoli, if the carrots aren't thinned, if the Brussels sprout while you're in Belgium and the beets green while you're floating the Snake River, all is not lost. There are still the onions and potatoes.

These vegetable-growers and their methods are presented as examples of what a gardener of a specific region might do to be successful. Some are city gardeners, some are rural; some are daring and innovative, some are conservative. The main point here is, what do they do when they go out there to get to work? What has experience taught them? What is there yet to be tried? What is new and useful, or old and still worth using? What is important to know about this climate, this soil, this place?

Of course gardeners possess diverse views, but they have one thing in common: they are practical. They do what works best for them. And what works best for them, in their particular gardens, may help you decide what will work best for you.

On the whole, these interviewees have earned their fine gardening reputations over long experience. Few gardeners rise as overnight sensations. Local gardening is an art and a lore and takes more than a season to learn. A serious mistake made one year can't be rectified until the next year. The wrong variety of corn, one day of soil moisture deficit, application of the wrong fertilizer, planting spinach in May or tomatoes in July — well, there is always next year.

A gardener learns patience.

Among the many virtues of these gardeners is their modesty. I doubt whether any of them would claim to be the best gardener in town. Every one of them wanted it known that he or she was "no expert," even though their gardens plainly belied their assertion. There are many other outstanding vegetable growers in the Northwest, they say.

So we won't claim they are anything but a select representation of the gardening populations of their areas. Still, their names are the ones that come up when one asks around for advice. And if they lived next door, they'd be delighted to help you out with very good advice on gardening, I know.

Read this section, then, for amusement and information, for hints and warnings, and for general garden wisdom, from people who could well be your neighbors.

REGION I

MT. BAKER

OLYMPIC MTNS.

Cascade Range

MT. RAINIER

MT. ST. HELENS

MT. ADAMS

Pacific Ocean

Coast Range

MT. HOOD

MT. JEFFERSON

THREE SISTERS

Willamette River

Deschutes River

John Day River

OCHOCO MTNS.

Crater Lake

Upper Klamath Lake

SISKIYOU MTNS.

Rogue River

Oregon

Washington

Idaho

Montana

Penticton

Osoyoos

Oroville

Okanogan

OKANOGAN HIGHLANDS

Okanogan River

Columbia River

Roosevelt Lake

Spokane River

Spokane

Coeur d'Alene

Coeur d'Alene Lake

Hayden

PURCELL MTNS.

Lake Pend Oreille

Troy   Libby

CABINET MTNS.

Kootenai River

Clark Fork River

Flathead Lake

Missoula

BITTERROOT MTNS.

Lewiston

Snake River

Walla Walla

Umatilla

Hermiston   Pendleton

BLUE MTNS.

WALLOWA MTNS.

Salmon River

Baker

Burns

Malheur Lake

HART MOUNTAIN

STEENS MOUNTAIN

Lakeview

Boise

Nampa

Vancouver

Bellingham

Victoria

Arlington

Marysville

Edmonds

Seattle

Tacoma

Olympia

Yelm

Strait of Georgia

Skagit River

Puget Sound

Wenatchee
Dryden

Ephrata

Moses Lake

Ellensburg

Yakima

Yakima River

Portland

Corvallis

Florence
Eugene

Redmond

Bend

Coos Bay

Gold Beach

Medford

Ashland

Columbia River

42

The North Coast

INTRODUCTION

The north coastal area is, for the purposes of this book, the land mass surrounding Puget Sound and the lower Strait of Georgia, with their islands. The terrain is thoroughly scoured, having suffered through several glacial advances. The last one, called the Vashon Glacier, pushed as far south as ten miles or so beyond Olympia, with plenty of glacial outwash extending farther than that. Most of the soils are thus made up of whatever the glaciers picked up, carried along and deposited. There is sometimes a top band of forest humus, if it has not been disturbed. The best soils can usually be found in river valleys, although their water tables are naturally high. At some depth or another, a hard layer of glacial till can often be found.

As to the infamous weather: over a fourteen-year record, Seattle-Tacoma received a yearly average of forty-eight percent of total possible sunshine. January has the least, at eighteen percent, and July the most at sixty-six percent. This is not a very high average: only Sault Ste. Marie, Michigan, and Pittsburgh, Pennsylvania, have forty-eight percent averages for the year, of the cities recorded. But statistics are only statistics, and that is not the whole story. This area receives more sun in July and August than Jacksonville, Florida, New Orleans, Louisiana, or Raleigh, North Carolina!

The rainfall averages not quite thirty-nine inches, almost exactly that of Washington, D.C. The highest precipitation is in December and the lowest in July. In other words, if you are a winter gardener your crops are going to get overwatered, and don't expect the famous Northwest rain to keep your garden watered in July or August.

Average yearly temperature is 51.1, with a high for July of 64.5 and a low in January of 38.2 (again, averaging daily Seattle temperatures over the month).

In this area, unless you live above one thousand feet, your average winter month temperatures will be well above freezing. That does not mean, however, that it will not freeze, as any experienced gardener can tell you. Indeed, it will freeze at unexpected and inopportune times, such as early April, just after you have set out new lettuce seedlings. Or mid-October, when you were thinking of bringing in the rest of the tomatoes to ripen.

Because the prevalent winter Pacific storm systems stretch over a broad area, temperatures differ little from south to north Puget Sound, from the coast to the lower-altitude inland. Only when retrograde airflows bring clear sub-Arctic temperatures from the interior, as they infrequently but still rather dependably do, will those who live closest to the main passes and valleys that connect the west side with the east side suffer markedly lower temperatures. This can happen in particular when cold air travels down the Fraser River and spreads into the Vancouver and Bellingham areas, or over Snoqualmie or Stevens passes into the upper Puget Sound valleys.

Fall gardens in this region do not succumb to frost so often as they dwindle in the shortening and graying days and increasing, chilling rains. The tomatoes and beans get late blight; the squash and cucumbers turn limp and scraggly from lack of sun.

At that point, the dedicated gardener does not throw in the trowel. It is the time to get something hardy planted for winter. Gardeners of the north coastal region, like those in the Willamette Valley, are learning to grow garden vegetables the year around, and that is an advantage that sets these regions apart from all of the others discussed in this book.

California it is not, but neither is it Minnesota. Binda Colebrook, in *Winter Gardening in the Maritime Northwest*, comments that northern Europeans have long been knowledge-

able about winter gardening, and have developed a tradition and a culture that could be useful to people here, as the climates are similar. Either their migrating relatives and descendants have forgotten this or they never knew it, for many people still use gardening methods better suited to the interior of the continent. Seed company catalogs and garden books, too, are predominately eastern and do not offer much advice for winter culture.

Referring to maritime climate opportunities for gardening, Steve Solomon *(Organic Gardening West of the Cascades)* says: "Twelves months of fresh vegetable harvest is possible most winters in most locations," and goes on to offer a veritable Ode to the Joy of Fresh Vegetable Eating, remarking that he cannot justify leaving his well-fertilized beds unproductive during any part of the year.

Of course, not everyone who *could* garden twelve months a year *will* garden that long. There is the simple matter of burnout. For many gardeners it is more exciting to get a fresh start each spring and give it a rest after fall harvest. Cabbage salad five days a week is not always inspiring. Gardeners interviewed for this section, however, have on the whole found ways to keep something — not necessarily cabbage, either — growing through most of the year without a lot of work.

Cabbage is grown commercially on the Saanich Peninsula of Vancouver Island, where cole crops thrive in the maritime climate and winter gardening can be successful.

VICTORIA: Dick and Rita Berry

Retired Victoria Police Officer

Dick Berry and wife Rita have a house that sits on the solid rock of Ten-Mile Point, as far east as you can get in Victoria. Their view is spectacular: across Haro Strait to San Juan Island and Mount Baker beyond, and north toward Vancouver.

Site and Soil

Dick: Our lot is gradually sloping, but the general impression of getting around on this rock is that it would help to be a mountain goat. If you get out in a boat and look back, you get an idea of how rough and rocky it is.

Not very many people along here have vegetable gardens. Most people think you couldn't. But we were lucky — the original owners brought in soil. They filled in dips in the rock, so some places the soil is very deep, although in other places I can dig down only a foot or so.

My dad was a gardener, and I've gardened for about 45 years, myself. I was born here in Victoria.

Rita: He's always had a beautiful vegetable garden. The soil is very loamy and good, but the drainage off the rocks above us keeps it damp rather late in the spring and I have to be careful where my first crop, the broad beans, goes. Too much rain and cold will rot them before they germinate.

Dick: One of our problems here is that we face northeast and the garden slopes in that direction. So our soil doesn't warm up as fast in spring as the soil of our neighbors around the south end of the point. We still get sun almost all day, because the slope is not very steep or high behind, but the very low angle of a late winter sun on a north-facing slope definitely makes a difference.

Our vegetable plot is so small we have little choice of where to put things, so I can't rotate much. We plant the broad beans in the same place each year because that spot dries out earliest. The beans don't mind it at all.

Conditioning

Dick: The soil that was hauled in was a good start, and I have added kelp. The winter storms begin in November and go on through January. They tear the kelp loose and wash it ashore. I carry it up and lay it on the garden and chop it up. When I want to plant in March or April, I dig it in.

The kelp doesn't seem to add salt to the soil. It lies out during the winter rains and gets well washed.

I also put manure on the garden. I get it from our kids' place out at Sooke — they have horses there. I bring it back in big feed sacks in the back of the truck and dump it on the garden, or make a pile of it to have when I want to side-dress something, like rhubarb. Rhubarb loves it. If I think the plants need it I also use a commercial 4-10-10 mix.

I don't know the pH of the soil. My vegetables tell me this is what they like.

I keep a double compost bin going. Everything I cut off or discard from the garden goes into it. I use a handful of Rot-It over the top, and a bit of soil over that. Then we use it as we need it around here — I can use every bit that we make.

We do have some problems. My favorite raspberry, the Cuthbert, has a root rot, and they say the only thing to do is throw it out and get a new variety, but I hate to lose it.

Planting

Potatoes are our main crop, and I haven't much choice of where to put them because they take up a lot of room. Another gardener I know had to throw his potatoes out because of potato scab. I haven't had any trouble with potato scab. Maybe the kelp gives them some protection. Maybe it's the sea air, or the salt spray. Sometimes during the winter storms I can see a fine white film

Dick and Rita Berry live on a rock that slopes to salt water. Soil was brought in to fill the dips and they add composted everything, including corn stalks and kelp. Dick also brings in truckloads of sacked horse manure.

of salt over the soil, there's so much of it. Whatever it is, I plant potatoes in the same place every year and I don't have any trouble with potato scab.

I hand-dig all the beds each spring, and smooth them out. Then I plant in rows, wide enough apart to cultivate between them with a Dutch hoe or cultivator. I don't need any power tools — there's no room for them.

We've tried a little companion planting but can't see that it is much help. The garden is so small everything is companion-planted, anyway. Of course, I always have to watch out. "Somebody" keeps trying to get a few flowers into the vegetable garden, but I won't let her.

We don't seem to have a need for mulch to keep the moisture in. I don't have much problem with watering as there is considerable underground runoff from above, as I mentioned. Since the garden seems to be in a bowl of soil, any watering we do in the back would naturally seep into it along the buried rock surfaces.

I may have to do a little watering in the driest parts of summer. Usually I water by hand, or occasionally use a sprinkler on an evening in August. I like the evenings because when the sun gets up here in the mornings, it is hot right away — the sun is slanted directly at us.

Climate Modification

The only help I use to lengthen the season is a tomato planting bed on the south side of the house, a lean-to with plastic over it, that will grow six plants. This fall I'm covering a couple of tomato plants in the garden with large clear-plastic bags to see whether it will help to ripen the tomatoes. I wait for the soil to dry and warm before I plant in the spring, but don't do anything special to hurry it up.

I've learned to talk to my plants, though. I tell them to get going. I read that Prince Charles talks to his plants, and if he can do it, so can I. Of course, I have to look around first to make sure my neighbors aren't listening.

The only plants I start indoors are the tomatoes. I got this seed from a Chinese commercial grower here about forty years ago. The tomatoes are resistant to rain damage, they are sweet, and they grow well in a greenhouse. I've never had any problem with leaf curl, either, until just recently. I can only hope it is a passing problem, because I like this kind of tomato. As far as I know, it has no name. We call it Our Own. I pick out a well-shaped tomato, not too big but a nice size, put it through a sieve and separate the pulp from the seed, then dry it, clean it and store it in a medicine bottle.

I germinate the seed on a heating cable in the basement, then move the seedlings to a light spot. When they're an inch or so high, I transplant. Or I start them in peat pellets so I never have to disturb the roots. We always have too many and give a lot away. They don't go outside until the end of April or first of May, and then they're under shelter in the lean-to.

Everything else is seeded directly into the garden, unless we buy a few cabbage plants at a nursery.

First I put in broad beans, about the first of March — depending on the weather and soil conditions. I may lose a few, but I can always sow a few more into the bare spots. The broad bean seed I save too, and we have a pink Portuguese bean we like. It seems a little hardier than the other.

After broad beans I put in potatoes — again, I will have saved some from the year before. Then come the peas, around the first part of April, as well as onions and beets.

You have to take into consideration that we are right on the water here. Not everyone around Victoria would plant like this. People farther inland can plant earlier. Other places are drier, or have better exposures to early sun.

We don't do any winter gardening here because it's too cold and wet, and I've generally had enough gardening to satisfy me by the time fall comes, anyway. My winter chores consist of laying out the kelp as I collect it and chopping it up.

Seed? I like to buy it from a local company that deals in seed, not somebody who sells nails and cedar siding too. Buckerfield's is a good place — they have their own seed. I also like Clark and Cordick, and Bordens. These are three well-established firms around here, and there are other good ones, I'm sure.

A tool I like the best? None of them. Well, perhaps the cultivator, the three- or five-pronged type. It gets right up along the rows and does a good job.

We have such trouble with the carrot rust fly that I've quit growing carrots. We can buy them fresh, grown on the island, quite cheaply. We do have some problem with black fly on the broad beans, which I use soapy water on. For slugs I use slug bait — especially in the lettuce. If we have a root maggot problem, I use a dioxin spray right around the roots.

The most difficult thing here, I think, is timing. You can have a week of the most gorgeous warm weather in March and you want to get started. But it will be followed by two weeks of downpour which ruins everything. It's an old story.

But to go out in the garden before dinner and say, "Well, we'll have this tonight, and that should be just about ready for tomorrow," and have absolutely fresh things to eat, that is the best of it.

My advice to would-be gardeners here is to first check that they have deep enough soil to grow a garden, because a lot of this area is very shallow and rocky. Then, if it looks good enough, or you can bring in some more soil to build it up, go ahead and plant. Don't let anyone tell you you can't grow things along the seaside.

Favorite varieties:

Potatoes:	Norgold or Netted Gem
Onion:	Yellow Danvers, good for drying
Green bean:	Roma — beautiful for freezing and eating green (Buckerfield)
Broad bean:	(saves seed from year to year) Portuguese pink type and regular
Beet:	Cylindra (Formanova) from Island Seed Co.
Radish:	Cherry Belle
Pea:	Green Arrow — goes to 5 or 6 ft., has a terrific yield, 9-11 peas to pod (Buckerfield)
Lettuce:	Buttercrunch or Butterhead

VANCOUVER: Rita Lehmann

Across the Strait of Georgia and a little north of Victoria lies Vancouver. Rita Lehmann's West Vancouver home sits between

Rita Lehmann, too, lives on a rocky slope where she had to gather soil and add organic matter, until now she has loam. She uses a greenhouse, primarily sun-heated, a coldframe and cloches to extend the growing season.

mountains and sea on a rocky, sloping lot. Like Dick Berry, she was able to find enough soil to make a beginning on a garden and has been adding to it ever since.

Site and Soil

Over the thirty-five years we've lived here I've added a great deal of compost, manure, seaweed, starfish, and chemical fertilizers of the general vegetable variety like 5-10-10. I've even done a little green manuring. It is in good enough shape now that I can call my soil loam. But soils around here are varied. There are many sandy areas along the shore and peaty spots in the Fraser River Valley. We have acid soils and find it necessary to test them by using a home kit or sending them to a lab. I apply dolomite lime for the *Brassicas* especially — in fact, most of the vegetable areas in my acid garden.

Conditioning

Compost is important for building up my soil. I use kitchen vegetable waste, weeds, soil, and seaweed in layers. It gets turned whenever my husband's feeling energetic.

Our garden is small and divided into many sections over a steep fifty- by one-hundred-foot lot, so it is hand-weeded and cultivated.

I like to mulch, and I gather grass clippings or eel grass from the shore in fairly large quantities. I also use compost. It helps to keep the weeds down, retains moisture, and as it decomposes, improves the soil texture and nutrient content.

My favorite tools are a good, strong trowel and fork, with welded handles, a ladies' small spade, best quality secateurs, and a stainless steel dibber.

I water with hoses and various kinds of sprinklers, and we have a small underground watering system for a few areas. In the hottest part of the year I water at least every other day and in the drier places I water every day.

Planting

I don't make a formal plan, but I do rotate plants according to annual growing conditions. I use all planting methods — scatter-seeding, raised beds, rows, and several large containers.

I use interplanting to get the best use of the space. I plant early and late varieties together — squash in my small corn plot, lettuce between late-flowering *Acidanthera* bulbs (as you see, I like vegetables and flowers mixed). I have not found interplanting to keep out pests very effective.

My schedule for planting goes something like this:
In the greenhouse:

    January: leeks, onions

    Late January or early February: greenhouse tomatoes

    Mid-February: broccoli

    February-March: everything else except the winter vegetables

In the garden:

    Early March: peas, lettuce, broccoli, spinach all go in the raised beds with covers.

    Later March: spinach uncovered

    Mid-May: beans, corn

Seedlings go out starting March 15 with the cabbage family, then the rest depending on type and how much heat is needed. I like the Vancouver store, Earthrise. They stock seed especially suited to Northwest gardens.

Climate Modification

Large plastic cloches that fit over two three-by-eight-foot beds are *very* effective for extending the garden season. We also have a nine-by-thirteen-foot greenhouse designed to be heated primarily by sun. We rarely need a heater in it, and we use it for just about everything — vegetables, flowers, bulbs. We also have a coldframe, wood with plastic windows, for wintering some of our half-hardy plants, and hardening off seedlings from the greenhouse, before they are put out in the spring.

I start all my own seed.

From mid-January sowing of tomato seed in the greenhouse I will get ripe fruit in June, and in September I bring in some plants to the greenhouse again. They give me tomatoes into December.

My special interest is vegetables that grow best in our soft Pacific Northwest climate, with special emphasis on the winter vegetables. Purple and perennial broccolis and winter cauliflowers get enormous and withstand some bitter winter weather. I grow several kinds of winter lettuce under the cloches and I like to try new varieties each year.

Growing of winter vegetables, it has seemed to me for many years, deserves much wider attention. (See recommended variety and seed source list.)

Pests and Problems

Pests in my garden and what I do? slugs — use bait; cutworms — apply Sevin; white fly — Ambush; carrot fly — Diazinon.

I have clubroot in my soil, unfortunately. This means I can't grow *Brassicas* for several years, until the disease disappears from

An energetic and systematic gardener, Mrs. Lehmann has tomatoes from June into December and Brassicas all year. She plants what grows best in the mild Northwest climate, with special emphasis on winter vegetables.

the soil. I grow some of my winter vegetables (the *Brassicas*) on borrowed plots because of it. The only way I can combat clubroot is with lots of lime and rotation.

There is both good and bad in our weather here. The bad is, we have cool temperatures most of the time, lots of rain, and a very short warm season. The good is, we have mild winters and year-around gardening is possible.

I have had problems growing beets, but with better soil they do well now. I have found cucumbers difficult.

When I'm on Master Gardener duty at the Botanical Garden I answer a lot of questions about horticulture. My general advice for new gardeners here is to use lots of compost and organic materials of all kinds; buy a good book, or several; grow the varieties best suited to this area; join a class — get to know other gardeners.

Recommendations

Rita Lehmann's Winter Vegetable List:

Look in the seed stores and catalogs for the following kinds of vegetables in varieties listed as winter-hardy:

Jerusalem artichoke — can be obtained as a root, no special varieties necessary as it is naturally hardy, can become invasive.

Beet, leaf — or perpetual spinach, of the chard family, available from Thompson and Morgan or Sutton's Seeds.

Brussels sprouts and cabbages; Broccoli, purple sprouting — planted in spring or summer to harvest in late February through April, depending on variety; needs lots of space, also comes in white, from Thompson and Morgan, Territorial Seed, Earthrise..

Winter Cauliflower — produces large heads from March through April; several varieties available from Thompson and Morgan, Territorial and Earthrise.

Celeriac — a slow-growing celery-type plant with large, rounded, edible root.

Rhubarb chard — attractive red-stalked greens from Dominion or Stokes.

Chinese cabbage, Siberian kale, collards and corn salad — very hardy, may be found in Stokes, Territorial, Suttons, and at Earthrise..

Endive —

Kohlrabi — a long-lasting cabbage family member, most seed companies; Territorial gives good directions and description.

Leek — Alaska or Siberia — available to harvest all winter.

Onion — Egyptian or walking type, White Lisbon from Territorial, Sweet Winter or June onion from Territorial, and Kaizuka from Abundant Life.

Salsify — or black-skinned *Scorzonerea,* a long, tasty root; seeds available from Dominion Seed Co. and others.

ARLINGTON: Ward Briggs

Along the rise of hills on the north side of the Stillaguamish Valley is the wide spot in the road known as Bryant, just out of Arlington. Right down the road from the Lost Dutchman Nursery and Trout Farm, Ward Briggs runs his little seasonal produce farm where you can turn in and get the freshest of sweet corn right out of the field and carrots straight from the ground. The prices are so low he might as well give the stuff away, but he says he only wants to make enough to pay for his supplies, and the rest is his hobby. In September you could get the following:

Carrots	25 cents a pound
Beets (with top)	25 cents a pound
Kohlrabi	15 cents a pound
Sunburst (squash)	15 cents
Zucchini	10 cents each
Spuds	(out, they were only volunteers anyway)
Tomatoes	35 cents a pound
Corn	Beacon Bi-color, 8/$1
	Golden Jubilee, 10/$1
	Kandy Korn, 6/$1

Ward Briggs makes a planter of plastic sheeting and pvc pipe. "Plastics can add three months to our growing season," said Briggs, who has written a pamphlet explaining how he does it.

Cukes . . lemon, 35 cents a pound; slice, 15 cents each	
Beans	35 cents a pound
Free	Oregano, Sage, Parsley, Chives

Ward says he plans to slow down, though, go more to corn only because people like it best. Instead of opening in June, he can wait until August and have more time to spend with his grandchildren, who come to visit him from the East.

Briggs keeps a 2.5-acre growing area going, including greenhouses. The season is shorter than it is in most of Puget Sound, but for four months, at least, he has vegetables growing outdoors, and the rest of the year he is experimenting with various ways to grow under plastic.

Ward is known locally for his expertise in plastics. He has written a pamphlet distributed by the Snohomish County Extension office which explains his various tests and conclusions over the years as he has tried out different materials.

Site and Soil, Conditioning

Briggs: My garden lies on the shore of an ancient lake bed. Just behind are stands of hardhack and cattails in a black muck. But some sand and gravel have washed in, in some past time, so there is good drainage. There is also a lot of humus, or I wouldn't be gardening here at all.

For eight years I have ordered chicken manure by the dump-truck, at $20 a load. It is steaming hot and has to be spread in January or early February so it cools down.

I buy steer manure by the truckload too. The place was a cow pasture before I turned it into gardens. There's little need for commercial fertilizer, though I keep a hundred-pound sack of 10-20-10 for special cases. It takes me about three years to use up a sack.

I take a rough pH reading from a meter, but I go more by what grows and what doesn't. A simple test for pH is to plant spinach and Swiss chard. Spinach has a very short range of tolerance, between 6.5 and 7. If it is growing well, you know that your pH is ideal. Swiss chard has a range of 5.5-7.5, so if the spinach grows poorly but the Swiss chard grows well, you know your soil needs some amendment to correct the imbalance. If neither one grows well, but apples, rhubarb and blueberries do, you can tell the pH is low and you need to add lime gradually.

We have acid soils here, to be sure, but most people are still adding too much lime. You don't need it every year, although if you use a hot fertilizer you need more. With twenty yards of chicken manure I figure I will need two hundred pounds of lime, or ten pounds per yard.

The people who lived here before me caused a problem for me by overliming the soil. They had hogs and threw on the lime to help kill the smell. The pH was so high when I changed the culture from pigs to plants that I couldn't grow anything at first.

Raw materials go right back on the garden in summer and are tilled in during the fall. I even put cornstalks on the garden. I use two 8-horsepower tillers, one a Troy-built and one a reverse tine. In the fall I borrow a heavy tractor tiller to take care of the big chunks of cornstalks and the like. But you don't need a tractor. In a small garden you can take a butcher knife and chop up the stalks, then till or spade them in.

Anything except paper, plastic or metal, I put in the garden. I even bury meat scraps and bones in such places as around the fruit trees.

I use a regular hoe, and I like my hand-push cultivator for getting out weeds after the plants start coming up. I adapted it so there's a little plow blade that pushes dirt over to the side, and automatically hills the corn and kills the weeds. Corn usually requires cultivation once a week to kill the young weeds and gradually hill the rows.

In my opinion, people here generally water twice as much and cultivate only half as much as they need to. You have to be familiar with how a plant grows — it needs air. Watering packs the soil down just like walking on it does, and increases the loss of moisture by capillary action.

When I water I usually use a hose and do it by hand. But you must realize that I have an extremely high water table here, at the edge of the old lake bed. Actually there still is a lake out there in the middle, called Bryant Lake. Once my vegetables get started, their roots don't waste any time getting down where the water is.

Planting

In the fall I draw out my plan for the next year, put down the dates I want to plant and when I planted this year. Then if I can't follow it exactly, I make a revised plan for future reference. I also keep a daily calendar on when I put things in, when something comes up, harvest dates and that sort of thing. I usually start the

Market gardening is a hobby with Briggs, who sells enough produce at near-giveaway prices to pay for his supplies. Here, squashes hang from overhead supports.

first of January with the calendar.

Excerpt from Ward Briggs's planting calendar:

Jan. 5: plant peas under tunnels.
Jan. 25: start tomatoes inside.
Feb. 10: tomatoes to 2″ pots in greenhouse.
March 1: till corn area, put in Crispy Sweet lettuce seed and soak parsley seed.
March 13: soak pumpkin seed, start on 15th.
March 14: transplant Roma seedlings.
        15: black plastic down.
        16: till bean area.
        20: more plastic for beets.
        22: carpet down, parsley up (18 days).
        24: transplant Patio tomatoes — greenhouse and tomato hut, both under tunnels.

Briggs's tomato hut, an outside growing box shown here in use at the Marysville Demonstration Garden, has polyethylene walls to be rolled up on hot days, left down when it's cool. See page 51 for diagrams and building instructions.

27:	rhubarb pie!
28:	black cloth down for 4 rows of corn.
31:	soak 250 Kandy Korn seed.
April 1:	more Kandy Korn to soak.
3:	plant 5 rows Kandy Korn; 4 black plastic, 1 tunnel.
4:	frost, 32 degrees.
6:	Roundup on east field, tilled for BiColor.
May 1:	replant Beacon corn
13:	start 10 zucchini in styro, 3 pumpkin in styro.
14:	cukes in spool, parsley in tub, zucchini in tile.
17:	start cantaloupe, transplant WSU tomato, lemon cuke.
18:	8 rows carrots.
20:	more corn.
23:	4 rows beets, 2 kohlrabi, tomatoes in carpet.
24:	1 row Oregon Giant beans; kohlrabi goes to garden.
27:	carrots up.
28:	start 20 spaghetti squash, 20 zucchini.
29:	row of Oregon Giant, acorn squash.

I know for sure that putting a couple of rows of bush beans in with beets between is a good idea. At the time the beans are finished you cut them down to soil level and let in the sun. Now you have nitrogen in your soil for the beets, which will just jump.

I have heard that planting garlic with beets improves their flavor. I wouldn't know, though, as I don't eat beets — I just sell them.

I rotate beets and carrots, but not the corn and beans.

I plant row gardens, but carrots and beets may be planted in very wide rows. I can kill the weeds first with black plastic and I never have to weed these rows after that because the plants come up so thick.

Climate Modification

The first thing after tilling is to lay black plastic down along the section I am going to plant, and leave it. Starting in about April, I will get enough heat under the plastic to germinate weed seed within three to four weeks. By June it takes only ten days. Of course the weeds can't grow under the plastic, so after a couple of weeks I have brought up all the surface weeds and killed them and am ready to put in my vegetable seed.

I've been able recently to get some big rolls of a woven black cloth for keeping weeds down. One side is fuzzed and rough, to keep the weed seedlings from finding their way through the fibers. It is expensive, but it outlasts plain plastic. I cut small holes for corn seed, then I can leave the plastic down in the corn rows the whole season. It helps keep the water in the soil. I am hesitant to recommend it, however, until I have tried it out for two or three years.

For a great mulch I don't think anything beats the old indoor/outdoor carpeting made of nylon, which unfortunately isn't made anymore. If I had a half-acre of it, I'd use it all. You can raise anything in it. You lay it down, cut a hole to put your transplant or seed in, and you don't have to worry much about that plant the rest of the year. The carpeting heats the soil as much as thirty degrees higher than the surrounding soil, keeps it moist, keeps out the weeds, and you don't get muddy feet walking down the rows. The best colors are black or dark red, but I would take any color I could get.

I grow almost everything under tunnels to start with. I use polyethylene, Reemay, corrugated fiberglass tunnels, poly-sided growing huts, fiberglass greenhouses, and combinations of all of them. I start nearly all my transplantable plant seed inside the greenhouse, and what I don't (for instance, peas), I start under tunnels and let them grow to three or four inches before I take off the cover. When I'm through with the peas I put the covers on the beets. I use many tunnels five times each year for progressively later-starting vegetables (e.g., peas to beets to carrots to zucchini to pumpkin).

I'm convinced that people in this area need to look into plastic culture further. You can start at least a month sooner, and can extend the season that much or more into the fall. With care you can extend your growing season three months. And that's a lot because we have only a 120-day average growing season here, with only 108 days that I can really count on — quite different from Edmonds or Marysville, where I have gardened. One year here I had bean plants frosted on the second of June. Another year I lost corn on the nineteenth of September for the same reason.

Dome-shaped or see-through greenhouses aren't much use here for vegetable growing. The best use of the greenhouse is from February to the first of June. The best is a lean-to type with a north wall painted either black or dark red to absorb the energy and give it back as heat inside the greenhouse. If you have a conventional-type greenhouse, you can make a noticeable difference in it by dropping a black plastic sheet from one of the supports at the north side.

I heat one greenhouse with an airtight wood stove, but use it

Ward Briggs's fiberglass tunnel

Rectangular panels at exterior plywood can be staked at each end to close the tunnels.

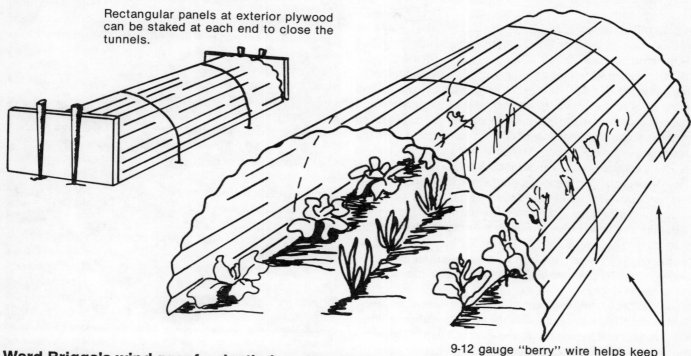

9-12 gauge "berry" wire helps keep fiberglass in proper tunnel shape — loops at sides can be twisted for easier handling.

Ward Briggs's wind-proof polyethylene tomato hut

Top = corrugated fiberglass or polyethylene sheeting

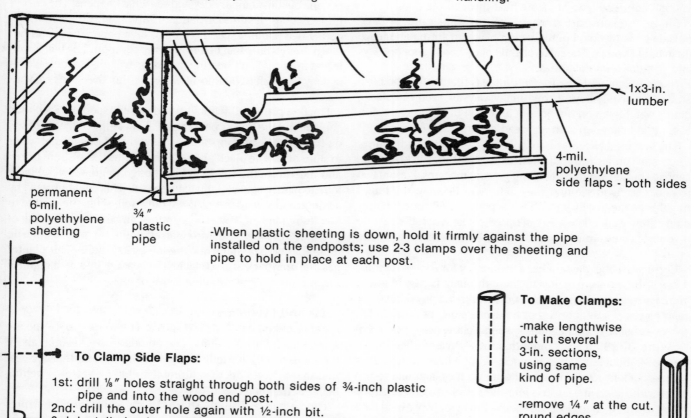

1x3-in. lumber

4-mil. polyethylene side flaps - both sides

permanent 6-mil. polyethylene sheeting

¾" plastic pipe

-When plastic sheeting is down, hold it firmly against the pipe installed on the endposts; use 2-3 clamps over the sheeting and pipe to hold in place at each post.

To Clamp Side Flaps:

1st: drill ⅛" holes straight through both sides of ¾-inch plastic pipe and into the wood end post.
2nd: drill the outer hole again with ½-inch bit.
3rd: install pipe by pushing screw through larger hole into smaller, then screwing into the wood post.

To Make Clamps:

-make lengthwise cut in several 3-in. sections, using same kind of pipe.

-remove ¼" at the cut. round edges, spread apart

only early in the spring when it might freeze after I've got seedlings started — maybe once or twice.

I start all my tomatoes inside the greenhouse, and I grow a lot of them there all summer. There are three greenhouses here, two with north walls: a 12'x12' Quonset-type, a 10'x16', and a 10'x30'. I keep something growing in all of them all summer — melons in the Quonset, Patio tomatoes growing in old sinks and Early Girls in the ground in another, and Patio tomatoes and lemon cucumbers in the last one. I keep water stored in a drum in the greenhouse. It not only retains the sun's heat, it gives me warm water for the plants. I've heard that watering a tomato seedling with cold water can set it back three days. I believe it. I think the bacteria in the soil go dormant so the plants don't get the nutrients they need to keep growing.

The plants from tropical regions, like the pepper and tomato, naturally love heat. I have proven by tests that these plants can tolerate temperatures up to 150 degrees F. *if* they also have high humidity. They won't set fruit at such high temperatures, however, so while they are blooming the heat should be reduced to under 95 degrees.

As another experiment I constructed a double-walled greenhouse, about fifty cubic feet, inside the bigger greenhouse. When outside temperature was 32 degrees the main part of the greenhouse was 48-52 degrees. Inside the inner greenhouse the temperature was between 98 and 106, with no heat other than the January sun. This would be ideal for some plants if there were enough light and a way to store heat through the night.

I have also constructed what I call the tomato hut, a large outside growing box. I put in young plants in spring and leave them until October. The sides, of 4-mil plastic, roll up for hot days and stay down for cool ones.

One problem with the tomato hut was that the plastic blew around on windy days. I tried many ways to keep the plastic down, weighted it on the bottom and all. Finally an extension agent and I came up with an idea that works: (see page 51).

The best use of Reemay is for cole crops, radishes and turnips. They don't mind the reduction in sunlight and it keeps the cabbage butterfly out so you don't get root maggots. I tested two rows of carrots to see how they did under Reemay, thinking I might keep the rust fly out. Well, it kept the rust fly out, but they didn't grow well. Since you can't predict just when the rust fly is going to come around, you may as well raise carrots out in the open.

Corrugated fiberglass makes a good cover for a lot of reasons. It keeps the moisture in, lets the light through, is easy to put in and easy to store when you are through with it. I buy the regular clear pieces at a lumberyard or hardware store, not the expensive greenhouse stock that nursery supply places sell. The dimensions are 26"x8'. It costs more than polyethylene sheeting, of course — about four times as much — but it lasts twenty times as long. For long rows I form the sheets over the plants and secure them with rigid wire pushed into the soil. I can add as many sheets as I need, then close the ends with a piece of plywood held in place with a stick.

One thing about the row covers: they bring on the slugs. Just

Water stored in a drum absorbs and retains heat and can be handy for hand-watering young plants. Tomato seedlings, especially, are retarded if watered with cold water.

put one out on a January day and see what happens. They're out there singing "It's June in January" and having a great time. I do my pea planting, get the ground all smoothed out and put down Corey's Slug Bait before I put my cover on. The bait is protected from pets and weather, but slugs will dig in. You get a lot of dehydrated slugs in there after a while, but they don't eat your peas.

I made a planting tub from a wooden cable spool. Black plastic goes around the hollow bottom and about fourteen inches of soil on the top. The bottom can be filled with plastic jugs of water to store heat. The black plastic alone warms the air from below and thus heats the soil. It is big enough to grow several large tomato plants, squash, or cucumbers in. This could be used by a handicapped gardener, if the spools were set in the ground to the desired height. For a top, a frame can be constructed out of pvc pipe and covered with polyethylene, or a clear plastic umbrella could be stuck into the soil by its handle. This planter has one drawback: it is so efficient in heating the soil, it requires much more water than other types of tubs.

Pests and Problems

I am not bothered much by pests. The worst two for me are slugs, which I use a bait for, and aphids. I use Diazinon above the ground only for aphids and the few insects that are real nuisances. Moles are also a problem, but I am slowly getting better at trapping them.

I have had a disease attack all my summer and winter squashes, including some vines nine feet in the air, and my cucumbers too. My solution has been to plant only cucumbers

listed as resistant, such as Marketmore-76. Also for this reason I raise lemon cucumbers in a greenhouse only. (The cucumber beetle introduces the bacterium, Ward — get rid of the bug or use some of your famous row covers.) The worst problem here is predicting the weather. And I used to be a meteorologist!

Recommendations:

I buy some of my corn seed from Vesey's in Nova Scotia, on Prince Edward Island. They have a northern Maine outlet too. They have about the same climate as we have and they specialize in short-season seed. Rather than trying to grow what is good in California or Iowa, get seed adapted to your conditions. Beacon and Bicolored Harmony are good corn varieties from this company.

I like to buy my bulk seed from the Marysville Feed and Seed.

Corn: Kandy Korn is everybody's favorite. It is a late corn — I can just barely get it to mature here, but that is probably a good thing because once my customers get a taste of it they don't want the other varieties. It seems to be weak-rooted and will blow over easily, so I top it once the ears are set. Golden Jubilee is an old late-season standby, and Seneca is another good variety. For early corn I like Vesey's Bi-color or Beacon. Corn seed is about the worst seed for faithful germination. I have had established varieties that germinated at less than eight percent, and two first-year varieties germinate at less than two percent. Now I won't plant corn seed until I test it by soaking ten or twenty seeds overnight, then keeping them warm and damp between paper napkins for three or four days. They pass my test if seventy-five percent sprout both a root and a shoot. You can get a head start if you sprout all the seed the same way. But sprouted seed is hard to handle, so I float them in a bucket of water. Then if you don't like to bend down, you can try my method:

I tie the bucket on a string around my neck, carry a one-and-a-half-inch plastic tube of the right length for me (about four feet), and walk down the furrows dropping each sprouted corn seed through the pipe exactly where I want it. I made up this method when my back was giving me trouble one June, just when I had to get things planted, and I still use it.

Tomatoes: Patio or Pixie are my favorites. Romas are great but require a very long growing season. I freeze Romas whole. The secret is in defrosting them. If you have a microwave, give them just a small shot of defrosting, so they are still solid, then cut them in pieces and lay on the drainboard for a little while. They don't look so good as a newly cut fresh tomato from the store, but they certainly taste a lot better. I save a lot of my own seed, and pick the biggest of the crop so the tomatoes are getting gradually larger each year.

Beets: I used to plant Detroit Dark Red only, but I tried the cylindrical type and found that people really prefer them. Now they are all I raise. They don't get woody, they slice uniformly, the tops stay good longer to use for greens, and they can be planted closer together.

Cole crops: I don't plant cabbage, broccoli or Brussels sprouts. I am a great kohlrabi booster. This is the absolutely best climate to grow kohlrabi, and don't let anyone tell you they don't get very big. If you can grow cabbage you will have no trouble growing this vegetable. You can have tender, sweet kohlrabi here as big as cabbages — some to ten pounds. The faster it grows, the better, and if it gets lots of water it will just keep on growing. It is perfect to start early and again in July for a winter crop. These will last into February or March, when they start flowering. Kohlrabi doesn't have the pests that the other cole crops have. I think it makes better cole slaw than cabbage (I have "educated" my customers, and they love it). There are two types available, purple and green.

Beans: Oregon Giant pole beans are very good, light-colored, streaked with red, very large, and turn green when cooked. I raise them on permanent eight-foot frames strung with fish netting.

Squash: Sunburst summer squash, acorn, vegetable spaghetti, Hubbard winter squash, zucchini.

Cucumbers: lemon, and green slicing.

Peas: Sugar Snap pole peas exclusively. Most get picked too early or too late. They are prime only when the peas have developed until they start to touch each other in the pod. After that starch forms instead of sugar and the flavor suffers. But at their best, they are very good. I see little children going out of here with some in their hands, eating them raw. Why bother with any other kind?

Garlic: Again, I had to educate my customers. Garlic leaves are the best part of the plant. Cloves are for winter use. The leaves are sweeter than the cloves and you can use them early. I plant twice as much as I will need so I can use the greens too. They can be used anywhere that regular garlic is used, in salads and sauteed under steaks. Some people even use them in sandwiches.

Look into the plastic culture, follow the new developments, try them out and see what works for you. This is the best way for a vegetable gardener to get a longer and warmer season for produce.

The Puget Sound climate is unique. There is no place like it in the United States. Most books and publications are written by "experts" in the East or California, and I find that only about ten percent of the advice is good for the Puget Sound gardener. The more local your information, the better.

MARYSVILLE DEMONSTRATION GARDEN: Beth Burrows

Beth Burrows calls herself an "assertive volunteer." She doesn't wait for others to initiate projects. She has been a gardener for about fifteen years; she got into it by way of a house plant collection in Michigan, where she was particularly proud of her five-hundred-plant succulent Euphorbia collection.

Since she gave away the Euphorbias and moved west, she has been putting in many hours at the Marysville Snohomish County Master Gardener Demonstration Garden:

Beth: I was one of the original eight or ten volunteers who arrived one day to begin pulling out the blackberries. It was hot and tiring and thankless work. A woman of eighty or more, who was working with the group, was accidentally struck across the face by a big blackberry cane and seriously lacerated. She cleaned off the blood and went back to work. Since she refused to give up, the rest of us could hardly complain or go home until the job was done.

The land had been used as a cow pasture, I think, because every once in a while we ran into a regular mother lode of manure.

This garden is run strictly on voluntary lines. Everything is done free. The seeds and supplies that aren't donated are bought with proceeds from a booth we run at the Tacoma Fruit Fair.

One of the sins of this garden is the lack (so far) of a compost heap. [Author's note: a compost demonstration area was added to the garden shortly after this interview.] I would like to feature composting in the Gourmet Garden, and hope to have something modeled on what they have done in Seattle at the Tilth Garden.

I like to emphasize the aesthetics of vegetable gardening. Too many suburban gardeners don't do some things that would benefit them because they don't look pretty and they might offend the neighbors. Big heaps of compost sitting around are not particularly pleasing. It is the same with row covers, even though they are worth using. So something less conspicuous is better for those who care about the aesthetics.

I am a subversive here. The extension agents know a lot more than I do about the basics of vegetable gardening, but there are some things I disagree with. They aren't totally devoted to organic gardening, of course. They aren't supposed to be. They are supposed to offer choices. But still it seemed to me they were using far more chemicals than were needed. Friends of mine were dropping out of Master Gardeners because they couldn't bring themselves to recommend chemical pest controls. I was considered to have sold out to the pesticide companies because I stayed on, but I stay, and I try to do little passive-subversive things like coming in early to pull the grass along the fence line so it won't be sprayed with herbicides.

Also I try to get new things accepted. One year I grew plants that our extension agent called weeds. He wouldn't let me leave them in long enough to go to seed, because he said they'd take over the garden. I have grown dandelions in containers, too (really an insanity with their long tap roots), just so they won't spread.

Planning here is done by committee, but it works. There are

Dedicated volunteers, working with Extension Service agents and Master Gardener coordinators, have developed a demonstration garden in Marysville. Volunteers learn the basics, try new methods, share their know-how with one another and with beginning gardeners. For whom to call about gardening programs in the various regions, see Appendix C. (Snohomish County Extension Agency)

many sections: the pest control section, the plastics, the herb garden, the 4-H garden, and a test row-cover area. But it doesn't leave much space for new ideas.

Our raised garden beds are exceptionally high in the gourmet section, probably because I have very energetic workers helping — they dig harder. The results are phenomenal. Everything here came up ahead of other beds this year.

One experiment I tried was to take some vegetable starts from a volunteer's greenhouse and put them in one row under a tunnel, and in another row I planted seeds under a tunnel. After six weeks or so the differences weren't noticeable. The seed-started and the start-started plants were about the same.

We begin about the end of April to put seed in, and go to early October, though last fall we left the radicchio in, cut it down, marked it so it wouldn't get plowed under, and mulched it. The second heads the plants grow are little maroon clusters of leaves

much desired for gourmet salads. Nobody works here during the winter so the radicchio was pretty much on its own. It did fine.

All Master Gardener trainees volunteer twenty-five hours of work a year here. We keep our donated tool supply in a shed right here for them to work with. I personally like working with my hands. I'd advise every gardener to get down to the level of the plant and hand-weed. That way you see what is going on, what bug is eating it, what pocket of soil won't drain.

We start with rototilling in the spring. I've heard that double digging by hand is terrific for the soil, but this depends on the gardener. If you tell a first-timer to get out there and double-dig the vegetable plot before starting, she's likely to tell you she'd rather sell her place. Experts sometimes forget what it is like to start out. You have to make things a little easy at first. And you have to make them look good so people will try them. A polyethylene lean-to doesn't look good on a $200,000 house. After awhile new gardeners aren't new gardeners anymore, and they don't care so much about easy or pretty as they do about good vegetables. And if the neighbors are still giving you a bad time about your garden, smile and give them some seed to grow, or some fresh produce.

I have a "death" speech I give. Something is bound to die. You could do everything to absolute perfection, the neighbors cheer you on, God could be on your side, and yet something dies. It is a shock. So I tell people about plant deaths, and that it probably happens for very good reasons, but not reasons having to do with them personally. Otherwise new gardeners may take it so much to heart they will give up.

We have tried unusual plants in the gourmet section. Salsify has been a terrific success, yet it was on an extension agents' list of weeds.

We have a yearly Munch-In to try out the produce we have grown, and everyone who tried salsify liked it, as far as I know. As a matter of fact, one mother who tried my mock oyster recipe (with salsify) told me the only vegetable her son ever liked was salsify.

Vegetable amaranth is under-appreciated. Cooked in a little butter, it is a great spinach-type vegetable. I think it far surpasses the New Zealand spinach. Amaranth will sit quite unmoving during cold weather, but give it some warm weather and it grows so fast you can almost see it change.

We have had some disappointments: jicama (pronounced HE-kah-mah) for one. By the end of the season we had just one plant surviving — a spindly little thing with a miniature root on it. I don't think it will grow here. The same with watermelon. Not enough heat. They grew big but they didn't ripen.

We have had some small cases of vandalism. Someone managed to do away with all the A-1 carrots, a new variety we were trying. Maybe they had a horse to feed.

The extension agent wanted us to do miniature vegetables this year, but I said we'd have to be here all the time to pick them at the right moment. Otherwise they wouldn't be miniatures. Still, we have been trying the new Japanese tomato called Rouge Ogura, which is a miniature and good for pots. The Japanese developed them for their decorative effect.

Systematic testing in the Marysville Demonstration Garden shows what doesn't work well, what does, and what works better. (Snohomish County Extension Agency)

Actually you don't have to have a garden to grow things to eat. I see no reason whatsoever to buy a quarter-ounce of dried herbs in a bottle for a couple of dollars or more when you can grow them in a pot on the windowsill for pennies.

I spend so much time here that I have a very small garden at home. It lines the driveway. But in it I grow salsify, carrots, zucchini, parsley, tomatoes, radishes, broccoli, herbs, winter squash and Egyptian Walking onions. I don't think the walking onions are much use except for people who drink martinis, but they are interesting.

People who come here for information and help often ask about house plants and lawns. They bring in a sick house plant that cost them $1.95 to buy and want a $3.00 spray recommended for it. I suggest that it would be a lot better if they threw the plant out and got another. The average house plant life is two years, I think they say. But people don't want to believe it. They say, "My Aunt Agnes had this same plant for forty years." But they more than double their cost and don't have a healthy plant.

And lawns! I once heard an "expert" telling a young couple they should dig out their front yard to a depth of eighteen inches and replace the soil. Here was a young couple who had just bought a new house and didn't even have the money to furnish it, and he's telling them to sink thousands of dollars into the lawn. Well, he may be right if you want a gorgeous lawn, but if you want a reasonably good lawn, there are easier ways to go. It's true of vegetables too. If you want perfection, you don't have to arrive there all at once, you can work toward it gradually and use a little common sense. I mean, why get your heart set on beefsteak tomatoes if you live in a cherry tomato part of the country?

It takes a core group of people to get a demonstration garden like this going. There were a few of us who really dedicated ourselves to it, with the help of the Extension Agent, the Master Gardener coordinator and a volunteer named Howard Bentley. We call him Boss Howard. The first two years of this garden, he

was our chairman and overseer. He worked so hard it almost killed him. You have to have committed volunteers or you will fail. We have some people who won't even take vacations in the summer, they're so committed. I say this garden is good because of the work put in it, but also because of the spirit of the place and the good vibrations from the workers. People I say this to sometimes back off, thinking I am saying something religious, but I'm not, I just believe in the efficacy of good people working together.

Recommendations:

Sugar Baby watermelon is not suitable for the Marysville area, even though it is supposed to grow in northern climates.

Sakurajima Mammoth Daikon radishes are not suitable as a summer crop . . . they bolt with hot weather. Grown in the fall they probably succeed. On the other hand, the Tokinashi type Daikon is recommended. Growing them under screened covers would eliminate root maggot problems.

Florence fennel is easy to grow and has no apparent pests, a good choice for people who like licorice. The seeds are good in certain cookies and cakes, and the tops are great on fish.

Corn salad is a success, especially if grown in cool weather or in a winter garden.

Salsify is a perfect summer crop with no problems. Raised beds help root development.

Tampala or Edible Amaranth is a most successful crop. It takes hot weather to develop and doesn't do well if planted too early. But the amount of edible material per square inch of growth space is incredible, and the plant lends itself to selective picking of leaves over the entire summer.

Herb Gardening:

In Marysville, the Master Gardeners have created an attractive

Why pay dollars for herbs you can grow for pennies? Perennial herbs in the Marysville collection please the eye and the nose as well as the palate, and could be grown on windowsills. (Snohomish County Extension Agency)

perennial collection of herbs within a couple of raised beds (actually one is called a mound, and one is raised with a rock border). These herbs are recommended not only for flavor but for scent and looks as well. This is a list of herbs that grow well here:

Bee Balm	Hyssop	Southernwood
Borage	Lamb's ear	Sweet woodruff
Chamomile	Lavender	Thyme, coconut
Chives	Moneywort	Thyme, common
Feverfew	Oregano	Thyme, golden
French tarragon	Sage	Thyme, lemon
Germander	Santolina	Thyme, woolly
Horehound	Savory, winter	Yarrow

SEATTLE: Dick Taber, with Pat

The Tabers live on the east slope of Capitol Hill in Seattle. From the street, the house snugs down behind its white fence and rose garden, looking modest. From the back, it rears up in a series of terraces, steps and stories to an impressive height. Gardening in such a spot might be thought pure folly, but the Tabers have been successfully raising their own vegetables here since 1974. To get down to the garden with the kitchen compost, they must open the door to the steps, go down an inside flight, go through an outside door, then walk down another flight, thence along the little path to the edge of the property and the compost bin. The return trip is an aerobic delight.

Site and Soil

Dick: We had a yellow clay here, a heavy, gummy, stuff that grew blackberries. Besides blackberries, the backyard had been the dump for all the remodeling and construction that had gone on for years. We had old wire and globs of stucco and used tiles and old cupboards. We first thought we'd make a run for our two dogs, and cleaned it out for that purpose. We fenced it, then made some beds around the inside of the fence for sugar peas and lettuce.

We used some of the lumber lying in the backyard to make planting boxes. The two outside dogs dwindled to one inside dog, and the garden has expanded every year until now it takes up the whole area.

Conditioning

Everything the soil is now, we owe to compost. It has been the major addition to the clay. We throw vegetable scraps into a bucket up in the kitchen and when one of us feels like coming down, we add it to the heap. I put down grass clippings or nitrogen-rich material, then a good layer of soil. When the composting box is full I dig a trench someplace in the garden to put it. There are two hog-wire cylinders for extra clippings, weeds and such, which I also throw some dirt on. By spring most of this is a good, granular humus that I spread around on the beds before I dig them up.

We get loads of plant material from our front garden, including leaves and tree prunings, that go into the piles. We've also put in some wood ashes from the fireplace, although we don't use it anymore so the supply has dried up. Crab shells compost very well. Actually we haven't put much else in, no sawdust or manure or fertilizers. There seems to have been an oil leak from the old storage tank under the house, but the potatoes grow right over it and don't seem to mind at all.

Planting

We grow tomatoes, rhubarb, cabbages, snow peas, sweet peas, bush beans, pole beans, broccoli, cucumbers, zucchini, basil, dill, carrots, sweet onions and potatoes, sometimes chard, and more — all in a twenty-by-thirty-foot plot of ground. Besides that, we have figs, strawberries, raspberries and an apple tree. The central path is paved with broken slate from a pool table that was in the house when we bought it. We have built each raised bed with whatever lumber we had handy, a few at a time over the years, and we don't change them. All we do is keep adding compost.

I dig the beds each spring standing on a one-by-twelve board about four feet long. This avoids compressing the soil, as it is so full of clay that any pressure on it makes it lumpy.

If you stand down in the middle of the garden and look up, you see that the houses in the neighborhood block the afternoon sun. We get morning sun, but by early afternoon, even in the height of the summer, the garden is shaded. The sections closest to the house are naturally shaded first, so we plant tomatoes and cucumbers out where they can get the most sun. I built a sort of prow over the garage below for some of those plants. If we wanted to expand again, we could put another terrace below that for squash and beans — maybe even corn.

We can't rotate much. We have such a small space we just plant where it's handiest at the time. We like to add flowers here and there, like the rose and hydrangea growing in among the vegetables. Anything that isn't thriving in the front flower garden comes down to the back. Anything that fails there goes to the compost.

We get our seed from any local market — we aren't choosy about the brand. We also buy more starts than we used to. One place we've found to buy plants is the Lake Washington Vocational Technical School, where horticulture students raise seedlings for practice and sell them at very reasonable prices. Nevertheless, I enjoy seeing things come up and we start such things as lettuce, carrots, cucumbers, snow peas and beans. We have an excellent growing spot on the south side of the living room, right over the boxed-in radiators.

I find it best to transplant in rather dry soil in this clay, then water afterward. Pressing down wet soil around the roots makes lumpy, impermeable material for starting plants.

Nothing we do has a regular program. We like to do so many things we can't stick to a regular schedule. We do what we can when we're around, and it seems to be enough. If we are going to be gone for a long time in the summer we get somebody to water the garden, but otherwise it gets a good dose of neglect.

Dick Tabor and his wife, Pat, garden on a steep-slope city lot, where they've turned clay into growing ground with compost. They raise roses and herbs in the front yard and in back, away down, vegetables, berries, even an apple tree.

Pat: If we had a serious schedule, we'd get too high-centered. We'd be spinning our wheels trying to get every little thing done and we'd never get away.

Climate Modification

Dick: We don't look for especially long-lasting varieties. We couldn't raise anything seriously in the winter since there is so little light, but whatever manages to survive into late fall, such as cabbages or broccoli, we take advantage of. We plant a late summer crop of lettuce to have in the fall. Carrots and potatoes last a long time, too.

One year we took advantage of our flat, sunny roof to grow peppers and eggplants, which won't usually grow in our short-day backyard. They did quite well, but I had planted them in ten-inch pots, not adequate for their root systems. With deeper planting pots or planters, we could grow quite a garden of heat-loving varieties up there, assuming the roof could take the weight.

Pat Tabor goes a long way up or down between her kitchen and compost pile, yet they compost all kitchen and front-yard waste, and Pat even tried roof-gardening.

Pests and Problems

We have no pests bad enough to drive us to giving up gardening. We have aphids on the Brussels sprouts, and we have slugs in the lettuce. For the slugs, which lurk between the boards of the planting beds, we use bait.

We have long, narrow lots here, with the houses shoulder to shoulder. What one neighbor does affects the others. Our near neighbor to the north discovered a rat in his blackberries one year and called in an all-purpose exterminator to get rid of the vermin and the blackberries. The "Agent Orange," as we called it, that was sprayed to get rid of the vegetation nearly exterminated our garden too. It drifted over to our side and wiped out the new plants I'd just set out. So I set out some more. They sprayed again, and again I lost them. This went on for some time. Finally I complained, though I like to think I'm not a complaining type. They apologized and said they'd pay for the damages. That was the year I found out how much my vegetable garden was worth. I got $15 in the mail from them. I don't know how they arrived at that, I didn't ask. We finally got a few things to grow, but it wasn't a great year.

Recommendations:

We like to grow herbs in the front yard with the flowers, where they are handy. We have — both back and front — mint, shallots, chives, garlic, marjoram, several kinds of thyme, basil, and cilantro (which slugs love). It is best to grow herbs where you can gather a handful at the last minute, to throw into a pot that's simmering.

One herb, rosemary, doesn't seem to do well here. There is a folk belief that rosemary thrives best in the garden of a home where a woman "wears the pants." Pat claims I secretly stomp it out when she tries to grow it.

Pat: We use or preserve all our produce. We blanch and freeze individual packages, just the right size for any dish we like to cook.

SEATTLE: Stan Gessel

Stan Gessel is a city gardener. His present garden started as a weed patch-cum-junkyard that required a summer of cleaning, digging and leveling before anything much could be grown on it. The weeds that came out were the start of the ongoing compost pile. Stan's position as Professor of Forest Soils at the University of Washington makes him a local expert on soil amendments and vegetable gardening as well.

Site and Soil Conditioning

I ordered a couple of yards of composted sawdust and dug it all in by hand, then added nitrogen and phosphorus and let it sit over the winter. The following spring I planted the first garden we had here. It has never been mechanically tilled or cultivated — everything has been done the hard way. The area is only fifteen by twenty feet, so hand labor is possible throughout. I hand-water as well.

We excavated under the back porch for more house space. The soil from that went into the garden, too, so it is as raised now as I want to have it.

All the compost goes into the garden. Now and then I have a sample of forest soil from an experiment I am doing at the university, so I throw that in. Also I get a bag of dolomitic limestone every two or three years to keep the pH down. I buy commercial nitrogen and phosphorus only — I don't think soils around here are much in need of potash so I add it only very occasionally.

The compost bins take up a lot of space, but are definitely worth it. I've built them of concrete blocks, the kind with holes in them, about three feet high. We throw in all the vegetable matter from the kitchen and the garden, both flower and vegetable. Grass clippings when we have them. Once in awhile I add a little urea to help it along if it looks as if it needs nitrogen. In summer I have to water the pile once in awhile to keep it moist.

In December or January, when the garden is pretty well

Prof. Stan Gessel grows tomatoes in containers. He has little gardening space, but he understands soils and how to get the most out of them. He starts tomatoes inside, from seed, and grows enough to give some away.

Chives and parsley, strawberries and kale grow in planters, peas and beans climb the fence, flowers are tucked in here and there, as the Gessels "try to make room for everything" in two thousand square feet. "Everything" includes dwarf fruit trees, some grass and a basketball practice court.

cleaned out, I spread compost over it all. Even the large materials that aren't composted go on, but if they don't decompose by February, when I'm ready to get the soil ready again for planting, I rake the pieces out and throw them back into the bin. The rest of it I dig in and smooth out.

Planning and Planting

The first seeds I put in — in March — are radishes, beets, lettuce, peas, spinach, and onion — both seeds and sets. We like different varieties of lettuce and peas so we try them all. The peas are trained up along the wall, the fence, or on stakes, to keep them up out of the garden and in the sun. At the end of June when the peas are finished I replace them with pole beans. Harvest of these extends through September or October. As some things come out, others can go in: cauliflower and cabbage transplants are added. Carrots and lettuce are re-seeded. In May we have to do away with the beet crop just because we need the room. Tomatoes are more important.

I raise tomatoes to a good size under glass before I set them out — usually sometime in May when the weather seems right. At that time they generally have flowers at least, and often there are small tomatoes.

I will stick a cucumber or squash plant in among the flowers when there is space for it. I don't let any room go to waste.

The last plants I put in are Brussels sprouts and the last lettuce. The lettuce lasts us through October and the sprouts will furnish us with a homegrown vegetable until December or later.

We try to make room for everything. We like roses and dahlias as well as tomatoes and cucumbers. We're trying grapes along the garage wall, with a good south exposure. There's also an espaliered pear there. Chives and parsley go in the brick planter. Along the back porch are dwarf apples and a plum tree. There is a patch of grass for open space, and a small basketball practice court. All this we manage to squeeze into the two thousand square feet of our backyard.

Pests and Problems

We get root maggots on the radishes, aphids on the broccoli and other cole crops, leaf miners on the spinach, and worms in the cabbage. Usually they aren't a serious problem. When I think they are getting out of hand I go after them with diazinon or malathion. The slugs in the lettuce are annoying and I put down a bit of slug bait for them.

Recommendations

Most of our seeds and seedlings come from local stores. We don't look for unusual varieties for a special purpose. It is a plain garden; we haven't room even for corn or potatoes here. What we need is easily purchased nearby except for the tomato seed. I like Burpee's Early Girl, Big Girl, Beefsteak and Big Boy, and it is the only vegetable I will start inside. I always have too many, so I give a lot of them away.

Other varieties that we like and always try to plant:
Lettuce: Bibb, Romaine and leaf
Peas: Edible pod, no special cultivar
Radish: Icicle and Red Globe

Since I have spent much of my life studying Northwest soils, people ask me what they should do to improve their gardens. I tell them to use nitrogen in the form of ammonium nitrate or urea, but I always warn them to use it very carefully because nitrogen in high concentrations burns the plants. Occasionally if the pH level is exceptionally low, it is necessary here to add dolomitic limestone. Gardeners also need to get phosphates into the garden soil. It is cheaper to buy these amendments separately and use them as needed than to buy the boxed mixes labeled "for tomatoes," or "for roses."

I recommend composted bark or rotted sawdust as a good source of organic matter, but even when it is aged it should not be added without a little nitrogen and phosphorus.

I know some people are against the use of chemical fertilizers, but when they are used intelligently they are better and less expensive than the alternatives.

YELM: The Rev. Harold Dawson, with Joey

Yelm is a small town southeast of Olympia near the Nisqually River, which rises in the glaciers of the south side of Mount Rainier. The Dawsons came to Yelm after years of serious gardening near Roseburg, Oregon. They've had other gardening experience in Spokane, eastern Montana and Sitka, Alaska.

Yelm prairie is a glacial outwash area with naturally rocky or gravelly soil. Like the other prairies of central-western Washington, it is well drained and dry in the summer, thus supporting stands of oak among the evergreens.

Site and Soil

Harold: When we moved to Sourdough Landing in 1980, our three acres were pastureland. We fenced in the yard and about 1,500 square feet for the garden, and during a few warm days that first February we worked up the garden space. When real gardening time came, the space was a sheet of quackgrass. I knew I'd have to win a major battle with that right away, or I'd be in for constant warfare.

We wanted to try Bartholomew's idea from *Square Foot Gardening* [see bibliography], so I divided the garden space into four-foot squares with pathways between. Then I built a sturdy screen of one-inch rabbit wire on legs to straddle a four-foot plot, dug deeply, and screened out all the quackgrass rhizomes along with the bigger rocks. It sounds like a tremendous task, but I did some each day for two or three weeks and called it my aerobic exercise. Since then, when quackgrass comes through I just pull it out, rhizome and all, no matter how long it is.

We've built up the garden beds with compost so now the soil is loose and workable. We don't use any commercial fertilizer — we're "health nuts," all-organic gardeners. We use horse, goat and cow manure, and chicken manure when we can get it, mostly composted first with grass hay, alder chips, kitchen garbage, winter cover crops, whatever. We layer the stuff, keep it moist, turn it occasionally, and make sure it's crawling with earthworms.

Joey: Harold is big on earthworms. He raised them for sale in Sutherlin, but now he buys them. They don't live in this sandy soil, but they thrive in the compost.

Conditioning and Care

Harold: I rototill the garden in the spring to get it ready for planting. After planting, we hand cultivate or weed. Sometimes we use a mulch of semi-finished compost on the garden to keep down the weeds, but usually the plants are too thick and close together to need much mulch.

We had a drip system one year, but the green plastic hoses invited algae growth, which plugged up the emitters. The supplier changed to black plastic finally to solve that problem, but by then I had pulled out my whole drip system. Mostly now I water by hand, banking up the soil around the plants to hold the water in. I liked the drip idea, and may get it started again.

Climate Modification

Harold: Our climate here is colder than we were used to in southern Oregon in the summer. We notice the difference mainly in the size of our sweet-meat squash. Ten pounds is good here, but we expected several thirty-five-pounders in Sutherlin. One has to be more choosy about varieties here.

We often use visqueen tents or covers over the eggplant, peppers, and tomatoes. We have a sun porch on the south side of our house, too. It is a light, sunny place for growing tomatoes, sunflower greens and some other things the year around. If it is cold, we leave the door to the living room open to get heat to it from the wood stove.

Joey: We got the idea of sprouting sunflower seeds from *Mother Earth* magazine. They're about as nutritious as anything you can eat, and they're delicious.

Harold: We grow the sunflowers about four feet apart along the fence, with petunias, nasturtiums, marigolds and a variety of herbs between them. We use a lot of the sunflower seed in the bird feeder, but most of them we sprout for ourselves. We soak the seed overnight, spread them thickly on sifted compost an inch

After many years in Alaska, the last of them as skipper and mate on a mission boat, the Dawsons anchored on the Yelm prairie and put a piece of it to food-growing. They're confirmed "health nuts" and strictly organic gardeners.

deep on trays, and cover them with several thicknesses of wet newspaper. When they raise the newspaper we take it off, and in less than a week of total time we have two succulent leaves from each seed plus four to six inches of equally tasty stem.

Joey: Sometimes the hull comes up on the leaves and has to be lifted off, but that's easy. The sprouts don't develop well from hulled seed. We have sunflower seed sprouting all winter in the sun porch. They make any green salad better, and if you're out of other greens, they make a tasty salad by themselves.

Harold: That same issue of *Mother Earth* gave plans for a harvester to hull sunflower seeds, but I never got around to building it and now we've misplaced the plans. I feel guilty about that because we always have plenty of seed, but we buy hulled seeds for cereals and snacks.

We raise most of our own seed and like to have it as early as possible. But people are surprised at our weather — we don't have Seattle weather here. We get a close-up view of Mount Rainier from our living room windows, but it brings us later and earlier frosts. We can have frost through much of May, but the cole crops are usually hardy enough to survive cold nights under cover. I start putting seedlings out sometime in April.

I plant garlic and some onion in the fall. More onion sets can go in the garden from February on. Peas can be planted then too. During March and April I seed in cabbage and broccoli. Carrots seem to be less bothered by the carrot rust fly if planted in June, and they do just as well.

For fall, I put in cabbage, broccoli, kale, chard, lettuce and onions. Sometimes onions, broccoli, garlic and parsley will survive through the winter. But some winters they won't. We have had zero weather here.

I winterize everything except the fall garden by planting a cover crop. I have used wheat seed just because I had it readily available, and it grows well.

Pests and Problems

The cabbage butterfly is a pest, especially in my wife's lavender plants. I go after them with a tennis racket — good exercise.

Root maggots are definitely pests, but we don't fight, we retreat by rotating their favorites to another spot. Rutabagas and turnips generally are infested with them.

Joey: Another little problem is the aphid population in the sun room. They like all the light and heat, I imagine.

Harold: We have a real problem with potato scab too. We keep the soil very rich with manure and perhaps potatoes are not so pleased with that kind of soil as some of the other vegetables are.

Harold built bird houses to attract birds and get their help with insect control. Most of the sunflower seeds are sprouted indoors for salad greens. The birds get the rest.

We find it better to buy the potatoes. Carrots too — we like to have enough to make carrot juice the year around. Hard experience has taught us to plant onions and garlic early and use mulch.

There are difficulties with trying to garden here: tomatoes seldom ripen much before frost. Corn is iffy. So are eggplants and peppers. But we have learned to enjoy the things that do well here. We are happy working in the garden.

Recommendations

Try sprouting sunflower seed for winter greens if you have any inside space. You couldn't use it to better advantage!

My favorite seed company is Territorial, in Lorane, Oregon. Locally, we've found Gordon's in Yelm to be the best supplier of seeds and other garden needs.

I am happy to take Territorial's recommendations on what to plant for most things. I have tried almost every kind of corn, but we always go back to the old-fashioned Golden Jubilee.

I think it is important to work out a plan for a garden that suits your needs, your tastes. It is also mandatory to have a good compost pile going all the time. Keep your eyes out for spoiled hay and other free materials that could be added to your pile.

Buy a start of good red earthworms and take the trouble to find out the minimum care for their continued existence. They are worth a lot in the compost pile.

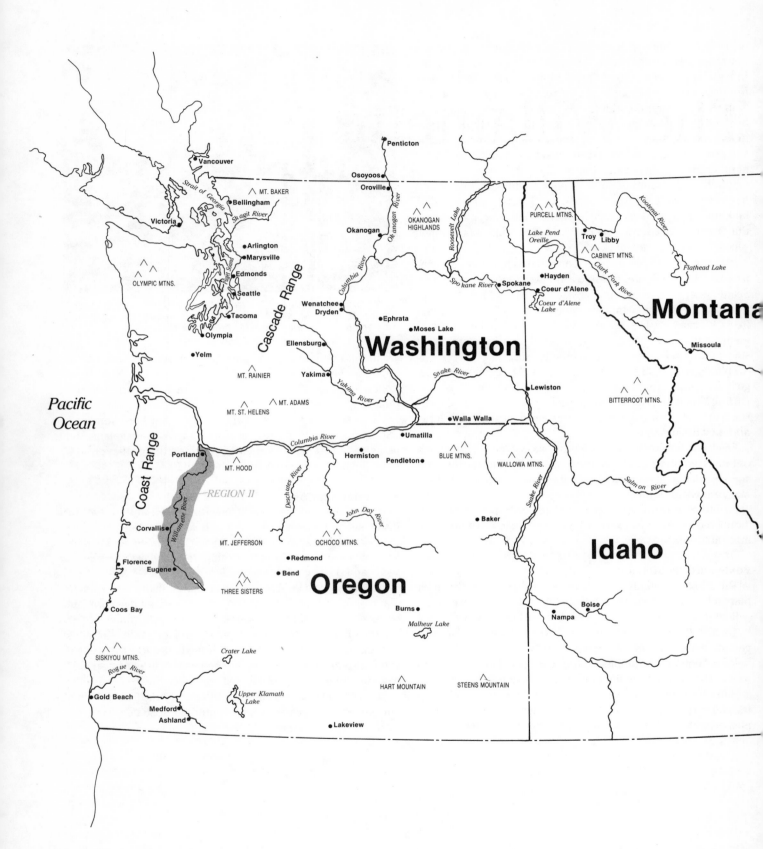

Pacific
Ocean

Montana

Washington

Oregon

Idaho

Strait of Georgia

Vancouver

MT. BAKER

Bellingham

Victoria

Skagit River

Arlington

Marysville

Edmonds

OLYMPIC MTNS.

Puget Sound

Seattle

Tacoma

Olympia

Yelm

Cascade Range

MT. RAINIER

MT. ST. HELENS

MT. ADAMS

Coast Range

Portland

MT. HOOD

REGION II

Corvallis

Willamette River

Florence

Eugene

THREE SISTERS

MT. JEFFERSON

Deschutes River

Redmond

Bend

Coos Bay

SISKIYOU MTNS.

Rogue River

Gold Beach

Crater Lake

Upper Klamath
Lake

Medford

Ashland

Lakeview

Penticton

Osoyoos

Oroville

Okanogan

Okanogan River

OKANOGAN
HIGHLANDS

Columbia River

Wenatchee
Dryden

Ephrata

Moses Lake

Ellensburg

Yakima

Yakima River

Columbia River

Hermiston

Pendleton

BLUE MTNS.

John Day River

OCHOCO MTNS.

Burns

Malheur Lake

HART MOUNTAIN

STEENS MOUNTAIN

Roosevelt Lake

Spokane River

Spokane

Snake River

Walla Walla

Umatilla

WALLOWA MTNS.

Baker

Snake River

PURCELL MTNS.

Lake Pend
Oreille

Troy Libby

CABINET MTNS.

Hayden

Coeur d'Alene

Coeur d'Alene
Lake

Lewiston

BITTERROOT MTNS.

Salmon River

Boise

Nampa

Kootenai River

Flathead Lake

Missoula

Clark Fork River

62

The Willamette

INTRODUCTION

Of all our Northwest regions, Nature has blessed the Willamette Valley especially. The temperatures are benign. Some of the finest soils are found there. Outstanding nurseries and plant stores abound. The valley teems with home gardeners and truck farms, with filbert and walnut groves, fruit tree orchards, grass seed farms, nurseries, Christmas tree farms — just about anything that can be grown in the Northwest can be grown here.

The Willamette is a broad, nearly flat alluvial valley with a scattering of low basalt hills. Elevation of the river increases from about 150 feet at Salem to around 400 feet at Eugene, making the flow rather too lethargic to interest even the mildest whitewater enthusiast.

On the west side of the valley are hilly extensions of the Coast Range. To the east, marine sedimentary rocks make up the near skyline. The valley was entirely flooded more than once during glacial times, with a resultant mix of usually silty deposits. Most of the valley bottom soils are sandy loam to silty clay loam, but clays may be found on the upper benches. Along the edges of the valley, soil parent material is igneous and sedimentary rock, and soils may typically be reddish brown, silty clay loam to nearly pure clay. Soils are generally acid and in need of liming to be suitable for vegetables and most other crops.

Weather records for Portland show that, for an average, it gets 49 percent of the sunshine which would beam on it through a year if clouds didn't get in the way. For comparison, the twin cities of Minneapolis/St. Paul, which lie at approximately the same latitude, get 58 percent. Boston, another latitudinal neighbor, gets 60 percent. Only a few U.S. cities get less than half the available sunlight per year. But Portland's summer sun is quite predictable,

and the lush productivity of the valley attests to the fact that there is ample sunlight during the important growing months.

Annual average precipitation (still in Portland) is 37.61 inches, very little of which falls in July and August. December is the average rainiest month of the year. Again, comparing Portland with Minneapolis/St. Paul, those two cities average 25.94 inches of precipitation per year, the highest amounts coming during the summer months (nearly four inches in June) and the least during the winter. Boston has 42.52 inches average, rather evenly spaced throughout the year.

Possibly to make up for less sunlight, Portland's yearly average temperature is higher: 53 — compared with 44 for Minneapolis/St. Paul and 51 in Boston. The gain comes in the mild winters, for Portland's average monthly temperatures never fall below January's 38, while in the Twin Cities, January brings a 12 degree average and in Boston, a 29 degree average. Portland's highest summer average is in July at 67 degrees, the Twin Cities, 72, and Boston 73.

Translated into vegetable gardening terms what does this mean? In the Willamette Valley, make the most of every ray of sunshine and preserve heat with the various heat-conducting and storage devices now available for all warm-weather crops. Don't rely on summer rains to water for you; plan an irrigation method. Capitalize on mild winters by growing the many cool-loving greens and root crops available to you.

If you are lucky enough to have some valley-bottom loam to garden on, enjoy it, add to it, and be grateful. If your soil runs to clay, amend, amend and amend some more, or fill raised beds with something lighter.

PORTLAND: Charles Bushman, with Marie

Chief of Utilities, Portland Veterans' Hospital (retired)

Charles Bushman is a happy man when he is figuring out a new and better way to increase the productivity of this city mini-farm, and the yard and house basement testify to his ability to rig up or build practical devices for growing, using and preserving their prodigious harvests.

Both Charles and Marie enjoy sharing their bounty and their expertise. He is involved in the Multnomah County Master Gardener program and volunteers time in teaching others to garden and to preserve. They brush up their own techniques in minicourses given by the local extension agents.

On one of their jaunts to some corner of the country, they are usually hauling along jars of jam or dried fruits and vegetables for distribution. They have an appreciative public in Hawaii just waiting for their apricot jam and dried foods when they get off the plane.

For the Bushmans are always searching for good buys on airline fares — it doesn't much matter to where. They will go to some new spot just because they got a bargain on the transportation.

Charles is only recently fully retired. Most of the work that has gone into this Portland yard and home was in addition to his regular work. Yet he has had time over the years to build and maintain the most thoroughly intensive garden covered in this book.

There isn't a single nonfunctional square inch of space in the Bushmans' 50-x-159-foot city lot. As you walk up the street in late summer you see the corn and sunflowers growing almost as high as the house, right there in the front yard with the roses. In the back, greenhouses, growing beds, a bee hive, fruit trees, compost and storage bins and a shed for the tiller, a patio and a small swimming pool, and permanent plant supports for beans, grapes, and the very tall September Red raspberries Marie Bushman has to pick from a ladder, give the visitor a sense of being in a much larger place: how is it possible to get so much into such a small space?

The Bushmans moved to this house in southeast Portland in March, 1940, and immediately set to work to improve the clay that had been excavated for setting the foundations of the house. Not only was the soil undesirable, the backyard was full of junk that had to be hauled out by hand. But to Charles it was inconceivable that they should not have a garden. He was gardening when he was six, "under coercion," and by the age of fifteen he was planting and selling produce for pocket money.

Site and Soil Conditioning

Charles: I've done a lot of digging around here. All the planting areas have been double dug at least twice. I dug the swimming pool by hand. It started out to be a wading pool for our daughters. As I was digging I got to thinking, those girls are going to outgrow a wading pool by the time we got it built, so I kept digging. We did all the reinforcement and concrete pouring too.

We started with clay and added manure by the six-yard truck-

Charles Bushman, confirmed innovator, tried growing squash in the compost bin, but "production hasn't been great." Starting in 1940 with clay and junk, he has developed a prodigiously productive urban mini-farm. Neighbors don't mind the permanent bean supports (below), as the Bushmans share their harvest.

load, sometimes chicken, sometimes horse. Now we use cow manure. And we buy sand by the ten-yard load. Always ask for construction sand. You get a better-quality, sharper-edged sand. Even now, after 46 years, I add sand.

We've added so much to the soil here we are two feet above the grade of the rest of the neighborhood. The fruit trees grow in pits in the soil. I also use rye for a winter cover crop and green manure and till it in when spring comes. Then I use a triple-14 fertilizer, extra potassium and phosphate as they are needed. I like to keep the pH at about 7. I check it in the tomato beds every year.

Everything but kitchen waste goes into the compost: wood ashes, apple pulp from the cider press, garden debris. Coarser waste goes through the chipper first. I've tried growing squash in the compost bin — but the production hasn't been great.

The finished compost is an ingredient in Bushmans' Famous Homemade Potting Soil:

1 part peat moss
1 part perlite
1 part vermiculite
1 part coarse sand
½ part finished compost, sterilized with Vapam

This is used for all potted plants, seed starting, greenhouse beds, top dressing on newly planted furrows outside, and mulch.

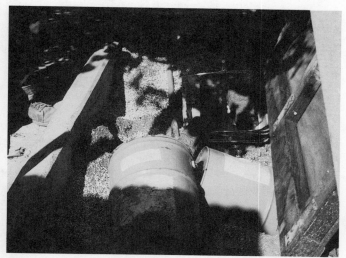

Bushmans' Famous Homemade Potting Soil, one of their shared secrets to success, is mixed in an underground bin, hand-dug as is the swimming pool. Charles does "a lot of digging."

Planting

I keep a detailed journal of the year's garden. That way I know what was planted, what we especially liked, what the weather was doing at various times of the season.

Some crops are rotated. I started out moving the bean frame from front to back every two years. Somehow it got heavier over the years, and I don't do that any more.

The BCS tiller, with a pivoting handle so it can be run with the tines in front or at the rear, is my favorite tool. All planting beds are prepared with it. It can be run backward, so at the end of the row there are no footprints in the bed!

All our weeding in the intensive areas and the greenhouses is done by hand. Rows of corn and cabbages are rototilled.

Other tools I use are a common hoe, a flat-bottomed, long-handled spade good for chopping, a power chipper and a power sprayer for the fruit trees.

Our beds are all raised — in fact the whole yard is raised. Those in front are permanent concrete structures. I plant corn and cole crops in rows, but carrots and radishes I often scatter-seed. Tomatoes and cucumbers go inside the two greenhouses for longer production.

We went into companion planting for pest control for a while, but the marigolds and nasturtiums looked so bad with all the bugs on them, I pulled them out.

Greenhouses have automatic drip systems, and some of the outside beds are also automatically watered. The system is in operation every day during the hottest weather, cut to every other day or less as cooler weather comes on. Corn is watered with hand-set soakers between rows, and soakers are used on asparagus. Sprinklers are set by hand for the rest, when they need watering.

Our planting schedule is something like this:

All seed except beans, corn, peas, radishes and carrots are started in the greenhouse in flats. In January I put in the lettuce, cabbage, cauliflower and kale seed.

Also the last part of January, peas go in the front bed outside, if the weather isn't too bad. We cover the rows with potting soil, as it seems to keep them warmer and doesn't freeze so easily.

The first of February the tomato seed goes into greenhouse flats. Seed potatoes are cut and sprinkled with sulfur and allowed to set 24 hours, then planted about the same time.

In late February, Marie starts her flower seed.

The first part of March I start cucumber and squash seed in the greenhouse.

Believe it or not, the first corn planting is usually in early April, and again we cover it with potting soil.

Then I start some more cabbage and cauliflower seed so we will have late crops. About this time, more corn goes in.

Everything is out by the first part of May. Tomatoes and cucumbers are permanently placed in their greenhouse beds, or in pots outside.

The late cabbage, cauliflower and lettuce seedlings can go in again in August. If they survive, great. If not, we're only out the seed.

We don't grow beets. Even pigs won't eat beets. Neither of us likes broccoli or Brussels sprouts, so we don't grow them either. We like to buy our Walla Walla sweet onions by the 25-lb. bag. We grow kale instead of spinach or Swiss chard because the leaf miners don't get into it.

With all our fruit trees, we don't get enough sun here for melons or for peppers, so we don't even attempt to grow them anymore.

Climate Modification

Number 1 greenhouse is a double-walled (acetate and fiberglass) structure built in 1954. This is where the longest-lasting tomatoes grow, a ground cherry bush makes its home, and tropical varieties of flowers from Hawaii stay all year around. The building is heated with a couple of Titan 1500-watt heaters except in the coldest weather, when I bring out a heavy-duty 5,000-watt heater. In summer, I pull sliding screens over the roof to keep it cool.

Number 2 greenhouse is lighter and a well-vented structure, not kept going during the winter. It is primarily for growing heat-loving plants such as tomatoes and cucumbers during the spring, summer and fall.

I put up a pea frame, which is easily taken apart and stored, in the front yard in late January or early February. After the crop is finished, I knock down the frame, put it away and plant corn.

The bean frame, which used to be portable, is made of sturdy lumber soaked in copper naphthenate. To soak it I use 4″ plastic pipe propped in the ground with a cap on its bottom. I pour the wood preservative in around the length of lumber to the top of the pipe. After several hours or overnight I turn the piece over and do the other end. This way I get the best possible protection for the wood and I don't waste the preservative.

Pests and Problems

We get aphids on the beans and corn. I use small applications of malathion if necessary for the beans, but not the corn when it is flowering, because it is lethal to the bees.

Cabbage worm — For this one problem, I will use Sevin, but I do not like to overuse this bee-poisoner.

For root maggots I will apply a commercial pesticide such as Dursban.

The crows and jays have a great time in the corn, and we put out Crow-Chex. It seems to discourage them. Human intervention is the only sure way to keep them off. Since our corn patch is right outside the front door, it is not such a great problem as long as we are home.

I have a good remedy for yellow jackets: hang a mixture of cat food and diazinon in a cottage cheese container or can from a low tree branch, where animals can't get into it. The yellow jackets take the poisoned meat back to their hives and share it around.

I use a commercially made lid that fits on a small-mouthed jar for flies. The jar is baited with a small amount of meat and partly filled with water. Flies can get in but not out again. It looks rather awful, but it traps a lot of flies.

We made a discovery when St. Helens erupted. We got fallout here and found that the ash was a good insecticide, especially for the apple trees. We had no coddling moths that year. One of the big difficulties in this area is getting the crops in early. Too much rain makes the ground cold. The best remedy is an extremely light, loamy soil.

Early fall frosts aren't a problem. If a cold spell hits, it won't be until late November at the earliest and by then we have the garden area battened down, with most produce stored or preserved and the remaining greenery in the greenhouse.

Marie: There isn't enough room for flowers. Charles likes them, but he doesn't think they are useful enough to waste much time and space on. If we have to choose between flowers and food, the food will win.

Recommendations

Charles: We are partial to Park Seed Company, but also like Liberty, Burpee, and Harris.

I raise exotic plants such as orchids and night-blooming Cereus and long ago applied for an Oregon nurseryman's license. I have number 013, which makes me an old-timer. I can buy plants and equipment from the wholesalers, Alfred Teufel Company, in Portland. (also in Everett, Washington — ed.)

Bushmans' Favorite Varieties:

Park's Greenhouse tomato — highly recommended for the greenhouse; excellent flavor and production

Red Express tomato — in pots outside

Better Bush tomato — in pots outside

Raider cucumber — strung up in greenhouse with tomatoes

Butternut squash

Oregon Giant pole bean — half our crop is grown for seed for the next year; we dry it on a screen in the garage

Alderman peas — grow very tall

Early Flat Dutch cabbage

Corn — Sundance, Honeymoon, Sugar Loaf, Early Sun Glow, Golden Jubilee

Pioneer carrot

Ground cherries — we grow one in the greenhouse

Kale

If you are moving into this area and want to start a garden, first get some herbicide like Roundup and get rid of the quack or Johnson grass. Then if you have clay, order 20 yards of coarse sand, spread about three inches over the entire surface of the garden area, and on top of that the same amount of cow manure. Store whatever you have left in the backyard for future use, because you won't have perfect soil the first year anyway. Rent or buy a good tractor-tiller and mix all this together thoroughly. Good soil is the main thing.

CORVALLIS: Homer Twedt

Fresh vegetables from the Willamette Valley show up in the markets of Corvallis, Albany and Salem, and are available at grower-operated produce stands such as that of Homer Twedt.

A former high school chemistry teacher, Twedt found that each year he was drawn farther into his summertime produce-growing, and decided to devote full time to it.

Soil and Site Conditioning

I now farm about 110 acres in disjunctive plots at the edge of town. Not all of it is in vegetables — 60 acres are in filberts and

Homer Twedt, chemistry teacher turned market gardener, farms 110 acres near Corvallis, 30 in vegetables, the rest in berries and filberts. He sells from a roadside stand next to his home.

15 are in berries. About 30 acres are devoted to vegetables. The soil is some sub-series of Willamette Valley loam that turns under the plow in such a lush, curling dark wave, it is a sight to make any gardener's mouth water.

Commercial vegetable raising is a different matter from regular home gardening. On 30 acres of land, there is less opportunity for manuring or adding organic matter to the soil. I use a commercial fertilizer which contains boron: Willamette Valley soils need boron.

Preparation of the soil is done by tractor, with a rotary disk plow. Fertilizer is added as side dressing during seeding (corn) or when the plants have begun to grow. Melons are fed by a fertilizer solution run through the drip irrigation system.

I'll tell you what I like to use for getting up the weeds when they are small: a hand-push cultivator. Even in such large areas, this method is far better than rototilling, and a rather simple matter if the weeds are not allowed to get out of hand.

Planting

I usually write out a plan beforehand, so we know how the land is going to be used. I try to keep the crops moving around, rotating to stay ahead of some of the particular pests. I'm careful to rotate tomatoes and melons.

By interspersing one crop with another, putting in the same variety of vegetable in different spots, I can cut down on the losses I might have if I were to use a monoculture-type of planting for each vegetable. Thus one large field will have a couple of long rows of broccoli, a couple of onion rows, then perhaps a section of melons. This way we stagger our plantings to lengthen the season of each variety.

I also like to locate some vegetables, such as tomatoes, beans and pumpkins, close to the sales area for the convenience of U-pick customers.

I'm enthusiastic about drip lines and I use them extensively. The problem with them is clogging. The intakes must have proper filters, which have to be cleaned often. The drip lines supply constant water as needed, with no waste, and that is a basic consideration. Fertilizer and water are the most important things.

Climate Modification

Another thing I am concerned about is the weather. Corvallis generally has a long growing season, but more often than not the length is determined by a late fall season rather than an early spring. Recently, spring has been a fickle ally, with possible frosts in May after tomatoes have been set out. A home gardener can tempt fate by putting out a few early plants, saving the major part for a week or two more. A commercial gardener is torn between the anxiety to get the tomatoes on the market first and the thought of the disaster of losing hundreds or thousands of seedlings on an unseasonably cold night. I can't run out and throw row covers over my tomatoes the last thing in the evening. There are just too many of them.

Row covering is getting more and more popular, however. It is a good way to beat the early cold and get a good start on the

Plastic row covers give Twedt's plants the early start a commercial grower needs. Drip lines supply water without waste. He plows with a tractor, but uses a hand-push cultivator and gets the weeds while they're still small.

vegetables. My row cover frames are made of 2-by-4 lumber with holes drilled every four feet for pvc pipe, joined together at the top angle. White plastic is used over it.

Many of the vegetable plants in my fields originate in local nurseries, such as Tom VerHoeven's Peoria Gardens. My principal concern is getting the plants early enough to get a head start. In commercial produce growing, the first one out with the produce will be the most successful, as everyone is eager to buy what is newest on the market.

I am growing and selling vegetables from April through October. I plant peas in early March, start the greenhouse plants in March and April. Other times, I keep busy pruning trees and caning berries.

Pests and Problems

As for pests, my worst enemies are nematodes and symphylans. Every gardener needs to know the sign of nematodes in the garden, and to identify symphylans by sight. Get down there on your knees and look. I use a commercial growers'

Many of Twedt's seedlings come from local nurseries. A market gardener, he's torn between the need for an early market start and the fear of losing thousands of seedlings to a late frost.

pesticide, such as Lorsban or Difonate. Slugs congregate under the plastic row covers, but Lorsban takes care of them too.

Recommendations

Pick Red and Jet Star tomatoes,

Super Sweet corn (planted well away from other varieties, to keep it from hybridizing)

  Other tomato varieties: Early Girl, Moreton Hybrid
  Other corn varieties: Beacon (early), Reliance (next early), Silver Queen (white), and Golden Jubilee
  Cucumbers: Raider, Lemon
  Broccoli: Premium Crop
  Cabbage: Market Prize
  Beans: Day Bush Snap Bean
  Melons: Burpee hybrid, Harper hybrid, Ambrosia, Huogen

For many of the vegetables, there are so many excellent ones I hate to name just one.

Most of my seed I order from the catalogs — usually Harris and Burpee. Some, such as corn, peas and beans, I buy in bulk.

I get very good technical advice from the Extension Service. When I'm stumped by a disease or insect, I go to them for help.

For those who might think of following my way of life, I'd give them this advice: go slow, don't try to do it all at once, add a little acreage at a time, and diversify. If one crop doesn't do well, you will have another to make up for it.

EUGENE: Pat Patterson

In the Lane County Extension office by the fairgrounds in Eugene, you might be able to find this gardening expert tending to her duties as a Master Gardener coordinator and part-time fill-in horticultural extension aide. Or again, you might find her at home on her 9.64-acre farm outside of Eugene off the highway to the coast, with husband Robert, tending to 2,000 square feet of raised beds, as well as to the orchards, greenhouse, solarium, Japanese garden, livestock, pasture and wildlife refuge. She might even be in the house preparing fruit and vegetables for storage in the root cellar. There is a hot tub, too, but it is hard to imagine when anyone around there has time to relax in it.

Site and Soil

I have been gardening my whole life, although only seriously since 1975, when we moved here. We began with bare clay used to run cattle on, with no earthworms, no squirrels, no birds.

The general origin of soil in the hills west of Eugene, where our place is located, is volcanic. There are 200 soil types in the valley around Eugene, and ours happens to be yellow clay. Raised beds are a necessity. Still, it is better than the local blue clay, which is a thick, sticky mess most of the year. Anyone with blue clay has little choice but to use raised beds and order a truckload or two of better soil to put in them.

We started with three beds, or about 300 square feet. Since then we have expanded to the present 2,000 square feet.

Of 200 soil types around Eugene, Pat and Bob Patterson drew yellow clay. Better than blue clay, Pat said, but even so, raised beds are a necessity. The Pattersons floored their beds with chicken wire to solve a problem with rodents.

Conditioning

The first year we hauled in old hay from people's barns — about 30 tons of it. We put this into the pasture, the orchard and the Japanese garden and worked it in. For the beds, we saved all the manure from our own animals and have used it as the basis of the material in the beds. We also use manure on the beds after they are cleared out for the season.

At one point we owned two hundred rabbits. To make use of every bit of rabbit manure, we built bins under the cages and added earthworms. The rabbit herd has dwindled now, and goats and sheep are our major manure source. Those are the three best sources — high in fertilizers and low in weed seeds.

We don't use sawdust for soil amendment, as it takes too much nitrogen to break it down, but we do like a commercial bark mulch for fluffing up the beds.

When we started the pH of the soil was 4.5 to 5.2 — far too low for much besides blueberries. We have raised it to a healthy 6.5 or higher.

We seldom add lime now, but since the natural tendency of soils in the Willamette is to become acid, we test occasionally to determine lime need. Vegetables that readily show lack of lime are beets, which will exhibit zoning in the root; and cabbage and spinach, which become lax, leggy and of poor quality.

We make compost of any healthy organic matter available except kitchen scraps, which are recycled through the livestock first. We have carted materials from Eugene's leaf dump, but the city officials are getting wise and making their own compost now, which they sell by the pickup load for a nominal fee. We do not use wood ash in compost; we either dump it on the weeds or use it in spots around places that need a little extra potash.

Bone meal — steamed to rid it of impurities and pathogens — rock phosphate, fish emulsion kelp spray, cottonseed and blood meal are other fertilizers we use. Kelp spray and fish emulsion is a remedial foliar treatment for plants that need specific and immediate help. Also, the potassium and trace minerals in kelp increase cold hardiness in plants. Kelp can be used wrong. We never use kelp meal because there is often a problem with heavy-metal pollution, and a growth analog in kelp, if overused, will cause hairiness in root crops and even retard growth.

We don't need machines for cultivation in the raised beds. We do it all with light handwork. Vegetables are grown close together to keep the weeds out. By now, the soil is loose enough to allow hand-digging of potatoes.

For favorite tools I'd have to mention a Warren hoe for furrowing and covering the seed when planted, a pitchfork for moving hay and straw, a flat-nosed shovel, a hula hoe, and a couple of trowels, one narrow and one wide.

We double-dug our beds at first, or dug them very deeply and thoroughly. But we had a rodent problem so we laid one-inch chicken wire in the bottoms of the beds and haven't been able to dig farther than that since.

Planting

We keep a careful journal of each year's garden and farm activities. We analyze the good and bad of the preceding year and

In Pat's beds, narrow because she is short, vegetables are close together to keep out weeds. Each bed is numbered and she keeps computer records of what to repeat or replace. Plastic jugs on the numbered posts (below), bottoms cut out, are for protecting individual plants from sudden frost.

decide what to repeat and what to replace. We have the luxury of a computer to keep these records now. A card file will do as well — the cheap computer. I recommend this to everyone. No one's memory is complete, of course, and putting pieces of information together for several years is the best way to find a trend.

We rotate mainly to avoid diseases. We are especially concerned about scab and careful to move the potatoes around. We don't rotate to get away from insects, as I don't believe it helps. Insects move about very well, that's how they've been so successful.

Our beds are laid out more or less rationally, and are numbered and lettered, so Bed 1-A is the first section of the first bed and so on. That way we can identify where things are planted as we keep up the journal records. The beds are all three feet wide because (a) I am lazy, and (b) I am short.

Transplants are set out in a diamond pattern, although I think

The Pattersons practice polyculture, the art of planting herbs, flowers and vegetables together. She hasn't found many antipathies among plants, and as for trap-planting, "It's hard to trick insects—they've been around too long."

the ideal pattern is the beehive hexagonal, if I could just manage to keep track of how it goes as I set out the plants. Sometimes I scatter seeds and then thin, but that's hard to do — killing all those little seedlings.

Our schedule:

January: Cole crops and other cool-season vegetables are started in the greenhouse.

February: Start the first tomatoes, make a second planting of January seeds, and flowers.

March: Get serious about warm-season starts, except for melons, which will not do well if left too long in the greenhouse.

April: Peppers, squash, cantaloupe and further seedings of the early crops.

May: Everything goes out by mid-month except melons and peppers, and a few of everything else just in case. Early tomatoes and peppers in pots go on the house deck.

June: Start seed for fall crops (collards, lettuce, chard, carrots, beets).

(It should be noted here that the Pattersons' garden is in the

hills, at over 700 feet elevation, so they are likely to get later and earlier frosts than Eugene itself.)

We have water rights for pumping irrigation water from Long Tom River. We use a 5-horsepower pump and water with Rainbird sprinklers. If I had my choice, I would have a drip system, but even with the sprinklers the filters plug up fast. We simply can't use the drip method of watering. Some people in our area have difficulty getting enough water from their wells, so we are lucky to have the river.

Climate Modification

I use the deck, the enclosed hot-tub room, and the garage-cum-solarium for potted plants. At one time we had three greenhouses for bromeliads and orchids, but we have now reduced that to one, which is close enough to the house to tend easily. It is heated with a wood stove, and, yes, we do take turns getting up on cold nights to keep the fire stoked.

Heating mats are handy for propagation. These mats are obtained from a California wholesaler, and have double thermostats for extra protection from shorts. Everything except beans and root crops is started on the mats in Speedling flats — a foam compartmented tray shaped so that it automatically root-prunes the plants as they develop. The plants pop right out at transplanting time.

Reemay and polyethylene row covers are used for weather protection from February to June, and again from mid-September on until the last crop is gone. Beds have permanent frames and the covering material is ready to throw over them so we can run out and cover them at midnight if it feels like a sudden frost. We also use plastic jugs as supplementary protection for individual plants.

We don't use mulch extensively as it tends to cool the ground — we don't need that. The one thing we will go out of our way to get is hardwood shavings from a local furniture factory to use for mulch on potatoes and Jerusalem artichokes. We may use black plastic around the eggplants, melons and okra for soil heating.

We find that hot-weather vegetables, when they mature in this climate, often don't have the taste we like. We have to compromise by choosing borderline varieties and giving them all the help we can by various season-extending tricks.

Pests and Problems

We practice polyculture, or the art of putting a variety of vegetables, flowers and herbs together. I don't find many antipathies in plants. Anyway, it is hard to trick insects — they've been around too long. They know what they want and where to find it.

It's possible to use trap crops such as nasturtiums for flea beetles, or calendulas for cucumber beetles, but then what do you do with a bed of flowers full of bugs?

In diseases, we have nothing much that can't be dealt with by keeping weeds out and the area clean. There are some viruses and blights that cause a few problems — not serious.

For weeds, the first year is going to be the worst no matter what. The second year, if you are using raised beds and planting them intensively and hand-weeding, you are going to have a much

better situation. By the third year your bed should be in good shape, providing you don't add more weed seed in an uncomposted mulch or amendment.

Slugs are our worst problem. My answer to that is sourdough. Use any sourdough recipe to get a starter and let it work until it has a clear, alcoholic liquid on top. Stir this in, then put some of the mixture out in the garden in a cottage cheese container with holes big enough to let slugs in. They love it, like beer — and it kills them. Of course it doesn't hurt animals. If you add cornmeal and molasses you can attract and destroy cutworms as well, but there is a danger of attracting ground beetles. Since ground beetles are good guys, keep a close watch, and if you find them in the sourdough, discontinue treatment.

After slugs come aphids. We also get flea beetles at some point in the season, and leaf miners get in the chard, spinach and beet leaves. Once in awhile we get cucumber beetles, and on an extra dry year, some white fly.

My first choice for treatment is insecticidal soap. If that doesn't work, I use Bt *(Bacillus thuringiensis)* mixed with soap. If that doesn't knock them out, I try rotenone. But I consider rotenone a very toxic substance — worse than malathion, though it doesn't last so long.

We never use a powdered insecticide. It is not specific enough. It spreads to other things. I am very careful of chemicals; I have a lot of respect for them.

Even the insecticidal soap can be lethal to the wrong thing if used at the wrong time or in the wrong proportions. It can burn tomato seedlings, for example. Whatever I use, I always try it out on one or two seedlings before I spray everything.

We don't use garlic or cayenne sprays — they don't seem to do much good, and if you read the recipe you'll see it calls for the addition of soap anyway. Why not just use soap?

Recommendations

If it works, don't fix it. If you really like what you have been growing — if it works for you — then keep ordering more. But try something new, a couple of varieties a year, at least. That way you can keep up on the new cultivars offered by the seed companies. If you find one you like even better than the old one, don't be in a hurry to throw the old one out. You might have had an unusual year. Try it a couple or three years before making up your mind. Only you can know what varieties are best for your particular tastes and garden.

We look for the qualities of flavor, vigor, appearance and production. We can't use very large, space-grabbing varieties because we have a finite area for growing. We like to look for new and unusual plants to surprise our friends.

Variety List

Bean	Beurre de Rocquencourt wax
	Royal Burgundy bush
	Oregon Giant pole
Beet	Jacob's Cattle dry
	Formanova
	Ruby Queen

Tropical ornamentals, wintered in a greenhouse, get summer space in the Pattersons' 2,000 square feet of raised beds. They pump water from Long Tom River and irrigate with sprinklers. Pat would prefer a drip system, but even with sprinklers the filters plug.

	Winterkeeper (Mangels)
Bok Choy	
Broccoli	Purple Sprouting
	Green Goliath
Cabbage	Baby Badgerhead
	Chieftain savoy
Carrot	Royal Chantenay
Celery	Dinant (slender, for seasoning)
	Utah improved
Chard (Swiss)	
	Geneva
	Perpetual
	Ruby Red
Chinese Cabbage	
	Monument
Collards	Blue Max
Corn	Bicolor Sugar Dots — a "corn's corn," stays well on the stalk
	Golden Jubilee — for drying, grinding and canning
	How Sweet It Is — almost like candy, you can eat it raw and it's good frozen
Cucumber	Burpless Bush
	Sweet Slice
	Sweet Success
	Lemon — pick while very young
Kale	Konserva
	Blue Knight
Kohlrabi	Winner
	Grand Duke
Lettuce	Royal Oakleaf
	Continuity
	Red Salad Bowl
	Black-seeded Simpson

Onion	Spartan Banner
	Spartan Sleeper
Mustard	Tendergreen
	Kyona
Parsnip	All American
Pea	Oregon Sugar Pod
	Sugar Ann
	Sugar Daddy
	Rembrandt
Parsley	Paramount
Peppers	Early Thicket
	Early Bountiful
	Italian Sweet
	Gedeon
	Hades Hot
	Staddon's Select
	Thai Hot
Potato	Finnish yellow
	Peruvian blue
	Red Pontiac
Radish	Champion
	French Golden
	Cherry Belle
Rutabaga	Best of All
Spinach	Melody
	Long-standing Bloomsdale
Squash	Ponca butternut
	Gold Nugget
	Vegetable Spaghetti
	Delicata
Sunflower	Sunbird
Tomato	Celebrity
	Early Cascade
	Sprinter — good for both cooking and slicing, more meaty, not so juicy
	Gold Nugget — a favorite from OSU
	Fantastic — medium to large, grows well for us
	Ropreco — hard-to-beat sauce tomato
	Early Girl
	Longkeeper
	Willamette
Zucchini	El Dorado
	Round
	Onyx
	Burpee's Hybrid

Working in the extension office has given me a good overall picture of gardening problems in the Eugene area. The worst ones have to do with cold soil and poor drainage. Those are problems to be solved over time by soil amendments, use of season-extending materials, and physical labor.

"The soil is everything," says Master Gardener Pat Patterson, who has built her soil out of "any healthy organic matter available." Her advice to the new gardener is to study the soil and use the Master Gardeners program where "there's a lot of help to be had."

Other commonly asked questions about vegetable gardening have to do with aphids and root maggots in the cole crops. For these, I try to preach what I practice: the use of mild insecticidal soap, and row covers for the time when the cabbage butterfly is at large.

To a new gardener, I would say: What is your soil? It is everything. Go to the soil service. Look at the soil maps for your area. If you can, spend one whole year just keeping records for your place — what the weather is, what happens in different spots, what warms up fastest, where the most sun shines, what drains well, what doesn't. After that, start planning the garden.

And use the Master Gardener program here. There is a lot of help to be had from us.

The Rogue

INTRODUCTION

Big Butte, Little Butte, Elk and Bear creeks form the upper Rogue River a little north of Medford, in the southwestern corner of Oregon. The Rogue then winds its way along the foot of the Siskiyou Mountains and through the Coast Range to reach the Pacific Ocean at Wedderburn and Gold Beach.

To the traveler moving out of the Willamette Valley south of Eugene, the land begins to take on a different aspect. For one thing it is higher, and inland it is a lot drier. Around Ashland and Medford the natural vegetation is often chaparral — a scrubby, dry association of low trees and bushes — or pine-oak forest. Toward the coast, where precipitation is higher, the forests are a denser, mixed evergreen type.

Medford, at the center of the inland Rogue, sits at an elevation of 1,300 feet. Average annual temperature is 53 degrees F., with a July average in the low 70s and a January average of about 38 degrees F. Yearly precipitation is 20 inches, with no very significant amount occurring in the summer.

On the whole, the Rogue Valley offers good conditions for vegetable gardeners, with warm and sunny summers and a long enough season to produce most of the vegetables in the seed catalogs. Winter gardening is a definite possibility here, with the use of protective materials. Cold air drainage off nearby mountains may cause some very cool nights, summer or winter, but most often the effect is felt in spring and early summer when plants may be set back by low night temperatures.

The fog and damp air of the coastal region keep back the frosts of winter but make summer gardening problematical, with a slim supply of heat units for vegetables that particularly like heat. Enthusiastic use of new heat-enhancing materials and all sun-trapping strategies will benefit the coastal garden. Gardeners around Coos Bay and Gold Beach may gain more from Willamette Valley gardening data than from that of Medford/Ashland, with some allowance for local adaptations. Soils, particularly those around Florence, are apt to be very sandy, and need large doses of amendment in the form of organic matter.

For the gardener, the southern inland and southern coastal areas are two quite separate areas with separate environmental factors to consider, but they are still both part of the same valley: the Rogue.

ASHLAND: Marjorie and Jim Luce

The pretty town of Ashland sits in a bowl of the Siskiyou foothills. Marjorie Luce and her husband, Jim, a retired surgeon, live just outside of town on the southwest slope of the bowl, looking through the pines on their property to the east side of the bowl. They have preserved much of the natural vegetation and have collected and added native species and flowering plants to what was there. A path meanders around the gardens, allowing a leisurely tour from the front door out over a dry stream, through small woods, past the herb garden and around to the workshop and the shaded garden patio where indoor plants can be set during the summer and, when it is hot, one can join them for a rest in the shade. There is a deck that goes nearly around the big house, allowing views over the tops of the pines to the valley and hills beyond.

But no vegetable garden?

Marjorie: We've had vegetable gardens, but not here. Since we've been in this house we've raised a few things in pots, but it is too shady, and we like the trees. We had a farm for years,

The Rogue River in southwest Oregon rises in the Coast Range, skirts the Siskiyous and enters the Pacific. Gardeners in the upper and lower valleys contend with distinctly different conditions.

down the valley. I also gardened when we lived in Medford, and I had an herb garden long before it was popular to have herb gardens. I've raised vegetables since 1950, and worked at it with my mother when I was a child. Now I spend a lot of time with the Jackson County Master Gardeners' group. We have one of the most active groups in the state. Maybe even *the* most active. I've been president of the group here, and vice president in charge of promotion for the state organization.

We put on a Spring Fair as an educational project for local people. Gardening and nursery companies from Ashland, Medford and other nearby towns take part, put up booths — Jackson and Perkins, for instance. We offer help on starting plants, pruning, composting, raised beds, winter gardening and that sort of thing. Then in the fall we put on another fair, with the Master Food Preservers, to help people learn how to harvest and store their crops.

We put out a calendar which contains all kinds of tips for people gardening in this area, from Roseburg to the south, out to the coast. We also have a book on family food production.

Site and Soil

Jim: We have fertile soil here, mostly deriving from decomposed granite. There is a lot of clay, too. On the east side of the valley farmers run into a black, sticky clay, nearly impossible to work with. On our side of Bear Creek we have lighter soils. For some reason there was less granite on the east side during the last geological upheavals, and more deposits of the very fine stuff.

In the valley itself, on either side of Bear Creek, there is a typical sandy loam, seven to ten feet deep in the most favorable spots, and some gravelly places. Glacier action brought some fourteen different types of soils into the valley from volcanic pumice to gravels. On our ranch north of here, we had a twenty-acre field with that many soils in it. How can you farm that?

The upper end had to be irrigated by pumping water from the river, and the lower end was always wet and sticky.

Because of the soil types the best way to garden here is in raised beds. Otherwise there is no question we have good conditions for gardening, and an adequate growing season.

In general, up on the hillside here we have rather acid soils because of the pine and oak leaves, although there are local areas with pHs of up to 7.

We have our own rain gauge here. In the valley, the average rainfall is 13 to 18 inches per year. For every one hundred feet of rise in elevation, there'll be another inch of rain per year. We are at 2,500 feet or so, and I have recorded these total rainfalls since we've been here: 1982-83: 46.85 inches; '83-84: 35.5 inches; '84-85: 28.14 inches; and '85-86: 36.35 inches. Well, you can't grow on an average, can you? You have to deal with what you get in any particular year. That does show you how precipitation varies according to your location, however.

Conditioning

People here can get redwood bark for their mulch and soil conditioner. We can also get fir bark, but redwood decomposes much more slowly, thus using less nitrogen at a time. We can get rice hulls, too, but I don't recommend them as an additive. They sprout. Aged sawdust is easy to come by here, and we can buy a good composted mixture from the Hilton Wood Company. There are many kinds of manure; sheep is the best because the seeds are more fully digested so they aren't sprouting in the garden. Manure is usually mixed with straw or sawdust.

We irrigate our gardens from a well on the property. We're lucky in this area to have some very fine artesian-type wells.

Everyone makes compost — that we can all agree on, though we have different ways of going about it. A lot of people use the three-bin method, and buy shredders to cut the wastes up as small as possible before they go in. We had a regular compost-maker going here for a while. It is a self-contained plastic bin three and a half feet across and three feet high, with holes in the bottom. We used a commercial compost starter; kept it well mixed and the temperature up to 140 degrees F. It takes a lot of work. Did you know, incidentally, that you can get a compost deodorizer if you think you need it?

The best gardens in this valley are on the best soil, no doubt about it. Most people are conservative, do row gardening. Many have rototillers and all the machinery necessary to do a big job. Families cooperate by buying a piece of machinery and passing it around.

Planting

Marjorie: People start gardening here by growing starts inside in March. We try not to start too early, as we may have a late killing frost. Seed can go in the garden around the first of May, usually. Peas go in earlier. Here on the hill where we are, we are warm later in the fall, but cold later in the spring than in the valley. Even so, we don't get some of the frosts they do, since the cold air drains right on past, so our crocuses are

Dr. Jim Luce and his wife, Marjorie, have grown food crops elsewhere, but on their land near Medford they have preserved natural growth, added more native species and flowers, and buy homegrown produce at nearby truck gardens.

out the cabbage butterflies and the fly that produces the root maggot.

Walls-o-Water are very popular here.

Our own most intensive efforts now go into our pots: pots of flowers, herbs and a few vegetables. I have tried the drip irrigation method in a pot of zucchini, but it is a lot of trouble.

Jim: For our planters, we mix some of our own soil, some commercial potting soil and some triple-13 or, more likely, slow-release fertilizer. We won't use the liquid fertilizer. When I stood there and watched it drip out the bottoms of the pots onto the decks, I decided we didn't need it. We have brackets on the deck pots now, so the pots can be swung out away from the deck when we water, to avoid staining the wood.

I designed a couple of tables for putting our plants on. We can set the scented geraniums and many of the plants we have outdoors in summer on these rolling tables, keep them in the insulated garage where there is enough heat from the big freezer to keep them from being destroyed in the coldest weather, and on warm, sunny days we can open the doors and roll them out.

Pests and Problems

Marjorie: Besides having too much shade for gardening, we have a lot of deer. I don't want to discourage them but of course they eat any tender greens they can find. I've grown squash in pots, and tomatoes, but the deer will come up and shake the fruits right off the bushes. Herbs work out better. The deer don't seem to care for most of them.

There are many organic gardeners here who won't use commercial fertilizers or any pesticides, and a few have dropped out of the Master Gardener program rather than recommend to others the use of chemical pesticides of any kind.

Recommendations

I would recommend Nichols Seed Company very highly for herb seeds. Other people here like Park as a good general source of seed. Gurney's seems a particular favorite with the organic gardeners. We like Territorial Seed Company. Steve Solomon (owner of Territorial Seed) comes and talks to our Master Gardener group.

There are many good nurseries and seed stores in this area: Ashland Greenhouses, the Grange Co-op, Stage Coach Farms, Valley View. Bish's does a lot of commercial herbs. Most people know about the Siskiyou Rare Plant Nursery, but they are open by appointment only.

It is popular to grow sweet potatoes here.

Dillard (up near Roseburg) is the best local spot for melons. Everyone knows about the Dillard cantaloupes. They are on the Umpqua River, down in a little valley, where it is quite warm.

Roseburg is also famous for a coreless carrot. Everyone loves to grow it.

We grow the Medford variety tomato in our pots.

Jim: The most difficult thing about gardening here is the soil. It is best to make raised beds, making sure there is good drainage underneath. If necessary, buy the soil ready-made. It will be worth it.

often out earlier — sometimes the middle of January.

Herbs are very good for interplanting in both flower and vegetable beds. They can go along the sides as borders, or right in among the other things.

We are spoiled now, not raising anything but a few tomatoes, and buying excellent home-grown produce at a famous truck garden not far away: Hanscomb's or another place. We do our own picking. Hanscomb's is located right on Bear Creek, on excellent soil. They don't seem much bothered by pests there and they think the presence of lots of trees and blackberries along the creek keeps the bugs in the brush and not in the garden. Some weeds are well known for attracting certain insects: nightshade draws the potato pests; prickly wild lettuce will draw the bugs that like greens.

Climate Modification

People are beginning to use the Reemay-type cloth for keeping

Ordinarily we have 170 days of frost-free growing weather and, especially in the valley, very little snow in winter. Lately, though, we have had some very uncertain spring temperatures, though there is no way of knowing if it is a permanent pattern.

MEDFORD: Jackson County Master Gardeners

Rogue Valley Vegetable Planting Schedule, from The Master Gardener's Calendar for the Rogue Valley, Oregon and Environs, *Jackson County Extension Service, 1986.*

January: In light, loamy soil areas, peas can be planted this early. Suggested varieties: Aspen, Aurora, Corvallis, Dark Green Perfection, Green Arrow, Laxton Progress, Little Marvel, Oregon Sugar Pod.

February: Start seeds for all *Brassicas* inside; start tomatoes.

March: Dig vegetable garden and prepare soil for planting; plant more peas, as well as lettuce, cabbage, onions, potatoes, kale and chard, weather permitting. Start squashes, cucumbers, melons inside late in month.

April: (average last frost date this month) Plant *Brassicas:* cauliflower, kohlrabi, more cabbage and broccoli (suggested broccoli varieties: Green Comet, Waltham 29). Plant more onions, carrots.

May: Time to plant and transplant all beans, Brussels sprouts, cantaloupes, cucumbers, dill, eggplant, kale, peppers, pumpkins, squash, late potatoes, corn, tomatoes and watermelon.

June: Plant rutabagas, late crops.

July: Plan your winter garden: beets, carrots, cauliflower, lettuce, broccoli, cabbage, collards, peas, kale, kohlrabi, parsley, mustard, spinach, radishes, turnips, Chinese cabbage. They should be ready by October.

August: Plant peas for late harvest. Fertilize squash, melons, cucumbers and broccoli for further growth.

September: Pick and store winter squash; green tomatoes for ripening inside if frost threatens; beets, cabbage, collards, kale, kohlrabi, mustard, spinach, Chinese cabbage can go in for early spring harvest; bring in a few chives, parsley plants, other herbs, for windowsill gardening over the winter.

October: Plant garlic for next year; dig and store potatoes; harvest all remaining squash and pumpkins; plant more crops for early spring.

November: Divide and mulch rhubarb; mulch asparagus beds; spread manures, mulches over vegetable garden area.

December: Plan next year's garden.

REGION IV

The Okano(a)gan

INTRODUCTION

Here we examine the river valley and the adjoining hillsides only. The land away from the settled parts is generally rugged and very little suited to gardening. The higher areas can have frosty nights nearly any time of year. The natural vegetation is a forest and grasslands mix, with ponderosa pine a dominant tree. The valley from beginning to end has been glacially scoured many times, with a resultant jumble of soil types—or no soil at all. Much of it is coarse and very well-drained material. A good source of irrigation water is very important to the gardener.

The *Okanagan* Valley lies north of the border beyond Oroville, Washington, and Osoyoos, British Columbia. It has been the fruit basket of western Canada for some time, although many "For Sale" signs are noticeable on the orchards along the roads. With the new interest in wine producing, some of the orchards are being converted to vineyards. The valley, with its many lakes and its reputation for sunshine, is a favorite place for summer recreation. The towns are thriving and busy; the countryside is beautiful. The best agricultural land and climate lie within a short distance of the river itself and the lakes it drains, a band narrowing from a widish corridor at the border toward Penticton and Summerland, and stretching through Kelowna to Vernon.

The *Okanogan* Valley of the south is merely an extension of the same river, spelled with an o instead of a second a, on its last miles toward the Columbia just south of the town of Okanogan. Except around Lake Osoyoos prosperity is less evident and farms are fewer. Some fruit orchards dot the sides of the valley up through Omak and Tonasket, but not in abundance as in the valley farther north.

Lacking the fine, long lakes of the upper valley, this area is less popular with summer recreationists. Nevertheless, in the fall hunters from far afield come to search for its herds of mule deer, and most of the year individuals looking for open spaces and scattered high lakes are attracted by its wilderness country.

Annual precipitation in the Okano(a)gan Valley runs about 10 or 11 inches, but those in the northern parts will receive slightly more. Most of the precipitation comes in the winter, and all Okanogan gardeners must face the fact that their gardens need considerable irrigation.

Temperatures vary significantly, with cold air drainage from the high ridges an important factor, but the large lakes add their ameliorating influences. On the average, Penticton gardeners can expect about 140 days of frost-free growing, from early in May to the first of October. As in many places, but especially here, Nature may throw a monkey wrench into the works with a June or September frost, and it has been known to freeze as late as the middle of June. Hope for everything, but count on nothing! Keep a few tomato and pepper plants in a safe place until it looks as though summer has certainly come.

The same advice goes, and double, for those who live on the fringes of the Okano(a)gan highlands. Here it is advisable to search out the warmest spots, where the snow melts first, for a garden. All expectations should be tempered by the knowledge that frost can hit at any time. On the other hand the high, dry hills are likely to be parched by mid-July. The summer sun will draw moisture out of the soil at prodigious rates. With luck, there will be about 100 days of good gardening time.

Eggplant matures for Earl Chambers in Penticton, where 100 good growing days are expected. Irrigation is imperative here, as the summer sun is hot and summer rainfall is next to none.

PENTICTON: Joyce Brown, Marg Penny, Earl Chambers

Here is an introduction to three energetic, innovative and civic-minded gardeners of the town of Penticton, which lies between two lakes in the Okanagan Valley.

Joyce Brown has lived in the same house in Penticton since 1950. There was no soil whatever for gardening when she came, but she is a determined and active person and she wanted a garden. By bringing in an initial layer of topsoil, then returning every scrap of good organic matter to the garden, she has literally created soil where none existed.

The large backyard garden under the care of Marg Penny extends from the back door, under an enormous walnut tree, to the chicken house at the alley. Marg keeps busy canning and freezing her produce, besides running an agricultural exhibit for the area in the fall. There are 3,000 exhibits, from Apiaries to Youth, and she is in charge of the whole thing.

Earl Chambers runs the quintessential intensive garden. His ideas for space-saving strategies ought to qualify him as gardener on the first long-term space flight. In the six years he and his wife have lived in their present house, he has developed a system for efficient and low-care vegetable growing that makes the best use of their city lot and still gives them plenty of room for grass and flowers. The vegetables themselves take up 20 × 36 feet of space.

Site and Soil Conditioning

Joyce: We had a creek running right through the front yard for years, until the city engineering department diverted it. The spring floods of the creek scoured out the soil and washed it downstream, so we were on rock and gravel.

In general, the Penticton area has alkaline soil. Keeping up regular additions of compost keeps my soil at a good pH.

I'm not good at composting, but I'm dedicated. I either dig the waste right back in as is, or throw it in the bin for later use. I never throw out a scrap that is usable in the soil. The larger material I shred with the lawn mower if I can, and sometimes I use a commercial composter named Rot It.

The size of the vegetable garden is only about a tenth of an acre, or less. I conducted morning and afternoon kindergarten classes here for 25 years, with as many as 86 children at a time. I didn't have time for a lot of gardening. I enjoy having flowers all around, and keep much of the yard in perennial beds.

Marg: Our soil is sandy. We have added a lot of composted chicken manure (it must be composted to get rid of the weed seeds). We keep a large (four by eight) composting bin going all the time. We have enough organic material in the soil now, we don't have to water more than once a week—except the raspberries, which take more while they are producing. Watering is most important, though. You can plant all the seeds you want, but if you don't give them water to start they won't do a thing.

All the digging is by hand, a little at a time. I garden in blocks, or plots, and dig one plot at a time. I try to get it dug a few days ahead to let it settle. Then I rake it out and plant it. I plant in short rows within each plot.

I start out at six every summer morning in the garden. The Lord gives you good ground to work with and it's hard to resist it. But it isn't always easy. Lately I've taken a lesson from a gentleman next door who was gardening in a full body brace. He lowered himself to a pad on the ground and gardened from that position. I make myself a quilted pad or use a couple of folded feed bags, and it is a lot easier than stooping over. Of course, you have to get up every now and then and move the pad.

Earl: We have a glacial deposit here of sand and silt, no stones. The original pH was very high, about 8.2, but now it is down to 7 where it belongs. I have squeezed a compost bin in between the garage and the edge of our lot, where I put my grass and leaves and encourage my neighbors to leave theirs too. It makes a humus quite fast and I have put it all into the garden beds to build up their organic content. I also use a little triple-7 commercial fertilizer when needed, and have double-dug many times. Now I hand-weed the beds.

Planting

Joyce: I was brought up on the prairie of Saskatchewan and learned to grow food in rows, so that's how I did it for many years. Now I've learned to use the wide-row, scatter technique because

it is easier and keeps the weeds down. I think the plants like the company, anyway—they like to cuddle up to one another.

I like the idea of companion planting, especially of putting flowers with the vegetables. My father thought I was nuts, though. He could grow everything, even in the very short seasons in Saskatchewan, but he never mixed vegetables and flowers.

Earl: I make sure we rotate our vegetables around the different plots for a change of scenery.

Joyce: I have the best luck just putting seed in the ground, not transplanting. If they fail, I buy some replacements. A couple of hot spring days may cause the ground to dry out very quickly if I'm not watching carefully.

Since my soil is shallow, I've not had good luck trying to grow root crops. The best things for me are the vines: squash, melons and tomatoes. Our hot summer weather makes them thrive. But I must tend to the watering very carefully. The shallow soil means the roots can't grow deep and they dry out easily.

Marg: The first things I plant in spring are the peas and broad beans, perhaps by the end of March. Did you know that if Easter comes early, it means an early planting season? I grew up on a farm and learned all that lore. The signs of nature, and planting by the moon, were all important.

After the peas and broad beans, the potatoes go in. Then the carrots, beets, parsnips and any other root crops, probably the first part of April.

There is a gap after this, before the lettuce and early cabbage, which have been started in the coldframe, are transplanted to the garden. That is usually early May. About May 15, beans, corn and tomatoes can be put out. So can melons and squash, a bit later.

I can get beets and carrots through October, and the late corn will last into October. So will the potatoes. The best kind for me are Norlands. Pontiacs are a good late variety.

Earl: I make a written plan and follow it, but there are always changes to make at the last. I like the idea of raised beds and am going to be doing that more, planting my seed in blocks.

My first seed, onion, is planted on March 1, inside the coldframe. On March 15 or thereabouts, I plant cauliflower and cabbage seed. Tomatoes get their start the middle of April. They won't be put out until the first of June, so I don't want them getting too big and hard to take care of beforehand. The onions go out on April 10 and the others go out the latter part of April.

I start seed in the garden by the first of April. Usually it will be carrots, peas, spinach, radish and lettuce. April 10 I seed parsnips and set out potatoes. Corn and beans I'll plant May 10, and cucumbers and squash by mid-May.

I have part of the garden fixed up with an underground drip system. The average rainfall in this area is eleven inches a year, so during hot weather I irrigate every second day.

Climate Modification

Joyce: We always have "unusual" weather here. When I first came, it was hot and dry in the summer, as it is now. But lately we have had colder and rainier springs, shorter summers, and early frosts. On the whole, we have moderate winters. The storms

Chambers gives his tomatoes an April start in coldframes heated with 25-watt light bulbs. The plants go outside in early June.

come from the coast, to the west. Our major winds blow either up the valley or down, north or south.

It is possible to have late fall or winter gardens here by putting in carrots, lettuce, beets and such, but few people do. One must wait until it begins to cool off again, as the seeds don't germinate well in the hot weather. Some people will grow a small amount of produce in their greenhouses all winter.

Earl: I don't have a greenhouse—there really isn't room.

I use cloches to get my soil heated and the young plants started. I do use a coldframe, made of old storm windows. In the early part of the season, I heat them with five 25-watt bulbs strung in each one. I guess you could call it a hotbed, in that case. I start onion, cauliflower, cabbage and tomatoes in these beds.

We overwinter carrots, parsnips, celeriac and beets by leaving them in the garden and mulching them with leaves.

I plant a salad garden in a large wooden box sitting on an old lawn mower. This way we can wheel it around to convenient spots, where the sun is shining—a portable salad garden.

Joyce Brown, Marg Penny and Earl Chambers bring gardening experience from widely different areas and now, in Penticton, they pool their know-how and encourage other gardeners. Their tastes run to flowers as well as food crops.

My underground drip system comes from a 50-gallon drum set up at the end of the garden. I fill the drum with water from the hose and let it warm up. The plants get gravity-fed, heated water any time I want to turn on the tap.

Pests and Problems

Joyce: The worst problems here have to do with weather—frosts at the wrong time, or intense summer heat that dries things out. Water just disappears. I would put in a sprinkling system if I were to start over—although there's a lot to be said for hand-watering. You get time to plan and think about your garden. You enjoy your garden at the end of a hose.

Our insect pests include aphids. I brush some diazinon on the barks of trees to keep them off because they are worst there. Earwigs come and go and aren't too serious. A climbing type of cutworm strips plants at night and is annoying. My worst enemy is the grasshopper. Now I don't do much but worry about them,

though back on the prairie we used to do something awful like put out DDT mixed with sawdust to get rid of them.

Earl: Our worst pest was the wireworm. I got rid of them by digging everything over a dozen or so times and picking them out. For root maggots I've used a collar about six inches in diameter slipped around the stems of the *Brassicas.* For aphids, I use Safer's Insecticidal Soap.

I think the most common problems gardeners have here are the very hot summer weather, the soils—which have to be amended — and some of the insects. But on the other side of the coin is the long growing season: 142 days frost-free.

Recommendations

Joyce: My favorite sources of seed are Ontario Seeds, T and T of Winnipeg, or Burpee. I think seed or plants bought from places as close as possible to your own environment are the best.

Earl: My favorite seed companies are McFayden, where I can save a great deal on costs, Dominion, and Stokes. As for a local nursery, I would recommend Knapps.

Humus is the single most important thing to put in the garden: three or four inches every year. I would start a new garden by having my soil tested by an expert, then learn to test it myself every year to make sure I have the required ingredients.

Joyce: I think the newcomer here should consider first what soil he has, as it is the most important ingredient. It should be developed in any way available to the gardener, with a lot of organic matter.

As in many things, getting together with people who like to do the same thing often accomplishes a lot. We have a garden club here (I am now president) that has developed a rose garden near Lake Okanagan. We also sponsor a lawn and garden competition for the city of Penticton. The members volunteer to judge different aspects of gardening over the seasons. We have an Early Spring Garden award, Rose Gardens, Street Fronts, Vegetable Gardens in August, Late Gardens and Fall Gardens in September and October. We began by giving out silver cups or plaques, but people were lukewarm about that, so now we have heavy plastic plaques printed with the words "Penticton Beautifidtion Council Award" and the date. They can be put up on a fence or gatepost and are very popular.

I am also a member of the Beautification Council, which makes suggestions to the City Council about how to improve the looks of the city. Our current project is walking paths—not sidewalks but dirt paths. The City Councilors didn't understand why sidewalks weren't just as good, but when you're a bulldog or a terrier you don't give up on your ideas. We wanted real walking paths, and we are beginning to get them now, with little wooden footbridges over the creek.

Earl's Variety List:

Cabbage:	Golden Acre
	Houston Evergreen
Carrot:	Scarlet Nantes
Cucumber:	Straight Eight
Onion:	Riverside Sweet Spanish

Potato:	Red Pontiac
Radish:	White Icicle
	French Breakfast
Tomato:	Pink Delight
	Delicious

Space Saving (Earl Chambers)

1. Along one end and one side of the garden I string chicken netting, and sow a double row of peas along it.
2. In the centre of a bicycle-wheel rim I place a 12-foot 2-by-2 planted about 2 feet into the ground. On top of this I fasten another rim. The holes are already drilled in the rims, so it is easy to string wire from bottom to top and down again. I use wire out of an old electric blanket. This is my pole-bean planter.
3. Cucumbers can be trained to climb a coil of cement wire 3 feet in diameter and 6 feet high.
4. I can grow Hubbard squash on a trellis made by stringing line from the bottom to the top of a rectangular wooden frame. I use netting for other likely climbers—for instance, cucumbers.
5. I divided my garden by a fence made of stucco wire, so I can have more climbers and flowers in a small space.
6. I sow seeds the same distance in all directions: carrots 3 inches apart in block planting, Spanish onions 4 inches apart. There is no walking on the plots and no hoeing.

Most recently, Earl has changed to raised beds and square-foot gardening, as advocated in the book, *Square Foot Gardening,* by Mel Bartholomew (Rodale Press, 1981).

First, Earl took out his hedge on the east edge of the garden to let in more light. Then he created his beds, each 16 square feet in size (4′ × 4′). Each square holds a certain number of plants: 16 carrots, 4 leaf lettuce plants, 1 cabbage, for instance.

To aid in planting, Earl constructed square-foot planting boards by drilling holes at assorted distances apart: 16 holes for small plants, 9 holes for plants needing four inches of space each, 4 holes for 6-inch spacing, and 1 hole for a large plant.

The new square-foot beds are just south of the long, east-west rows of peas and corn. A path divides the area to give access to the beds (see diagram).

"This is the best garden I ever grew," he maintains. It's a good example of the restless spirit of the never-quite-satisfied gardener—always looking for a new and better way to raise vegetables.

VEGETABLE VARIETIES RECOMMENDED FOR PLANTING IN THE SOUTHERN INTERIOR OF BRITISH COLUMBIA HOME GARDENS *(from a 1980 Provincial Government Publication)*

Asparagus:	Martha Washington, Mary Washington
Beans:	
Pole:	Scarlet Runner, Blue Lake and Romano

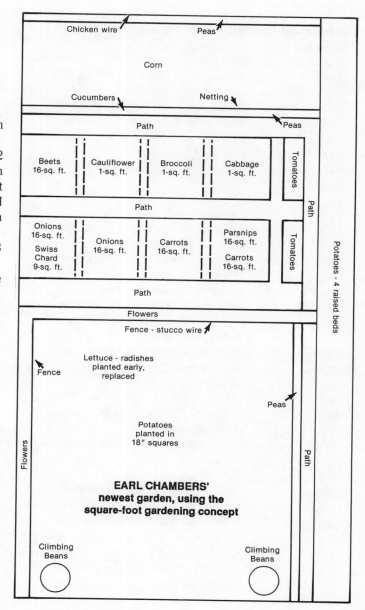

EARL CHAMBERS' newest garden, using the square-foot gardening concept

Bush, gr.:	Tendergreen and Executive
"wax:	Puregold, Round Pod Kidney Wax
Beet:	Ruby Queen for mucky soil, or Detroit strains
Broccoli:	Waltham 29, Italian Green Sprouting, Premium Crop and Hybrid Southern Comet
Br. Sprouts:	Jade Cross F and Long Island Improved
Cabbage:	
Early:	Early Marvel
	Early Wonder #1 and Stonehead
Mid:	Emerald Cross and Market Topper
Late:	Pennstate Ballhead, Danish Ballhead and Houston Evergreen
Chinese Cab.:	Michihli, Crispy Choy, and Burpee's Hybrid

Cabbage, red:	Red Acre or Mammoth Red Rock
Cabbage, Savoy:	Chieftain
Cantaloupe:	Honey Rock, Canada Gem, Harper Hybrid, Far North, Gold Star or Gosc
Carrot:	Hipak, Hybrid Spartan Sweet, Super Nantes, Gold Pak and Scarlet Nantes
Cauliflower:	Super Snowball, Snowball Y—late, Imperial—early, Igloo—late
Celeriac:	Prague or Large Smooth Prague
Celery:	Florida 683, Utah 52-70 or Clean Cut
Chicory:	Witloof
Corn:	
Early:	Garden Treat or Sunny Vee
Mid:	Earliking, Morning Sun, Sunburst, Extra Early Super Sweet or Golden Beauty.
Late:	Jubilee, Stylepak and Seneca Chief
Cress:	Extra Fine Curled
Cucumber:	Marketer, Challenger Hybr. or Marketmore. Pickling: National or Pioneer. Greenhouse: Faribo (Long Engl.) or Burpee Hybrid
Eggplant:	Black Magic or Black Beauty
Endive:	Green Curled
Leek:	Unique
Lettuce:	
Head:	Pennlake, Great Lks., or Ithaca Butterhead
Bibb:	Buttercrunch, Butter King, Dark Green Boston
Leaf:	Grand Rapids, Salad Bowl or Prizehead
Onions:	Spring seeded: Gringo or Riverside Sweet Spanish (sweet Spanish type for autumn) Storage for winter: Autumn Spice, Improved Autumn Spice, Yellow Globe Denvers, Autumn Splendour, Stokes Exporter. Pickling: White Portugal, Silver Queen
Green Bunching Onions:	White Lisbon, Beltsville Bunching, Southport, White Globe, Japanese Bunching
Parsnips:	Harris' Model, Model, Hollow Crown Improved
Peas:	Laxton's Progress, Progr. No. 9, Onward, Tall Telephone, Laxton's Superb, Dw. Telephone
Edible Pod Peas:	Dwarf Gray Sugar, Little Sweetie, Mammoth Melting, Super Sweet-Pod, Snow Peas
Pepper, sweet red:	Vinedale
Pepper, green bell:	Liberty Belle
Pepper, pimiento:	Perfection
Potato:	
Early:	Warba, Fundy, Early Epicure
Mid.	Norland, Norgold Russet, Kennebec,

	Pontiac
Late	Netted Gem, Kennebec (Norland, Norgold Russet, and Netted Gem are scab resistant)
Radish:	Cherry Belle, Champion, Comet
(fall)	Japanese Nermia, Long Black Spanish
Spinach:	Northland (Viking), King of Denmark, Longstanding Bloomsdale
Squash, acorn:	Table Queen, Royal Acorn, Table King
banana:	Banana
Turban:	Buttercup, Perfection
Hubbard:	Baby Hubbard, Golden Hubbard, Blue Hubbard, Green Hubbard, Warted Hubbard
Gourd:	Butternut
Zucchini:	Hybrid Zucchini, Golden Zucchini
Summer:	Golden Nugget, St. Pat Scallop, Early Summer Crookneck, Vegetable Marrow Bush
Swiss Chard:	Lucculus, Burpee's Rhubarb Chard
Tomato	
Bush	Earlirouge, Fireball, Bush Beefsteak, Starfire
Vine:	Early Red Chief, Stokesdale
Staking:	Early Giant, Ultra Boy, Wonder Boy
Gr-house:	Vendor
Turnip (Swede):	York, Altasweet, Laurentian
Vegetable Marrow:	Whitebush, Green Trailing
Watermelon:	New Hampshire Midget

OKANOGAN: Steve Harman, Linda Heaton

On the slopes off the road to Loup Loup Pass, almost 2,000 feet above the valley, Steve Harman and his wife, Linda Heaton, have

The only abrupt change is the spelling where the Okana(o)gan River crosses the International Boundary. The Okanagan Valley (Canadian) has slightly more rainfall, more orchards and more prosperity. In both, climate and soils are best close to the river.

spent the years since 1981 building a home. It has been 99.9 percent hard labor and determination. They came in an economically flat time, when unemployment was high, and found part-time jobs pruning apple trees and cleaning motels.

Since then things have improved and they have full-time jobs they enjoy, but their jobs and the travel to and from Okanogan each day take a lot of time, and the work on their hillside ranch goes slowly. In their "spare" time, they have built their sturdy, weather-resistant new home around an existing small cottage.

The 50 × 100-foot garden is surrounded by an eight-foot deer fence, a necessity here. In the late summer it is a patch of green in the golden hillside, tempting to wildlife. They located it in a flat pocket of deep soil with a small aspen grove on one side.

Site and Soil

Steve: We started our garden a couple of years after we moved here from Seattle. I rototilled, then brought in horse manure from a place up the road. Later we added sheep manure from another farm. I assume the soil was acid to start with. It is generally a forested area, which indicates a low pH.

Planting and Planning

The more we garden, the less we plan. We know how much and where we want to plant without thinking so much about it. We do keep a weather diary, so we know exactly what we are dealing with here. Our high so far has been 104 in July or August, and our low −25 in January. We are convinced that you can learn more from your own personal records of the microclimate you deal with than you can from weather forecasts or radio reports.

When the snow is off Omak Mountain, they say around here, it is time to put out the tomatoes. Usually early to mid-April is the date for cabbages and peas. From then to mid-June we plant a succession of crops, the late corn being the last to go in. We plant carrots in mid-June because we find we can avoid the carrot rust fly that way. On November 2 we pulled up about 150 pounds of carrots with no sign of maggots, and no chemicals used. That was real success. We have never had lettuce bolt or go to seed here, though it is a common complaint down in Okanogan. Our last crops will be out by the first of November, except parsnips, which go from Thanksgiving to February.

We do everything here equally, but Linda may weed a little more equally than I do. We have different ideas of what weeding is. Linda is neater. I tend to let them grow under control, which means I don't weed thoroughly where they aren't crowding the vegetables.

We have worked out a drip irrigation system that comes from the well. The tubes deliver the water exactly where we need it, and there isn't any waste. We get down and place the lines precisely where we want them and get a chance to look at the plants from ground level when we do. I think it is a good idea to see what is going on from that perspective.

Climate Modification

We use black plastic mulch to warm the ground around tomatoes and peppers and at the end of the season we cover them

A tall fence protects the Harman-Heaton garden nearly 2,000 feet above the Okanogan Valley, where a spot of green on the golden fall hillsides draws deer and elk. Steve and Linda started in 1981 and built up their ranch by hard work and determination.

with a clear plastic to keep them around a week or two longer. By October we pick the remaining tomatoes that look as if they'll ripen and pack them in boxes. We manage to keep at least 80 percent of them that way, and can have fresh tomatoes right through the fall. This year we harvested 75 pounds of tomatoes on October 12, some of them to put away for later ripening.

Pests and Problems

Other than deer, which we control with the fence, our problems are gophers, mice, grasshoppers and aphids. We have tried gopher traps, which don't work, rat traps, which do work if you direct the gophers' paths by placing obstacles such as cinder blocks in the way, and propane gas. Gas is the easiest—I stick the nozzle down the hole and turn on the gas. Just about anything seems fair to me when I find a whole row of nice, fat carrots chewed off underground nearly to the soil line.

We have found literally swarms of praying mantises at the PUD parking lot in Okanogan. We collect them and let them loose in the garden. At least some of them manage of leave egg cases to produce another generation the following year. We are quite sure they have reduced the grasshopper population.

Grasshoppers don't like squash vines, so we plant the squash around the edges of the garden. Grasshoppers work from the outside toward the center, at three or four inches a day. Squash leaves slow them down. Also, red cabbage seems to get less attention than green. Maybe they don't like the color.

Our worst problem may be our own attitude in the early spring when we should be starting seed. Everyone around here gets the winter blahs about February. Ice and snow for so many months, little dirty-snow paths around the place, and the lack of different activities eat away at your sanity. We've been taking a big vacation in a hot, sunny spot at that time, but it means being behind with our garden planning—and just about everything else—when we get back. We get casual about it, I guess. Then when it thaws and

the hills begin to green up, everyone cheers up and gets going again. And we wish we'd started our seed earlier.

Recommendations

In this area the first thing a gardener should do is observe his own microclimate. There are places nearby where our neighbors cannot grow corn or tomatoes because of cold air drainage. They grow very fine broccoli, cabbage, cauliflower and Brussels sprouts because their site is much cooler all summer, but it would be too bad if they had planned on a large corn crop. People who are considering a move into new land around here would do well to watch the area over a whole year to see just what goes on.

We buy our seed from Stokes, Seattle Garden Center and FM Seeds, the local feed store. Varieties we like:

Beans:	Tendercrop, bush
Beets:	Long Season
Cantaloupe:	Honey Rock
Carrots:	Danvers Half-long, Royal Chantenay, Imperator

Eggplant:	Ichibon, Japanese
Cucumber:	Burpee Hybrid
Cabbage:	Ruby Red, Early Jersey, Golden Acre
Broccoli:	Waltham
Cauliflower:	Snowball
Spinach:	Long Standing Bloomsdale
Onions:	sets of Walla Walla Sweets
Parsnips:	Hollow Crown
Winter Squash:	Acorn, Turban, Mimma
Summer Squash:	Patty Pan
Peas:	Sugar Snap

We plan for a fall garden, even up here in the hills. After frost has killed the summer crops we will have the following vegetables in the garden for late picking:

Cauliflower, broccoli and cabbages — a main crop for mid-October; **carrots and beets** — pulled around Halloween; **bok choy and parsnip,** covered and picked through the winter.

Penticton

Osoyoos
Oroville

Vancouver

MT. BAKER

Bellingham

Victoria

Strait of Georgia

Skagit River

OLYMPIC MTNS.

Arlington

Marysville

Edmonds

Seattle

Tacoma

Olympia

Yelm

Cascade Range

Puget Sound

Okanogan

Okanogan River

OKANOGAN
HIGHLANDS

Columbia River

Roosevelt Lake

PURCELL MTNS.

Lake Pend
Oreille

Troy Libby

CABINET MTNS.

Kootenai River

Flathead Lake

Spokane River

Hayden

Spokane

Coeur d'Alene

Coeur d'Alene
Lake

Clark Fork River

Montana

Missoula

Wenatchee
Dryden

Ephrata

Moses Lake

Washington

REGION V

Ellensburg

MT. RAINIER

Yakima

Yakima River

Snake River

Lewiston

BITTERROOT MTNS.

Pacific
Ocean

MT. ST. HELENS

MT. ADAMS

Columbia River

Walla Walla

Umatilla

BLUE MTNS.

WALLOWA MTNS.

Coast Range

Portland

MT. HOOD

Deschutes River

Hermiston

Pendleton

Willamette River

John Day River

Baker

Snake River

Salmon River

Idaho

Corvallis

MT. JEFFERSON

OCHOCO MTNS.

Florence

Eugene

THREE SISTERS

Redmond

Bend

Oregon

Boise

Nampa

Coos Bay

Burns

Malheur Lake

SISKIYOU MTNS.

Rogue River

Crater Lake

Upper Klamath
Lake

HART MOUNTAIN

STEENS MOUNTAIN

Gold Beach

Medford
Ashland

Lakeview

90

The Upper Columbia River Basin

INTRODUCTION

The north-central basin of the Columbia lies wholly within the state of Washington. Deep layers of basalt from the massive lava flows of geologic times underlie the region. Some of the area, known as the Channeled Scablands, is deeply cut with dry coulees and shallow, stony soils. The dominant vegetation type is grass, or shrub/grass in the lower parts and scattered mixed ponderosa pine stands in higher elevations along the edges of the region.

Precipitation is highest on the edges of this basin and lowest in the middle, and as a result soil types have been formed from the basalt or wind-blown parent materials. In general, the soils are high in mineral content but very low in organic matter. They are likely to be coarse in texture and require a lot of water to be rendered productive.

Climate can be harsh—from above 100 degrees F. in summer to well below zero in winter—and winds don't help matters. Spokane's highest recorded temperature is 108 degrees F. in August, and the lowest ever recorded there is a minus 25 in December. Spokane's growing season is about 140 days, from early May into September. Summer sun is abundant, but winter days can be gray. Summer temperatures average 65 to 70 degrees.

On the western side of the basin, the cities of Ellensburg and Wenatchee are influenced by the mountains at their backs. Winds can be fierce in Ellensburg as air pressure differentials of the coast and inland attempt to sort out their disagreements.

In Ellensburg, there is a 25 percent chance that the temperature will go down to 32 degrees during a mid-May night, and the same by September 19. From May 31 to September 8 there is very little chance of frost. In Wenatchee the best growing season extends from May 16 to September 31, with ever-decreasing numbers of days available as elevation increases up the Wenatchee River valley toward Leavenworth.

Ephrata, sitting well out in the basin away from the mountains, has a longer growing period—usually from early May to late September. Precipitation here is even less than can be expected in the outer circles of the basin, but the amount of rain that usually falls on the Columbia Basin in summer is too little to keep anything except bunchgrass and juniper happy. Irrigation for all crops is absolutely necessary over the entire region.

WENATCHEE AREA— DRYDEN: Robert and Adele Samuel
(Market Gardener)

When Robert Samuel was only six, he was pestering his mother for a little space for a vegetable garden of his own. After putting on a few years, he is still an enthusiastic gardener who works hard in his two large sections of garden, growing for his family, his neighbors, and the county fairs at the end of the season.

Adele: In our entire married life on the ranch we have never had to buy either fruit or vegetables. We can and freeze for the winter, and during the spring and summer we eat fresh veggies from Robert's gardens. We also sell surplus vegetables to the local residents and to cafes, to supplement our Social Security.

Robert receives a hundred or more ribbons a year at the fairs for his fruit, vegetables and flowers. He has so many ribbons our daughter made a large wall hanging of them—and she won a blue ribbon for that.

Robert Samuel, gardener since age six, has won so many ribbons for his fruits, flowers and vegetables that his daughter made some of them into a large wall hanging, and won a blue ribbon for it!

Planting

My schedule will be something like this:

Late April: onions—both seeds and sets, lettuce, spinach, peas, snow peas, carrots, beets, parsnips, Swiss chard, Jerusalem artichokes, salsify, kohlrabi and eight kinds of potatoes. Also cabbage, broccoli, and cauliflower. Then there is a bit of a lull. Perhaps about then I will also put in celery. When all danger of frost is over, tomatoes, bush beans, lima beans, three kinds of corn, cucumbers and fifteen kinds of squash. June first or a little later, the okra, seven kinds of peppers or more, eggplant, cantaloupes and watermelon. I will usually put in a late planting of redleaf lettuce and spinach for a fall crop. I grow sage and dill for herbs, as they are usually in demand around here.

Adele takes orders over the phone and pins them up by the back door. I fix up the orders. People come by to pick them up later. Some of them order the same things all the time, so all they

In the foothills east of the Cascades, Robert Samuel has turned 18,000 square feet of hard clay into garden soil, where he grows produce for his family and for sale. He starts some plants in a coldframe (below), then uses it with the lid up to grow tomatoes.

Site and Soil

Robert: When we came here in 1966 we had a grass field, nothing else. In one place there was a horse corral. Gravel had been dumped there—to keep it from getting muddy, I suppose. I don't mind some rocks, however, as they help drain and warm the soil. To prepare the garden, I first had a bulldozer scrape off the sod, then I rototilled with a tractor.

Our soil is basically hard clay. Every year after the crops are finished, I put horse or chicken manure mixed with sawdust on the garden and till it in to get it ready for the following year.

Conditioning

We keep a compost pile going, but one section of the garden gets more compost than the other because it is closer. I make up for it in the other section with the sawdust/manure mixture. The compost is kept in a bin and I turn it every time I think about it—about once a month. It gets watered whenever the sprinkler is over there, and I add some ammonium nitrate once in awhile to keep it working.

One garden section is 125 × 125 feet. The other one is 50 × 50. That's more than 18,000 square feet of garden to tend.

I never put lime on the garden. The native pH tends to be high in this country. With manure added, it grows good vegetables just the way it is.

I do put on a side-dressing of triple-16 fertilizer after the plants have been in for awhile. It takes about two eighty-pound sacks to the do the whole garden. I water it in, and that does it for the summer.

I work the garden just as soon as the snow is off and the soil has dried enough. Usually I start planting around the latter part of April. I plan it out in my head and know what I am going to do with it — no sense in writing it down. I never grow anything in the same place twice in a row if I can avoid it.

do is pick up the phone and call in for "the usual," like a regular customer at a restaurant. They appreciate having freshly picked produce.

The first part of September I pick out the very best specimens for the Chelan County Fair, in Cashmere. We also like to take some of our best gladiolas and dahlias.

I start a lot of my plants in a coldframe, on the south side of the tool shed. I've used a cable in the frame for thirty years—a lead coil with a thermostat, to give bottom heat. Unfortunately it quit on me last year. I made do instead with fresh horse manure in the bottom. It was satisfactory. After I am through starting plants in the coldframe, I use it with the lid up to grow some of the tomatoes and other plants.

After the plants start growing well, I can use the rototiller with the outer set of tines off to go between the rows. It tills an 18-inch width with the tines removed. I grow everything in rows. We grow so much it is easier to tend that way.

I water with overhead sprinklers. I don't like to water in very hot weather, 90 or 100 degrees, as it will burn the leaves.

My favorite tools are a scratcher-type hoe, a six-tined hand cultivator, and my power tiller. I don't think a person could keep up with such a big garden without some mechanical help.

Climate Modification

The past few years there have been frosts here up to around the first of June, but that isn't supposed to be usual. The season should start a week or two earlier. It seems to us the general weather pattern has been changing, getting colder in the winters and drier in the summers. We usually have a killing frost the middle of September at least, but it is sometimes the only one and will be followed by several more weeks when something could be growing. Of course some crops, such as carrots, beets and chard, will survive. After early October, it is time to put on a layer of compost and manure and till it in, to get it ready for the next spring.

Pests and Problems

We get a lot of slugs that hide in the rock wall of the terraced garden, so we put out bait for them. We get the green cabbage worm too. If it isn't bad, I will handpick it from the young plants, but if it is too much to keep up with I dust the plants with wood ashes. I won't use poisons on the cabbage. Cutworms I do spray for if necessary. I use malathion or Sevin. It seems to get the younger generations but not the tough older ones.

I have tried interplanting with marigolds to keep out bugs, but the bugs ate the marigolds.

Recommendations

We order our seed from Burpee, Harris, Henry Field, Gurney or Nichols. I like to try the newest varieties, the earliest hybrids, to see how they will do here.

Potatoes: Red Norland, Kennebec are best for the area; also Netted Gem, Burbank Russet, White Rose, Irish Cobbler, Red Pontiac, Red Lasota and the Yellowmeat or Finnish potato.

Bush bean: Top Crop
Lima bean: Christmas
Corn: Quicksilver, Golden Jubilee, Silver Queen and How Sweet It Is
Squash: zucchini, yellow zucchini, scallop, crookneck, Marblehead, and gourds
Peppers: green bell, jalapeno, cayenne, red chili, Hungarian wax, Anaheim chili, hot Portugal
Lettuce: Bibb, Red and Great Lakes
Tomatoes: Early Girl, Burpee Delicious, Beefmaster, Rushmore, yellow pear, yellow plum, red cherry, and a special variety developed by Samuel, with a red and yellow streaked fruit. All tomatoes are staked.
Cucumbers: Burpless, trained up a fence, Marketmore
Cabbages: red, Early Jersey Wakefield, Copenhagen Market

CASHMERE: Dave and Joyce Wooldridge

For several years Dave and Joyce Wooldridge had two homes, and divided their time between Seattle and this large, comfortable A-frame on the bank of the Wenatchee River. Now they are glad not to be making such frequent, long trips over the passes. Dave, a retired forest hydrology professor from the University of Washington, has been supervising a research project in Thailand.

In 1973, as commuters from Seattle, the Wooldridges started developing their property on the Wenatchee River. Now it's their full-time home and their once rocky soil is productive.

That has cut rather severely into their gardening schedule over the last three years. But that is something they work around. It doesn't keep them from gardening, any more than the rocky soil of their Wenatchee River home.

Site and Soil

Dave: We are sitting on a rock pile. Overall, 90 percent of the soil particles in a handful of our dirt are greater than two mm

in size. There is a band of finer texture, two to three feet deep, which we have incorporated as part of the garden.

We started the garden in 1973, in a pasture. We borrowed a plow—the old, horse-drawn type—and hooked it behind a Ford tractor. The land had been cultivated only slightly. I think somebody had tried growing strawberries on it, but not successfully.

Joyce: We took out at least ten tons of rock, no doubt about it. Since then, though, we just till it.

Dave's stepfather warned us when he first came and looked at this place that we wouldn't be able to grow a thing on it. But the first year we took a wheelbarrow-full of tomatoes a day out of the garden for several weeks. We sent him a 13-pound zucchini 33 inches long, just to show him he was wrong.

Conditioning

Dave: We add wood ashes, leaves, grass, and whatever we pull out of the garden and don't use—weeds, stems, roots, leaves, whole plants. No compost. We add triple-16 commercial fertilizer when the plants look as if the mobile nutrients are moving out of the older foliage—you can tell by looking at the leaves. We got hold of some 60 percent nitrogen slow-release fertilizer, which is supposed to be used on forest trees, and used it here, but we can't see that it is a lot of help to us. We use superphospate where needed, too. We have a trouble spot we have to avoid when planting. We think it may have been an area where I had a very hot fire going—a stump burned for ten days. Tomatoes definitely won't grow there.

We have an acre and a half in all here, and about a quarter of an acre is in vegetable garden. To improve the soil we had what is thought of locally as topsoil brought in, but it is a fine-grained material—80 percent silt and 20 percent clay—that does not drain easily. The soil that was here, with some organic matter, actually does better than the "topsoil." The original soil also is well stocked in micronutrients and calcium, having formed from a matrix of sandstone.

Our problem with the topsoil demonstrates very well what happens when you have soil layers of different textures. The fine-grained material has a pore size considerably smaller than the coarser sand below. Water does not move readily from one pore size to the next, so the fine-grained soil will become saturated before the moisture begins to move down into the coarse gravel. I get Aqua-Gro in gallon bottles, which I dilute and put on with a sprinkling can. It is an organic detergent—rather expensive but it goes a long way. It helps water flow between soils by breaking the surface tension.

All we really need here is sun, fertilizer and water. We get plenty of sun. We add fertilizer as we need it. And we have water rights to irrigate from the river. We figure it takes about two or two and a half hours of watering to apply about two inches of water. In the ordinary native soil that goes down 18 inches, well below the rooting zones of our crops.

Planting

We plant when we think the nighttime temperatures are going to stay mostly at 50 degrees F. or above. The last freeze here is

After taking out tons of rock and deep-plowing, the Wooldridges have soil that needs only tilling, fertilizer and water. Below: Asparagus is allowed to mature and develop seed.

supposed to be mid-May, and we wait at least that long, or longer. You can work your tail off getting your garden in earlier, but it doesn't grow.

We are in a frost pocket here, with noticeable differences between our area and those up and down the river from us. Stine Hill, behind us, traps the cold air coming down the valley.

Joyce: I do the garden planning, but I don't go by any book. I get frustrated by the books. They tell you everything but what you want to know, like how to get really big heads of broccoli. We don't rotate on any schedule, but do try to remember from year to year where something was before and put it somewhere else.

Dave: I don't think the nitrogen-fixing qualities of beans and peas have much influence here. It gets so hot in the summer that much of the nitrogen is oxidized from the soil.

Joyce: We seed the garden directly for most of the vegetables.

Some vegetables are started in the greenhouse. Most are seeded directly, but not before mid-May. "We're in a frost pocket here behind Stine Hill," Professor Wooldridge said. "There's no use trying to get your garden in early."

although once in a while we get tomato starts from a friend. If we are around, we may use the greenhouse to start some of our plants, but often we are away at just that time. If we start them in the greenhouse we use a slow-release fertilizer to make sure there are enough micronutrients, and we transfer them to the lath house before they go outside, to harden them off.

Pests and Problems

Dave: Insects can be a problem. The orchard sprays in the valley kill off everything, good and bad, and upset the whole balance of nature. I think we have every insect in the world here. There is no use in our being organic in such a chemically saturated area. We use diazinon, malathion and chlorban, if we have to, for soil insects. We also have grasshoppers, and we have aphids that collect on the aspens and cottonwoods along the river. Then there are the gophers. They seem to float down the river and hop off wherever they see a likely spot. I've trapped them, but don't find the traps much help. The gophers push their piles of soil ahead of them as they dig, and set off the traps before they get to them. There are two types of gophers here, light and dark. The darker ones are harder to trap than the lighter ones, for some reason. All in all, I think it is easier and more effective to gas them.

Recommendations

Potatoes:	Kennebec, Red Lasota
Bush peas:	Little Marvel
Cabbage:	Copenhagen Market
Beets:	Detroit
Carrots:	Danvers half-long, Nantes
Corn:	NK-199 (a 90-day commercial seed that Joyce got from her sister in Colorado), Kandi Korn
Tomatoes:	Big Boy, Early Girl
Squash:	Vegetable spaghetti, zucchini, yellow summer, pink banana (better pumpkin pie from this than regular pumpkin)
Swiss chard:	Rhubarb
Onions:	white and yellow sets
Lettuce:	red leaf, green leaf
Peppers:	sweet green

Tomatoes are picked by mid-September and all nearly ripe ones are washed in a weak bleach solution to sterilize them, then wrapped and stored. They taste much better than anything you can buy at the store, so it's definitely worth the effort. It's better than pulling up the vines and hanging them in the garage, which we have also tried.

EPHRATA: Elaine Porter

Across the Columbia River the land begins to smooth out, with small outcrops of basalt and sudden slashes in the topography known as coulees. Ephrata is a small town between Sun Lakes to the north and Moses Lake to the south, sitting well out in the open high desert of the central Columbia. Elaine Porter has a neat, rose-decked bungalow set back near the west edge of Ephrata, along a whole street of well-tended houses and lawns.

Site and Soil

When my husband and I moved in here 35 years ago we had a bare, sandy city lot. Some of this area is rocky, where a flooding creek washed the soil away, like the upper lot where I now have the vegetable garden. I was lucky because a retired friend offered to "rock out" the garden for me for something to do, and now I can rototill it with no problem.

The soils here are alkaline. Some have silt and loam in them, depending on what was washed in, in past times. The native soils

Tomatoes and corn thrive in Elaine Porter's garden in Ephrata, where summers are hot—too hot by June for some crops. Elaine finds that carrots do well with both corn and peas.

Herbs get the edge spaces in Elaine Porter's garden. She likes lamb's quarter and the tender leaves of dock, so she lets those weeds have some space too.

are actually high enough in nutrients that a person could raise crops with nothing but water for the first year.

Conditioning

Of course I have added a lot of mulch and organic matter over the years. I especially like rotted alfalfa hay, which is easy to get here. It adds nitrogen to the soil as well as organic matter. I also compost lawn clippings, weeds and other waste vegetable matter on the soil. If I have a lot of kitchen waste, I will dig a trench, bury the material and let it compost right in the garden. This is what my German grandmother did. She called it mulching.

I like to use horse manure, which is easy to get here from nearby riding stables. I also use some triple-16 commercial fertilizer, but not a lot. I will usually broadcast it over the entire garden area after tilling, using a hand-type whirlygig applicator, going crosswise, then up and down, and raking it in when I am finished. That is all the commercial fertilizer I put on for a year.

Planting

I like to draw out a map or plan for my garden each year. It is useful at the end of the season to see what has turned out well. I use the legal-size yellow sheets, letting the lines represent the rows. Then what I have liked that year I will order again, and what I don't like I leave out of the plan for the next year.

I rotate my vegetables, but I take into account my watering systems. Some watering is hand-done and some of it is overhead. I don't like to water tall plants with an overhead sprinkler as it weighs them down, so I group my plantings accordingly. Corn is a good example of a crop that should not be watered by sprinkler, if it isn't necessary. I irrigate the soil around the roots. The best watering system for that would be along shallow ditches. For watering here, I like the morning—especially if there is any problem with mildew. Evening is next best as less water will be lost to evaporation then. The worst time is mid-day or afternoon, when moisture barely has time to get on the ground before it is sucked up into the dry air. Leaves with water on them can burn then, too.

There are certain plants that get along better together than others, I think. I do know that strawberries cannot be grown where potatoes have been growing—at least for a couple of years. I grow carrots in the corn, a row of lettuce and a row of radishes with a row of melon between—the melon vines fill in after I use the lettuce and radishes. I think carrots and tomatoes do well together. Peas and onions, on the other hand, don't make good neighbors.

I plant in rows, as it is easiest. I have herbs around the edges: parsley, dill, chives, mints, thyme, oregano, borage, hyssop, catnip, garlic, sage, coriander (especially good for fresh salsa), comfrey, sweet basil and lavender.

Climate Modification

My children built me a very nice little greenhouse as a present. It has water and electricity in it. I start my plants in it, from seed I buy at the store or order from Burpee's. Sometimes I use electric heating pads covered in plastic for starting my tomato plants, keeping the heat on low overnight. This isn't a recommended

It takes water in prodigious amounts to make the desert bloom. Elaine waters by hand or with overhead sprinklers, and plans her garden by what can and what can't take sprinkling.

procedure, however: you may get a short. There are any number of ways to get in trouble by mishandling the heating apparatus in a greenhouse, and you must be very careful to know what you are doing.

I start my tomatoes about the first of March, inside. I also start peppers, celery, cabbage, cauliflower, Brussels sprouts, broccoli and annual flowers, all about the same time, in the greenhouse. That's about when the tulips bloom. I like to have my annuals started then so I can fill in the beds when the tulip bulbs are mature enough to cut the green tops off.

I plant lettuce, peas and spinach in the garden as soon as I can work the soil easily. About two weeks later, I plant carrots, radishes, beets, onions, kohlrabi, potatoes, parsnips, shallots, onions, salsify and turnips. When the danger of frost is past I plant everything else and set out my starts from the greenhouse.

While the garden is getting started, I am enjoying Jerusalem artichokes, asparagus, bunching onions and lamb's quarter—a delicious weed. These are my earliest crops.

A real freeze will probably come along and take care of everything in the garden by the end of October, but until then I can enjoy rutabagas, carrots, and Jerusalem artichokes from it. Around the first of August I start fall cabbage, lettuce and Chinese cabbage and that will also be growing through early fall.

Our weather may be too hot for many vegetables in summer, and the winds we get here will make the soil dry out very quickly. It is hard to keep enough water on the garden. Mulches will help then. I use pieces of old carpeting for one kind of mulch, and a layer of grass clippings that can be dug in later. Some things, like peas and lettuce, it pays to get in as early as you possibly can—because it will be too hot for them by June.

Pests and Problems

If there is a plant to grow, there is a bug to eat it.

I get the root maggot in my radishes and turnips, and I will use Chlorban or diazinon granules to get rid of them. Those are handy for any soil pest problem I have. Diazinon is good for cabbage worms and aphids also. I dust with Sevin or a general vegetable-garden powder for potato bugs or squash bugs. For all pesticides, I always tell people the most important thing is to read the label.

I cut the tops and bottoms from half-gallon milk cartons to use as three- or four-inch collars for my cabbages, broccoli and tomatoes—any individual plants I put out, setting them partly into the ground. It keeps the cutworms out and also protects the young plants from wind.

Recommendations

In our Master Gardener office, people often call about problems that have to do with watering. Tomato blossom end-rot is caused by uneven watering. It is important to keep the garden uniformly moist to the depth of all the roots and below. I also tell people to keep their weeds out, keep the rows clean, don't plant too thickly. Seed tape is useful for such things as radishes, as they are put in at the right spacing and there is no loss from thinning.

I am busy at gardening activities the whole growing season.

I have taken the Master Gardener course four years in a row, as I find that there are different speakers and I learn something new every year. We take turns, then, working in the Extension Service offices, doing our fifty hours of service a year. We do a horticultural section at the county fair at Moses Lake too, and I help judge. There are also horticultural courses offered at Big Bend Community College at Moses Lake. There is always more to learn.

Varieties:

Beans	Kentucky Wonder
Beets	Golden, Cylindra
Melon	Venus hybrid honeydew
Cantaloupe	Ambrosia hybrid
Carrots	Tondo
Corn	Early Sunglow, Honey and Cream, Silver Queen
Cucumber	Green Knight
Lettuce	Oak Leaf
Pea	Maestro
Tomato	Early Girl, Delicious

ELLENSBURG: Madeline Marsh

Like Wenatchee, Ellensburg is directly influenced by the weather which passes over the Cascade Mountains at its back door. A very noticeable aspect of that weather is the wind, a major environmental force which seems to come invariably from the northwest, from the mountains and along the corridor of Highway I-90. The Marshes' small spread sits west of the highway, on a section of the wide bowl of the Kittitas Valley, with endless views of the Mount Stuart range, the Colockum, the Naneum, the Taneum and the Manastash: high, impressive ridges that surround the valley and the Yakima River that flows through it. This is beef and alfalfa country.

The Fred Marshes have 5,000 square feet of their Kittitas Valley spread in garden—too much for two, Madeline says. Soils here are rich and deep, but near-constant wind from Snoqualmie Pass causes a watering problem.

Madeline loves gardening and likes trying new techniques and varieties. Here, she has Egyptian Walking onions, though she recommends Walla Walla sweets for the region.

Site and Soil

The soil here is called Manastash loam; it is very deep and rich, and probably originated as some sort of river deposit. Fred plows our garden area with a John Deere 50 horsepower tractor with a tiller. This is done once in the fall and a couple of times in the spring.

Our garden is really too big for the two of us now: about 50 × 100 feet. It started small, but we kept pushing back the pasture fences to get a little more space for corn or something we wanted. It is in sections, with permanent walks between them.

Conditioning

After spring plowing I throw out all the compost I have made over the year, putting it on the section nearest to the compost bin because it is easier. We also add all the hardwood leaves from the oaks, elms, box elder and the rest when they fall, letting them lie on the garden over winter. I also throw on some triple-13 fertilizer. This is tilled in again, and smoothed out to be ready for planting. We have no problem with the pH, though we have not had it tested. Generally around here the pH runs about 7.

My compost bin is constructed from metal fence stakes and wide-mesh wire fencing. I dump half-finished compost into that, from a free-form pile where the material is first deposited. I get the compost for the garden out of the wire container, then add more from the first pile.

We do most of our cultivation during the growing season with the tiller, but I do some hand cultivation as well. I have a favorite hoe that belonged to my Italian mother. It is pointed and feels good to work with.

Irrigation is a problem, with the wind blowing the water away as fast as it comes out of a sprinkler. For that reason I like a small sprinkler called "Can't Beat 'Em." It distributes the water evenly in a circle but does not rotate. Rotating types of sprinklers don't work here. We usually water all rows thoroughly once a week.

The soil holds the moisture that long. We pump our water from the irrigation ditch, and pay a one-time fee per year for it. Sometimes, when the farmers' fields are being irrigated, it will be cut off for a short time, but it is usually not an inconvenience. We couldn't use a drip irrigation system if we wanted to, because it would mean constant cleaning of the system. Irrigation ditch water is too dirty.

Planting

We don't draw a gardening plan out on paper, but we do talk it over and think it out. Since our garden is replenished and plowed every year, we start out with a clean slate, so to speak.

There is a problem with corn smut in the valley and because of it, buyers tell the farmers to move their commercial corn crops every year on this side of the valley. Home gardeners have less trouble because they don't practice monoculture. We plant in the old-fashioned row style, because it is easier to get the rototiller around during the growing season. My biggest interest is containers, however, and I am experimenting with them now. I hope to be able to raise flower pots to rent out for parties, weddings, rodeos and that sort of thing by next year. There is no reason I couldn't do vegetables or herbs as well. In fact, I am trying a nice mounded bush basil which can be quite a beautiful ornamental as well as a useful plant to grow. I have taken a strawberry pot, with its many openings, and put summer savory, lemon thyme, and rosemary in it. It seems to work well and look good too.

We start our planting here about Memorial Day weekend. Maybe a little before. I get everything of one variety in at once and don't do successional plantings. I think that is more for people who garden intensively or in square-foot gardens. I have so much space here I plant everything quite thick. Then I begin taking them out as they come up. We eat the thinnings and let the others grow larger. That is the way to have "baby" vegetables. As the corn and tomatoes grow, I side-dress with fertilizer again to make sure there are enough nutrients for them.

I have to make an exception to my one-time planting rule, however. I get Full-hearted Batavian Escarole from the Vermont Bean Seed Company and raise it for transplanting the middle of August. Small heads of it are then ready by fall. Also, I will put in curly endive for a late crop, and turnips for their late greens. These, along with the earlier root crops, will be in the ground until Fred starts up the tractor to plow, late in October.

I start a lot of flower seed, but of the vegetables I start only tomatoes and peppers. I do this on the bed in the spare bedroom, on an electric blanket with waterproof protection on it. I discovered this one day when I had left the blanket on by mistake. I sat down on the bed for a minute and a light bulb in my head flashed on: "Aha!" I said to myself, "This is what they mean by bottom heat." I just get them started there, then move them to a lighter place in the house until sometime in April when we repot them and move them to the greenhouse. At that time, we start heating the greenhouse with a 220-volt heater when it is needed.

Try using a damp sponge with a piece of felt over it for starting

seed. I set this in a tray and cover it with plastic. The sponge keeps it damp and the felt keeps the new root from digging itself into the sponge. I can see that way what is going to be a vigorous plant, what isn't, and what won't germinate at all.

We plant everything but tomatoes and peppers right in the ground where they will be growing. We put corn closer together than is recommended, at about 4- or 5-inch intervals, as close as can be managed and still get a good two-ear stalk.

I don't give my transplants any special handling; they go in as they are. One year I tried a gelatin and water mix recommended in a gardening magazine, but I couldn't tell that the plants did better than usual.

Pests and Problems

The worst pest we have here is the wind. We have set up big plywood panels along the north side of the garden as windbreaks. The hardwoods along that side also help, but nothing will really stop it. The corn at the windy end of the garden grows with a permanent tilt and grows more slowly than the more sheltered corn.

We have trouble with aphids. They seem to start in with the young alfalfa in the fields, then transfer to the young leaves of the hardwoods as the alfalfa is cut, and go on from the trees to the young vegetables. We use diazinon dust if they get too serious.

Root maggot is definitely a problem. Reemay should be a good solution here, to cover turnips and other root vegetables.

For the cabbage worm, we spray with diazinon. Same for the potato beetle, if we can't get rid of it by handpicking it. We get a little corn smut, but no corn earworm, which is surprising because other inland basin areas have a problem with it. We think it's thanks to our cool nights. Other parts of the basin have much warmer nights.

My most memorable crop failure was the year I overfertilized and burned all the tender new plants. I had to start all over that year.

Recommendations

Questions asked the Master Gardener office for vegetables most often relate to watering problems, or to such things as: "What do I do with all my cabbages?"

Favorite varieties:

Cabbage:	Golden Acre and Red Acre (both mature rapidly), Spivoy
Tomato:	Celebrity, Better Bush, Cougar Red, Early Palouse, Sweet Chelsea, Early Girl, Sweet 100, Spring Giant, Longkeeper (can be stored until at least December)
Potato:	Netted Gem
Pepper:	California Wonder, Ace
Leaf lettuce:	Red Sails, Oak Leaf (neither bolts early)
Carrots:	Super Nantes, Red-cored Chantenay
Beet:	Forminova
Cucumber:	Straight-8
Onion:	Walla Walla Sweet
Squash:	Golden Acorn, Sweet Banana, Hubbard

Herbs: I like to grow French sorrel, as my mother did, for making polenta. It is boiled and mixed with eggs and other ingredients as a side dish. Rhubarb could be used in the same way. Other herbs: chicory, summer savory, rosemary, rocket salad (really a green), chervil, bush basil, lemon thyme.

I also grow an ornamental pepper in a pot. The fruits are edible. I like to use an oak-leaf mold in my containers. It can be made by collecting oak leaves and putting them in plastic bags. It has taken me four years to get a good mold, however — longer than it is supposed to. I have made other kinds of compost with the plastic bag method too, but I find that the gases forming inside split open the bags, so they need to be punctured first.

The Master Gardener program and office in Ellensburg have been a real help to me, and I know that any gardener here would benefit from taking an active part in the program. I participated and enjoyed all the information I was able to get from speakers and materials made available to us. The office is open all summer to help gardeners with their growing problems.

I love gardening. I wouldn't garden if it was hard to do it. God gave us good soil here. We just take advantage of it.

SPOKANE AREA — TUM TUM: Wilson and Helen Bundy

If you turn off Divison Street in Spokane and travel northwest, you will drive through small forest and lakeside settlements. This pleasant, sunny northeastern Washington environment is attractive to retirees, with its unhurried and uncrowded way of life. The Bundys came from Alaska to their twenty-acre ranch only a year before this interview. They had had little time for settling in or learning the local gardening methods, yet they've created a thriving community of plants around their home. You get the idea, talking with Wilson Bundy, that he isn't exactly pursuing relaxation in his retirement.

Retiring and idling aren't synonyms to Wilson and Helen Bundy. One year after starting from scratch they had a thousand square feet of producing raised beds.

Site and Soil Conditioning

What was here before we moved in? Dog pens. The previous owners were dog breeders. They had staked and penned dogs everywhere. We started from nothing. But we have been gardening in Alaska, so difficulties aren't new to us.

The soil is sand, probably fifty feet deep. You could work it in a rainstorm. We sent in soil samples and got the word that our soil was low on the three major nutrients and that it had a humus content of less than one percent. So you can tell what that meant—I brought in truckloads of shavings from a sawmill nearby. I composted it with lawn clippings, and a fertilizer mix from a farm supply store, and ammonium sulfate. All this plus a two-inch layer of steer manure and an application of 10-20-20 was enough to bring the soil up to good producing quality within the first year. The one thing that was right from the first was the pH, at 6.5 to 7.0.

We worked the soil originally with a tractor, but after that by hand. I am gradually getting raised beds built and you can't very well get a tractor into a raised bed. We will use a spading fork, rake, hoe or hand trowel for most of the work, and I would like to find a good short-handled rake too. I figure we have about a thousand square feet of raised beds now, and the same amount in conventional rows, and we are adding more beds all the time.

I am not strictly an organic gardener. I have no compunctions about using commercial fertilizer, as I am satisfied the plant gets the same nutrients. But I do not use any more chemicals than I have to. I do not automatically get out a spray if something seems wrong. I am a great believer in a lot of humus. As these beds are built up with humus every year, I will need to use less fertilizer. Commercial fertilizers have the benefit of hurrying things along, getting your garden started, which is necessary for the new gardener. It is also easy to add when your plants are in and growing and seem to need a little boost of nutrients. I will also give my pumpkins and squashes an extra shot or two of fish fertilizer, at double what the label suggests, to increase their productivity.

Planting

I have had fifty years of gardening experience. I make a written plan for the year based on my experience and what I have read lately. I started my seed in the greenhouse the last week of February this year, but I think a couple of weeks later would be better. Our greenhouse is small and easily heated with a 1500-watt heater. I do tomatoes first, then ten days or so later I get the cabbage, cauliflower, broccoli and lettuce in. My tomatoes are a varied bunch. I have something like a dozen varieties to try now, and I will replant the ones I like the best next year.

With raised beds we often use companion planting. I plant radishes with parsnips—a short-term and a long-term crop together. At the front of the house we have large beds of flowers, but we are growing scarlet runner beans with them. They look nice there.

The beds are four feet wide so both of us can work easily across them. I think weeding raised beds is a lot easier than weeding in a regular row garden.

After fifty years of gardening experience, Wilson Bundy knows what it's about. To sand with less than one percent humus he added wood shavings, compost, manure and fertilizer to get good-quality garden soil.

Climate Modification

Our first fall frost this year came September 11, so we had a 112-day growing season. Even so, we ripened both Yellow Bell watermelon and Alaska hybrid cantaloupe.

Our beds are equipped with pipe supports for the polyethylene row covers. We can grow many things under cover. We can plant cabbage, broccoli, Chinese cabbage, lettuce and cauliflower seedlings in midsummer to have a late crop—they can be covered to withstand the first frosts.

We planted sugar pod peas, spinach, lettuce, radishes and carrots just before freeze-up. We hope for early vegetables from that planting next spring, after the ground has warmed.

Pests and Problems

So far our worst pests have been aphids, potato bugs and the cabbage root maggots. We have used Sevin for the potato beetle

Bundy reduces the gamble and extends the growing season with on-or-off plastic covers. Surplus produce, and there's plenty of it, the Bundys give to a senior center, where it's eagerly bought and makes money for center needs.

and diazinon for the maggot. We have often picked off the potato beetle by hand, but this time they got way ahead of us.

The worst problem here, I think, is that between the last expected frost in late May and the first one in mid-September, it could frost anytime. It would be totally unexpected, of course, and completely devastating, but it could happen. There isn't much to do about it. If you suspected it was going to happen you might try to cover everything possible. But gardening is a gamble.

Recommendations

Helen puts herbs in various beds with other plants. We have dill, sweet marjoram, basil, lavender, catmint, yarrow, oregano, sage, dock (sorrel), dill, thyme and some hot peppers.

Of course we can't possibly eat all the food we raise here. We never expected to. We take it to the Senior Center over in Ford and they sell it to make money for the Center. We had a good year for tomatoes this year. Many people lost their first planting during a late freeze and had to come back for a whole new crop of seedlings.

Favorite varieties:

Tomatoes:	Fireball, Early Girl, Early Salad, Yellow Pear, Early Cascade, Celebrity, Subarctic Plenty, Red Pear, Pixie, Early Pick, Earliana, Santiam, Oregon Spring Perpetual, Melody. In late July we were working on our third planting of spinach. Bloomsdale is too likely to bolt, but we find that Perpetual does not, and we also like Melody hybrid for freezing.
Spinach:	
Corn:	Early Extra Sweet, Honeymoon, a Burgess mix
Cabbage:	Early Flat Dutch, Stonehead, Copenhagen Market
Pumpkin/Squash:	Spirit bush pumpkin, golden zucchini, golden Hubbard, Golden Nugget winter (makes a nice size squash for just one person)
Cucumber:	Amira, White Wonder
Cantaloupe:	Alaska hybrid (Helen ate one and thought it was a strange, hairy cucumber), also Minnesota Midget

We try several new varieties of seed each year, and when we find one we really like we stick to it. For instance, we have found the very light-colored White Wonder cucumber that we especially like. Our favorite seed sources are Lily-Miller, Thompson and Morgan, Burpee, Burgess, Nichols, Gurney. We don't save seed, we order new every year.

ELK: Doris Delatte

Out on the northeast side of Spokane the land is more open than it is in Wilson Bundy's area. Among tree-scattered hills lie flat meadows — the remnants of ancient lake beds. Doris Delatte lives in a neat yellow bungalow down one of the dirt roads out of the very small town of Elk. The south side of the house has been extended with clear fiberglass and polyethylene to create a lot of covered growing space. This is home base for a commercial enterprise, Homestead Horticulture.

Doris: This is my walk-in coldframe. I don't have a real

Anything grows—almost anything—for Doris Delatte, who started her Homestead Horticulture in 1977. A dedicated organic gardener, she has taken some cues from Hmong refugees, who saw what chemicals did to their homeland.

greenhouse, but this does very well. I can start and grow seedlings from the first of February on. If it is absolutely necessary I use some small heaters, which cost me about six cents an hour to use, each one. I've used them this year a total of ten nights while I was starting my bedding plants. Eventually I intend to put in hot-water heat. Then I'll call it a greenhouse.

Outside are my non-permanent raised beds. Every fall I have those beds tilled, working in all the mulch I have laid on the paths over the summer. Other additives go on at the same time. I like alfalfa silage, a locally available organic product. It has a 16 to 1 carbon-nitrogen ratio, which is fairly close to the ideal.

Site and Soil

We've been in this place since 1977, but we have had gardens in many other places—both here and abroad. When we bought this house, there was very little water. The previous owners were trying to get along on a shallow well and having a hard time of it. We drilled a good, deep well to take care of the house and all of our garden needs.

The soil is sandy loam about four feet deep. We cultivate it with a big Troy tractor-tiller and a small power tiller, and use a 16-horsepower tractor for hauling soil amendments, pots and the like.

My garden is about one-half an acre, not including the growing house. That is a lot of space. I get help occasionally from volunteer apprentices who are part of the National Organic Gardeners' apprenticeship program. They are especially appreciated at seedling-transplant time.

Conditioning

I like to add manures from dairy farms, because there are restrictions on farmers as to the use of herbicides around the dairy area. I add grass clippings all summer, the alfalfa silage,

and the waste I throw back from the vegetable plants, which take nature's way of composting. I don't make a separate compost. I put manure in a ring directly around individual plants, so it doesn't touch the plants. It is the same principal as side-dressing with a commercial fertilizer. I do not dig it in; I want all the material right on top. If I dug it in I could not plant until it was rotted because it is too hot.

My soil has tested exactly neutral—pH 7. It is important that new gardeners in this area realize they do not add lime just because they did it in some other place. I have seen garden soil go to a pH of 8 because the owner had a fixed idea about adding lime.

Planting

Since we rotate our soil by tilling it every year and re-forming the raised beds, I don't rotate my plants by the commonly understood method. Instead, I always interplant, mixing flowers and herbs among the vegetables. One typical raised bed might include lettuce, celery, peppers, green onions, cabbage, petunias, marigolds, carnations, salvia, and chamomile. I use bedding plants because they allow me to space the plants properly while planting for a visual effect.

I think there are many attractive ways to diversify plantings using varieties you like, rather than trying to plant a limited-space garden full of varieties you don't particularly want but which are reputed to have beneficial attributes.

The raised beds are actually modified raised beds in that they aren't permanent. I build them high-sided so, when I irrigate, the water stays in the bed and drains down into the root zones rather than off into the paths. I water by hand or root-soaking, using sprinklers only when it's very hot and dusty. A heavy soak twice a week is usually enough. The organic matter and mulch help to keep it moist.

Climate Modification

The growing season here is only 85 to 90 days. It is colder than the temperatures given for Spokane, and we have to subtract about five to seven degrees from the radio announcer's low temperatures. During the day the amount of sun is about the same, but the city itself adds some extra heat from buildings. There really is no frost-free season here. One year a July 4 frost wiped out all our tomatoes and peppers. But I can extend the growing season quite remarkably with my enclosed growing house.

My main interest, besides organic gardening, is gardening in containers. That's where I do most of my experimenting. Right now some of us are trying to work out a good potting soil mix by using peat mined from the local dry lake-bed sources. Those lake beds have peat with a pH of 5 to 6.5 and some of the deposits are hundreds of feet deep. With vermiculite, perlite, blood meal, bonemeal, and other additives, we think we have a very good mix.

I think the container garden is the garden of the future.

For greenhouses, for people with no garden space at all, or no time, or weather problems, or trouble getting down to ground

level, this type of garden is ideal. It will also work for people who have only tree roots to garden in—they can use the paper-product pots set in the ground as far as they will go. The pot will eventually disintegrate, but it gives the plant a place to get started.

One problem with pots is watering, and that can be solved by automatic sprinkling systems, using drip irrigation, or with wicks for small pots. It's also important to start with good soil and large-enough pots. I use blood meal, bonemeal and good potting soil that is loose and holds water well—which means it contains peat and vermiculite or perlite, at least. Then I feed regularly with fish emulsion mixed with water. Even with containers, a gardener doesn't have to stay home all the time.

I give classes in container gardening here, or I take my materials and give demonstrations at club meetings. Also, people buy their starts from me. They know they will be hardy and well-grown since they will have been growing in my cool-temperature greenhouse from the start. My busiest season is around Mother's Day. People come to buy bedding plants and the larger flower and vegetable containers I have started.

People are usually intrigued by my mixed planters. In the salad planters I use four types of lettuce: romaine, red leaf, green leaf and butterhead. With them I put celery, green onions, garden cress, small parsley plants, bok choy and endive in various combinations. Peppers, tomatoes, cucumbers and large parsley plants get individual containers because of the space requirements for their roots. The containers can be quite as attractive as any flower pot, and more useful. If you want more color, nasturtiuims or marigolds can fit nicely into a pot of vegetables.

In the summer my greenhouse—or walk-in coldframe—is full of tomatoes growing right in the ground, cucumbers strung up trellises, peppers in pots. I picked 23 green peppers from one potted plant. I also have some late starts going for fall harvest.

It is important to remember, if you are new to this area, that even though you may have identical first and last frost dates, amounts of rainfall, high and low temperatures and numbers of sunny days, you can't grow the same varieties here in the same way you can in Des Moines, Iowa, for example. The catch is the matter of heat units. Everything else may be exactly equal, but Iowa has hot nights and we have very cool nights, even in midsummer. This is why your tomato plant needs all the heat it can get. They are tropical plants, after all, and don't much care for low temperatures. I prefer to grow tomato seedlings under conditions similar to what they will have to cope with in the garden. Daytime temperatures go as high as 85 degrees, nights as low as 45 degrees. The plants grow more slowly and remain stockier than those grown under warmer night temperatures.

I advise my customers to keep their tomatoes potted until the end of May, even if it means transplanting them to larger containers. Sun them outside during the day if it's nice, and bring them in at night when it's cold.

Night temperature dips into the 20s are not uncommon here during May. I believe temperatures around freezing will cause stress damage to hot-weather plants, though there may be no visual evidence. Such a stress might be a factor if some later

Though Doris is strong on container gardening, she has tomatoes planted in the ground in her growing house. They are tropical plants, and they don't cope well with cool nights.

disease attacks the plant. A stressed plant is a weakened plant, and very likely will be more susceptible to disease and insect damage.

"How do I get my tomatoes to ripen?" I'm most often asked. My advice may go against expert advice, but it works for me. The end of May I set out ten twelve-week-old plants two plants to a hole, staked. I prune them to two main stems per plant, then keep suckers removed during the growing season to force fruit to set on the main stems. Plants pruned to a single stem, one to a stake, tend to have a lot of split fruit and are subject to sun scald when too much foliage is removed. This method solved both problems for me. It can be used for indeterminate tomatoes only. We get vine-ripened fruit by mid-July every year this way.

Oriental vegetables are difficult if not impossible to grow in the spring here. The ground can't be worked until late in the season, when the days are long and warming up. By then these cool-

The raised beds in Doris's half-acre are tilled with organic matter and re-formed annually. She builds up the edges so water goes down to the roots rather than on the pathways.

season vegetables will bolt right away. It is possible and desirable, however, to plant them late in the summer and let them grow into the fall. I grow many crops of lettuce, from March to November, the early and late crops in containers.

I have experimented with lettuce, letting it go to seed in the garden. The seeds lie in the ground over the winter, then germinate very early in the spring, sometime in March—much earlier than the ones you would plant about that time.

Spinach is another plant that should go in very early or not until midsummer. If you plant it the first of August it will grow to about three inches before frost. It winters over at that stage under a mulch of straw and appears about the first of April. Three weeks later, you have spinach. I like Bloomsdale Longstanding for this method.

I use row covers for some of my outside crops. The melons and squashes are particularly susceptible to low temperatures and need protection.

Pests and Problems

I sell my vegetables to the organic food lovers. They are very choosy about what goes on their food. I normally use no pesticide except soapy water. If I do apply anything, even a generally accepted organic pesticide, I inform my customers what I used and when.

I've worked with other Master Gardeners to help the Hmong people from Cambodia who are now living in the Spokane area. They use city lots or pea patches to raise produce. They already know a lot about gardening, and in our case the students were sometimes teaching the teachers. I learned to ask myself, as they were asking us, why a plant needed a certain chemical. Was it for food or for medicine? They had never used chemicals and didn't know the methods. But they were very much aware of the defoliation chemicals used on their country during the war and what the effects were, so they were terrified of them. As far as they are concerned, any chemical is a medicine and not for use unless the plant is sick.

It takes some logic to get the best of garden pests. Often you can think of a remedy that doesn't involve the use of chemicals. For instance, keeping plants well fertilized is important, so they are vigorous and strong. Low nitrogen is apt to be the culprit in lack of growth here. A soil test will tell you. If that's the case, a shot of liquid fish emulsion will help a lot. Another example: we have quack grass. We get rid of it by repeated tilling and hand removal, rather than spraying.

I am committed to using the least "offensive" methods of plant production, but I also have a respect for technology. I believe the ideal method of growing will include the best of both the old organic and the new scientific methods. Ultimately, I think, it will come down to what works. How can you separate rotenone and pyrethrum from the chemicals? They are chemicals. What substance doesn't have a chemical composition? To try to describe organic as nonchemical seems to me a contradiction and is confusing. It seems to me there are as many different definitions of organic growing as there are people talking about it. At least we now have a law giving us some outlines for legal descriptions of organic and nonorganic.

Recommendations

I like to order my seed from Johnny's, Burpee, Park, Nichols, the Good Seed Company (Tonasket), Garden City (Missoula) and Les Jardins.

Varieties:

Cucumber	Sweet Success (for pots)
Pepper	Sweet Banana, California Wonder (for pots)
Spinach	Bloomsdale Longstanding
Squash	I like any variety of zucchini, and save some of the very large ones for the chickens for winter feed.
Tomato	Better Bush—I think it is destined to become very popular; an indeterminate with compact growth that makes it seem a determinate; large fruit on a relatively small plant makes it good for containers. Early Girl—good all around variety; sets seed at higher temperatures than many, so can be grown in greenhouse. Big Boy — for outside, very impressive. Sweet 100 — the only cherry tomato I like. Yellow Pear.

The Banana Belt

INTRODUCTION

Although this section of the Northwest belongs in the Columbia Basin, it is warmer than the upper basin and gardeners have slightly different conditions to face.

A soil feature of this general section is the Palouse Hills, with great deposits of a windblown, fertile soil known as Palouse loess. The Palouse Hills are generally described as rolling, and are filled with wheat farms. Not all of the Banana Belt is blessed with Palouse loess, however.

Walla Walla is south of the Palouse Hills, near the Blue Mountains and along the Walla Walla River. The town is directly on a line with the Big Bend of the Columbia River and its weather is influenced by warm, eastward-flowing air from the coast in the winter. This air has a definite ameliorating effect upon what would otherwise be a more frigid continental climate. Pendleton, Umatilla and Hermiston, Oregon, all receive similar general climatological influences. Hermiston, in particular, is known for its sweet watermelon, a fruit that takes a long, hot summer to produce.

Although much of the land is in farms now, the native vegetation runs generally to bunchgrasses, with few shrubs and almost no trees except along river bottoms, until the elevation begins rising near the Blue Mountains.

Annual yearly precipitation for Umatilla is about 8 inches, a little less along the lower Yakima Valley and a little more toward the Blue Mountains. Walla Walla's normal yearly average is about 16 inches.

Walla Walla's highest recorded temperature over 65 years was 113 in August; its lowest was −16 in January. Nevertheless, July temperatures average 75 overall, and January temperatures average just above freezing: 33.4. Amount of sunshine is 59 percent, 2 percent higher than Spokane's.

The term "banana belt" is obviously one bestowed for **relative** temperatures in this region. Walla Walla is hotter in summer than Yakima or Moses Lake. In winter it manages to stay above freezing more often, while Yakima's mean January temperature is 28 and Moses Lake's is 24.

The truth is out: bananas are not a big crop in Walla Walla.

WALLA WALLA: Otho McLean

Otho McLean, now retired, lives on a double corner lot in a pleasant house in a quiet Walla Walla neighborhood. He has spent his entire adult life in this small city and he knows its growing conditions intimately. He has emceed a local radio gardening show for many years and answered just about every question there is to ask about gardening in Walla Walla.

Site and Soil, Conditioning

In 1948 we decided to look for another house here in town. I carried a shovel around in my car every time I went out looking, because I wanted soil that would make a good garden. One place I especially remember because it seemed to have lovely rich, dark soil. I stuck my shovel down in it, though, and hit rock at four inches down. That can be true of Walla Walla. It has rock or gumbo, or it has good soil. I would still advise anyone looking for a home with garden here to do as I did, carry a shovel.

Finally I found a fellow gardener who was raising some fine corn and potatoes on a corner lot. I asked him whether he would

sell. He agreed, so we put our home up for sale and started over from scratch. But I knew we had good soil. I have had no regrets at all, even though I have been improving it ever since, with loads of manure and sawdust and compost.

Walla Walla's soils are alluvial, washed in from the springs and creeks that come down from the Blue Mountains. On the whole they are alkaline, rather low in nitrogen, and seem to have adequate amounts of potash. There are spots where the alkalinity is quite toxic. We call it a "black" alkali, although it looks rusty colored on the top of the regular soil, because most of the alkalinity is whitish. This black type is a magnesium product typical of the area.

Planting

My yard gets plenty of summer sun. In fact I use one of my big walnut trees — an old, ailing English walnut — as my lath house because its limbs spread out just right for shading my young plants, the fuchsias and some of the shade-loving varieties beneath it.

I am interested in trying many kinds of flowers as well as vegetables, and have bougainvillea and passionflower growing along the east side of the house with rhododendrons, azaleas and my rose garden. Another thing I like to grow are lilies — I start quite a few from seed in the greenhouse.

I can get a lot of my seed from Long's in bulk packages. If there is too much I can save it for the following year. Once in awhile I will save some seed from the garden, but not often. I must save my favorite tomato seed, The Queen, as it is not available commercially. I keep seed from the best and largest tomato. I have used seed from this tomato that was as much as ten years old. I believe, in fact, that the older seed came up faster than the newer, though I don't know why.

It takes a lot of water to keep the crops going in the Walla Walla summer. I use Andrews soaker hoses. They last me about five years before I have to replace them. I run them about half an hour

Otho McLean chose his Walla Walla home for its gardening potential. There the soil is alluvial, generally alkaline, and it may be good, or gumbo, or a thin layer on solid rock.

McLean likes to grow lilies, and they like the conditions he offers. He starts them from seed in his greenhouse. Late corn goes into the bed after the lilies are taken out. (O. McLean)

in each spot, then move them on to the next row. It costs us about $17 per month for water on the two lots in the warmest months, and I don't think that is excessive. Once in awhile I use a butterfly-type sprinkler, but I don't sprinkle the corn. It is too tall for one thing, and sprinkling washes out the pollen at the time of flowering and you won't get corn.

It is necessary to watch the soil for excessive drying out, with the hot sun and occasional winds we get here. My cabbage and broccoli will not do at all well if I let them dry out the least bit. Early drying in these plants will cause such stress they won't recover. They set flowers earlier than they should, and the flavor is not nearly so good.

Each spring I rent a rototiller, or hire someone who has one, and have the initial cultivation done mechanically. After that I dig and weed by hand. My garden size is 50 x 100 feet. It keeps me busy.

I start my next year's planting in September, when I put in the Walla Walla Sweet onion seeds. They get about 5 inches tall by November. I take them up at that time and reset them about 2 inches apart. If they aren't grown for awhile in the fall they will not reach a good size in one season. I do grow another kind, Fiesta, which will develop well in one season. They are a long onion, and they last well into the fall. I leave a few onion plants in the ground and the next year I have seed to plant.

For direct seeding I will start April 20 and plant steadily over a 25-day period, finishing up around the middle of May. All cabbage-related plants are put in together. When they come up and put on their first leaves I lift them and transplant them to the spots I want them to grow in. My last seeds to go in are beans and cantaloupe.

I consider rotation carefully. One reason is that the best way to avoid white rot in onions — a common problem here — is to move them around. The soil can be sprayed with a fungicide, too, if the problem is acute. It is especially hard on the early onions, like the Walla Walla Sweet.

Cantaloupes get ripe and flavorful in the hot Walla Walla summers. McLean cuts melon plants back after they reach maturity, so they put their energy into producing fruit.

Climate Modification

Our climate is not warm by some standards, but some winters the thermometer won't go below zero, and for an inland area at this latitude, that is relatively warm. Summers are hot by anyone's standards. You must watch for sun scald on tender young plants.

My greenhouse is built right into the ground and against the house, for maximum protection and heat retention. The heat is piped in from the house furnace. I also have a 280-watt element in sand which I use for heating my bench. If the temperature gets down to about zero I will turn on a small supplemental bathroom heater plugged into the thermostat that runs the heat cable. It is all double-glazed with glass outside and reinforced plastic sheeting on the inside. The way it is built, it is really more a walk-in coldframe with heat than it is a greenhouse. I could use a real coldframe, though, to put some of my cold-weather plants in, as they get quite spindly in too much heat.

I start my seeds on top of the hot water furnace. I've measured the temperature there at 70 degrees, which works fine for getting seed started. I start my tomatoes there the first of March, move them to light in the greenhouse or a house window, then transplant them after they are about an inch high into divided flats. I keep them in the greenhouse until the tenth of May, when they have pretty well filled out the rooting area and are ready to put in the ground.

I prune back my tomatoes and melons after the plants have reached maturity, so the vines aren't putting more energy into producing new shoots than they are into fruit. That means I cut my tomatoes off at the tops rather than pruning them laterally to one or two leaders.

We often have a good stretch of hot weather after an early cold spell and possible frost. I try to make the best of that time, so I put in a late crop of carrots that will mature after the others. I also have a last planting of corn about the last of June, in my lily bed, when the lilies are ready to take out. The corn, with luck, will be producing well into October. I don't care for the super-sweet varieties. I usually plant Golden Jubilee.

A stretch of hot weather often follows an early cold spell, so McLean makes a second planting of carrots as well as corn. Some winters here are freeze-free, but you can't count on it.

Pests and Problems

We have aphid and white fly problems. At times the white fly has been so thick on tomato leaves that I have to hold my breath while I'm picking the tomatoes. One of the ways to combat this pest is to keep the area entirely free of weeds, as they particularly like dandelions and buttonweed. Aphids come on the maple trees. I drench the leaves with Cygon to prevent a buildup of the population. Otherwise, I use as little pesticide as possible, perhaps very occasionally some diazinon. And some liquid slug bait keeps that problem small.

A late spring or early fall freeze is, of course, a problem that we have occasionally — as most everyone does. It is the unexpectedness of it that causes the difficulties.

Recommendations

I buy my hard-to-find seed from Burpee or Park, but do a lot of business in Walla Walla, especially from Long's Garden and Pet Supply.

Peppers flourish for McLean, as do other vegetables and flowers. He has gardened here all his adult life, and as host of the local radio garden show, he shares his expertise.

I have learned a lot from my work as the garden show host on Tuesday morning radio. We take questions right on the air and answer them at the time. Sometimes a local expert or county agent will come on, and we have two members of the Walla Walla Men's Garden Club each time (besides myself), so there is a lot of expertise to draw on. I think the most-asked questions have to do with *when* to plant (is it too late, too early) and where to get a certain variety or type of plant.

From my experience, I would advise a new gardener here to keep the garden small, and be careful about the planting times — not too early. Last, grow what does well right here in Walla Walla, not what you used to grow "back home in South Dakota."

Varieties recommended:

Squash	Butternut, more resistant to squash bug than Hubbard.
Beets	Detroit Dark Red
Carrots	Imperator
Radish	Cherry Belle, I've saved the seed from this more than eight years and had good germination.
Bean	(Pole-type) Burpee Tender Pod, also kidney beans
Parsnip	Hollow Crown
Cucumber	Burpless
Pepper	Yolo, Late Bell
Celery	Self-blanching type. I start the seed in the house. My wife uses it in what she calls her V-7 juice, made of mixed vegetables, based on tomatoes.
Asparagus	I've planted roots and I've had volunteers. The volunteers do the best.
Tomato	"The Queen" — got from a neighbor thirty years ago and seed saved since then — a low acid tomato; also Burpee's Delicious, uneven in growth but sometimes very large, and occasionally Early Girl, smaller than the other two.

Pea	Burpeeana, and occasionally something being tested for quality for the area.
Cabbage	Golden Acre
Cantaloupe	Burpee Hybrid, and a three-variety package with Crenshaw, Venus and the Burpee hybrid. Burpee sent me a package of small watermelons to try, but I don't think they can get beyond the pink stage before frost here. The season is hot enough, but not long enough.

WALLA WALLA: Sam Maxson

Sam Maxson has worked in horticulture most of his life: he was a major in floriculture and landscape gardening at Washington State when it was still a college and not a university, and he went directly into his father's greenhouse business from there. Until 1977 the Maxsons had a quarter-acre vegetable garden, but when it got to be too much to keep up, they moved to their present, smaller place where Sam practices his gardening skills in a 400-square-foot intensive bed, with a little extra for the corn.

Site and Soil Conditioning

This house wasn't built on very desirable soil. Years ago nearby Mill Creek was excavated, and the solid rock that was blasted out was spread out over the neighborhood. A foot of topsoil was hauled in to cover it up, then the houses were built. For the small garden I have now it wasn't hard to dig the soil by hand and get the chunks of rock out, put in some better soil, and then begin improving it from my compost heap.

Compost is the most important part of the garden. I watch my neighbors. If anyone is digging up sod I ask to take it off their hands. It's good for building up the bulk of the compost pile and the green grass adds nitrogen. I put in grass clippings and all the

For Sam Maxson retiring meant going from his greenhouse business into intensive home gardening. In his small backyard greenhouse he winters geraniums and starts all his seed. He makes his own potting mix.

A charming picket fence hides Maxson's compost pile, the "most important part of the garden," he says. He composts all healthy waste and adds nitrogen and superphosphate.

garden debris that isn't diseased. I also add nitrogen and superphosphate.

In our large garden we always had barnyard manure hauled in and spread to a depth of three or four inches, right over the entire garden. In the spring I supplemented this with a broadcasting of 16-16-16 commercial fertilizer.

Soil in this area has adequate potassium, but it is low in phosphates and nitrogen. In general the pH is about neutral, but the west side of town might be a half-point higher. That means keeping an eye on the soil so the pH doesn't get too high. I say this because the west side of town gets slightly less rain than the east side. Usually the more rain you get, the lower your pH. A few places there might run to pH 8, which is too high for an ideal garden.

The black alkali that we know here as a problem comes from the higher areas where there is a light, ashy type of alkaline. Water running through it washes out the various types of alkaline and settles it in the wetter, denser pockets along the valley bottom. Irrigation tends to bring traces of it to the surface, where it takes on a dark, rusty look. The city park, for instance, has a notable trouble spot in its southwest corner and iron must be added to the soil there to make it grow flowers. A good evidence of heavy alkali in the soil is the yellowing of plant leaves, because the plant can't use iron in the soil in this situation. A good way to combat it is to use a lot of organic matter.

Planting

I have a very relaxed attitude about planning my garden now, but when I planted a large one I was more careful. I knew then just how much seed I needed. But even in this small garden I try to rotate my planting. The best plan for me is to grow corn one year, a legume the next and an intermediate feeder the third year. As far as what to plant, I plant what we like best to eat. It is quite simple.

I think how you will plant depends upon what size garden you

are planting. When I was gardening on a quarter of an acre I used rows and cultivated with a rototiller. Now I practice block gardening and do all the weeding by hand. In my small space I can still raise enough for the two of us to eat during the growing season, and some things to put away for the winter. Of course, in the larger garden we had all we could use, all we could give away, and enough to fill a couple of freezers.

I do get concerned when I hear of farmers around here on food stamps. You can drive out into the Palouse Hills and see nothing but wheat farms for hundreds of miles. A tiny fraction of the land could feed a large family. So much food can be raised in such a small area, yet they don't seem to think in those terms. Farmers of all people should know how to feed themselves.

We start our seed in the little greenhouse at the back. I make my own potting mix:

6 parts rotted sod
2 parts aged manure or packaged steer manure
2 parts sand
2 parts peat moss

If it is lumpy I sift it through a screen. It is a light mix, and has a little nitrogen in it. If I am not going to grow my plants beyond their earliest stages, I don't add any more nutrients. I start just about anything in the greenhouse — even onion seed, corn — to get a head start.

If I'm growing in pots, I like to use Peter's fertilizer in solution. Also, after I transplant my starts into larger, six-pack type growing flats I use this fertilizer. When I put them in the ground, I add a small handful of a slow-release fertilizer — Osmocote, for example — to the bottom of the hole, covered slightly so, as the roots grow, they begin to pick up the nutrients. The whole garden will have had a triple-16 fertilizer added the week before planting.

My first greenhouse planting will be tomatoes during the earliest part of February. I intend to have tomatoes already set on the plants when I put them outside in May. The next seeds will get their start about the first of March. Those will be the cool-loving varieties, such as cabbages, that can be put into the ground the first couple of weeks in April.

Our last frost will normally be about the first day of May.

I order seeds from Park. I like them, and I think their packaging gives them an edge. I know the seed will be fresh when I get it, it germinates well, and it is always true. I don't usually save any seed. I order it fresh each year, and I try new hybrids because they grow faster and are more likely to be disease resistant than some of the old varieties. I do order from other seed companies too — especially Burpee.

Companion planting's a natural with small gardens. You can't really do anything else.

I use hand tools exclusively here — I have a narrow-bladed hoe I like, a "hoe down" fork, a pointed hoe for furrows, and a special hand trowel that I favor.

Climate Modification

Our weather in spring may bring long periods of cold and rain. Plants will just sit and do nothing in that kind of climate. Loose, light soil is best for early planting. Black plastic is good for

Maxson starts tomatoes in very early February and expects fruit sets by the time he puts the plants outside, in May. He starts other seeds about the first of March.

warming up the soil in spring, and for cucumbers and melons when they first go out. After summer comes we have the extremely hot sun to bring different problems. The soil takes a great deal of water, for one thing. There is no use heating up the soil then. It is better to cool it down, especially around the cole crops. That is the time to use an organic mulch. An inch of water a day can evaporate from bare soil during the hottest weather, and the plants will suffer if that rate isn't reduced or the water isn't replaced.

The weather service has an evaporation pan out at the Whitman Mission, not far from town. A local gardener can call the service to see what the ground moisture is actually doing at the moment. In the latter part of July and during August the temperatures can be expected to go above one hundred frequently, and any wind adds to the drying effect, although we don't generally have a lot of wind. Farmers dread the north winds especially because they are particularly drying.

Winters here are not severe. We get a relatively small amount of snow.

I keep the greenhouse going all year around. It is small enough that it is easily warmed by an electric heater. I have a hobby of raising geraniums and some rather exotic types of flowers, and

I keep them in there during the winter. In the summer I put them out under the partially shaded patio so they don't get sun-scald. I also like raising rock-garden plants and have some specially constructed rock mounds for them. That is where any herbs go — but they are more ornamental than edible.

Snap beans can be put in as late as the first week in August for a fall crop. Onion seed can go in about mid-August. Fall cabbage and broccoli will grow some years almost to Christmas before the cold weather gets them. They are often better then — the fall cabbages are more solid and make the best sauerkraut. Turnips can be put in up to the end of August and so can lettuce. Radishes might be another late crop to try, though I haven't done it myself.

Parsnips, leeks, and spinach are all good overwintering vegetables.

For an early vegetable, I recommend the English broad bean. I think it is a neglected crop and should be grown more often. It goes in very early in spring.

Salsify is another good, neglected vegetable. I especially like it in soups and with other vegetables.

Sweet potatoes do very well here if they are grown in a loose, sandy loam. I think they are a bit messy — they like to spread out to six feet or more and have to be hand-weeded. A specially-developed sweet potato for this area might be best, but I have selected sprouted potatoes right out of the vegetable bin at the grocer's with success. You must put them in a box of sand in a warm spot, and keep them slightly damp and half covered. As they sprout, you break them off and put them into the soil as rooted cuttings, not planted as a piece like a regular potato. After picking, they must be stored in a dry, warm place to cure. Otherwise they are watery and not very tasty.

Pests and Problems

Aphids are our biggest single problem here. I spray with diazinon or Sevin, depending upon the state of the crop. I also use Sevin for corn earworm, but I do not use it on anything in bloom because it is hard on the bees. My corn can often go unsprayed and be totally untouched by any pest. If an edible part of a plant needs spraying I use rotenone. Handpicking insects is the strategy of first choice. It is necessary to keep insects out because they spread plant diseases. With no insect pests you have much less trouble with other things.

We have an interesting insect around here called the leafcutter bee. It is essential to the farmer who grows alfalfa, as it is the primary pollinator of that crop. The bee, unfortunately, has the habit of cutting the edges off leaves to plug the holes where it lays its eggs. Each single egg is laid in a single hole and plugged with a piece of leaf. This means thousands of leaves are scalloped during a summer, although there isn't enough damage done to ruin the plant. It is a problem for rose growers, or people who are growing specimen plants for show.

Recommendations

I have worked on the radio show with Otho McLean, and find that we get a large range of questions from lawn care to peonies

(don't plant too deep or they won't bloom) to weevils and leaf-cutter bees. A lot of questions are asked about cultivation and irrigation, and about what can be planted late in the year. There are also the problems with chlorosis, stemming from the alkaline nature of the soil.

I would say to the new gardener to work your soil thoroughly and get it into the best shape you can before starting the garden. Don't buy your seed and plant it the same day. Use lots of compost, and if you don't have it, start making it. Get varieties of vegetables that work for your area, and that you know you will like. Some you can't miss on: cabbages, lettuce, tomatoes, corn and beans.

Ask questions of your nursery or seed store clerks, once you are sure they know their business. Most gardeners start out by planting too much. We all know about zucchini: two plants are one too many, but one plant will not be enough. Determine what you and your family like the best and plant that. Too big a garden will get to be a chore and may discourage you. I remember a man who came into the greenhouse once and ordered two flats of tomatoes. In those days, a flat held one hundred tomato plants. He couldn't be talked out of it. He planted all two hundred tomato seedlings six inches apart in rows. He got about as many tomatoes

as he would have with a fraction of that number of starts if they had been planted correctly.

Varieties:

Tomatoes: Park's Whopper would be my choice if I could choose only one kind. Also, Better Bush, Beefmaster, Golden Boy, Beefsteak and Sweet 100.

I got a hint once from an old-time seedsman in the valley: in this area we are short on magnesium. It is necessary to have magnesium to get a good pollen production in tomatoes and other plants, so to make sure there is some magnesium available. I have found that putting epsom salts (magnesium sulphate) into the soil of the greenhouse tomatoes before they go out will bring a quick set of tomatoes — up to a month earlier than others. A neighbor and I tested this by getting our tomatoes from the same greenhouse one year and putting them outside at the same time, treating them all the same except that I put epsom salts into mine. His plants were two to three weeks slower than mine in producing tomatoes. I don't think you can use too much of it — I never have had a problem with toxicity, but I put only about a level table-spoon around each plant early in the spring before they go out.

Corn: Golden Jubilee, Silver Queen, Butterfruit, How Sweet It Is.

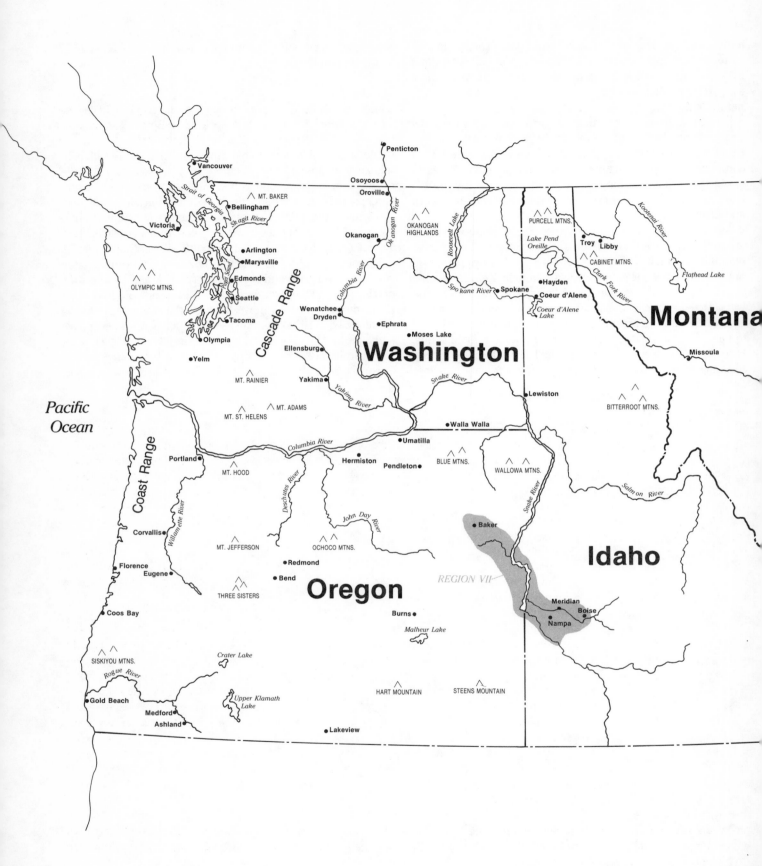

The Snake River Valley

INTRODUCTION

The central portion of the Snake River ties together this region of our Northwest gardening country. It is generally high basin country, between mountain ranges. Baker lies in the broad area between the Blue and Wallowa mountains, not far from the Powder River which drains into the Snake. The Boise-Caldwell-Nampa population center lies in a corridor between the Owyhee and Sawtooth ranges, where the Snake, the Boise and the Payette rivers run parallel before joining along the Oregon/Idaho border. The soils are generally alluvial in origin.

Natural vegetation ranges from grasslands to coniferous forests, depending upon altitude and precipitation. Juniper forests cover some of the drier uplands in the southern part of this region, and ponderosa pine can be found in large sections of the Blue, Wallowa and the Boise mountains. In general it is a vast and beautiful area of open forests and savannahs.

Temperatures can range from more than 100 degrees in summer to a cold minus 20 or lower in winter. Hot spells are certain but can be expected to be short. There is a considerable variation in the number of days between late and early frosts, depending upon location: in Boise the expected growing season is about the first of May to the first week or so of October. Sunlight is a plentiful commodity and precipitation is low. High winds are rare. Average summer temperatures are around 70 degrees for most of the main population centers, and in the 20s for winter. Precipitation is not much more than 11 inches for the year in the lower altitudes. Pacific storms have some impact on the mostly continental climate, delivering precipitation in winter months. Summers are markedly dry.

Gardeners in Region VII have to be alert and ready to take advantage of the early warm weather, remembering that frosts may yet pass through. Short, hot summers and early fall frosts call for an awareness of new varieties and special aids for growing. But where once local wisdom would have it that certain crops could not be raised, there is now a very good possibility of successful harvest of almost any garden crop. The use of plastics is part of the reason; a good attitude is another. The area is full of enthusiastic gardeners.

BAKER: Clara Hutchinson, Bill Stevens, Elaine Fillmore, Joe and Edythe Collinson, Edith Chadwick, Mary McCalden

This expert gardening group began its association through the Master Gardener program in Baker, directed by the county extension horticultural agent. Half of the group have been gardening a long time and the other half are relatively new at it. Edith Chadwick, for instance, has been gardening in the same location for sixty-four years, and Clara Hutchinson's garden has been going since 1942, while Mary McCalden has had a very short session with pulaski and shovel to get enough rocks out of her garden to find the soil. Garden size ranges from small beds scattered through the yard for easy access by the wheelchair gardener, Bill Stevens, to quarter-acre plots.

Site and Soil

Joe: Baker sits on an old lake bed and has a surprisingly high water table. One gardener, on an especially wet year, plowed in July and got stuck in the mud.

Our pH is very high. We have a definite alkaline problem and

Some of Baker's Master Gardeners inspect Helen Simmons's results. Here, gardeners of all ages and stages share their know-how, and by pooled effort they're propagating old-time varieties of fruits in a group-owned orchard.
(Maurice Mitchell, OSU Extension Service)

Planting

Planning and rotation depend on the size and type of garden: advice is to keep some kind of plan, to keep in mind the locations of crops from year to year. Most gardeners here practice rotation, especially for potatoes to avoid scab problems.

For easy access from his wheelchair, Bill Stevens uses raised beds and moves his crops from year to year with accessibility uppermost in his mind.

Other kinds of gardens: row, wide and regular row interspersed, intensive and a mixture of everything.

Elaine: our rule for planting is as early as the weather will allow, but it varies even around Baker. Usually we can put peas and potatoes out in early April. After that we can plant carrots, lettuce, beets, other early vegetables. Our last frost date is around May 20. Tomatoes can be seeded in a cold frame or greenhouse in March to be planted out the first of June.

We do a lot of our own seed starting under lights. Seed can come from the catalog companies or from the local store, sometimes it is saved from year to year, and sometimes Oregon State University comes up with some test seed for us to try here.

All: Favorite sources of seed: Burpee, Park, Gurney, Nichols, Territorial, Tillinghast.

Edythe Collinson's tomato plants look tall already? Here she shows how tall she expects them to get. And they used to say you couldn't raise tomatoes in Baker!

some gardeners add sulfur to bring the acidity up. Higher up in the hills there is a more acidic soil, but the weather is not so good for gardening. You can grow cane berries there, though.

Since the alkaline soils are deep we do not usually recommend double digging — it would just bring up more alkaline material to be corrected. Our methods include hand-spading, hoeing, raking, rototilling and, for extreme cases, the pulaski.

We always have to keep the pH in mind, and bring it down to near-neutral. We have some soil around here with a pH as high as 10. I have a spot in my garden that is especially alkaline. My pear tree shows severe signs of chlorosis. I am slowly working sulfur into the soil, but the roots go deep and it takes a lot of time. I hope I can save the pear tree.

In Baker, we can get a soil pH test from the county extension lab. There are also private labs where you can get an analysis from plant samples sent in. Cenex will provide a complete computer print-out of your plant nutrient content for about $25.

Edythe: Our problem here is that the TV garden program is directed to the Willamette Valley. When they say on the program to put on lime, our local gardeners go to the markets and ask for lime, so the markets stock sacks of dolomite lime with no information about its purpose nor when and how to use it.

Conditioning

Elaine: Composting materials: occasional piles of leaves, manure of all kinds, sawdust, wheat straw, grass clippings, nitrogen and phosphate, corn stalks, garden refuse. We put ours in a six-foot round bin made of fencing and turn about once a month. Squirrels and birds are attracted to the freshest refuse.

All: Soil amendments: compost, nitrogen and phosphate, commercial fertilizers of the 20-20-5, triple-16, or 16-16-20 variety; sulfur, barnyard manure, decomposed sawdust with nitrogen and compost, angleworms.

Flower and food plants mingle in Edith Chadwick's close-planted garden. The tires are part of the trick to raising tomatoes in Baker's three-month season.

Elaine: Any cheap seed — 1 garden to save money.

Joe: Seed from different companies is not always the same. For instance, Maestro pea seed from Territorial Seed Company is quite different from that put out by Burpee.

Clara: My favorite tools are a new finger hoe, onion hoe and an old hoe my father gave me.

Bill: Mine are hand tools that my brother made especially for me to garden from the wheelchair with.

Mary: I like an action hoe and a push-type cultivator.

Joe: The secret to a good garden is hoe, hoe, hoe.

Some people here — especially those with plenty of water from artesian wells or other sources — like to use flood irrigation, running water full blast down the deep furrows between their rows. The problem with it can be that some plants get too much if there are slightly lower spots, and others won't get enough. It takes a lot of water in the summertime here, however you irrigate. It may mean watering all day every day, rotating the hoses around the garden.

Climate Modification

Edythe: Baker's temperature in the late spring and summer will go from the nineties in the day to the forties at night. The growing season is three months—June 1 to September 1 or a bit later.

Mary: Spinach can sometimes be planted for a fall crop, but it is often too hot to start cool-weather vegetables in the summer. Lettuce, herbs and even squash sometimes reseed the following spring, although the squash can turn out to be a strange hybrid. We put all our vegetable garden in at once, but as an early crop finishes—peas, for example—we let the squash vines move in and take over.

Clara: We have a short, short season for growing. We have to plant seeds for transplants early to be ready to get them into the ground. Then we might have a bad hailstorm or a late frost and lose them anyway. We have hot days in the summer, but cool nights. Early freezing in the fall is a problem too.

Bill: For wheelchair gardening, I use large tractor tires as raised beds—they warm the soil early and make nice, large planters. I get them free.

Elaine: One way to beat a frost overnight is to get up very early in the morning, about 4 a.m. on an unusually cold May morning, for instance, and spray the plants with water. Putting on the sprinkler until the sun is up will often prevent damage to new seedlings.

We use a lot of special devices for beating the climate: grow lights, Walls-o-Water or old windows set around the plants, tires, blankets in the fall, sheets of black plastic, hot caps, coldframes, and greenhouses.

Edythe: Our Master Gardener group here makes money selling Walls-o-Water from the manufacturer in Salt Lake. We get $.60 - $.80 per sale from them for our own purposes. We raised 650 tomato plants last year to sell. Everyone is impressed — the community, the company that sells them, and we're impressed too. We use the money on development of an orchard up on the hill on some land leased from the city. We collect old-time varieties of fruits and propagate them by grafting. We have 150 to 175 trees there now and hope to get more. Watering is a problem — we would like to put in a drip system.

Joe: We plant our tomatoes in the Walls-o-Water set inside tires that are thirteen inches rim size, on black plastic. The plastic is cut out of the middle of the tire and the tire is filled with good soil or compost. A six- to eight-inch tomato is transplanted with some of the stem buried; bamboo stakes are put around the inside of the rim to hold the wall out. When the wall is set on and filled with water, it sits right on the bead of the tire. I stake the whole thing down too so the wind doesn't blow it away. It works very well. After the plant gets up beyond the height of the wall, we take it off. It really takes two people to do this, because they are full of water and heavy, and you don't want to drop them on the tomato plant. There are three gallons of water in the wall. After we are finished with the wall, we rinse it out and hang it upside down to dry, so that mildew won't get started inside. At that point, we set in a wire frame to keep the tomato plants up off the tire.

I know for certain that this method will bring us tomatoes two or three weeks earlier than any other method. We are gradually converting all the local gardeners to this way of growing tomatoes.

I also top my tomatoes, from about August 1 on, because I don't want any more of the plant's energy going into producing new flowers and fruit that won't mature before frost.

Edith: They used to say you couldn't raise tomatoes in Baker, but since Walls-o-Water made its entrance here it has been a different story.

Joe: Did you know you can take cuttings from your best tomato plants, root them, and pot them up? If you have an indoor growing area or heated greenhouse, you can get very early starts for the next year that way.

For successful gardening in the Baker area, plant only the earliest varieties. Plant as early as possible. Be sure your garden is set in the sunniest location.

Edythe: Even with all our precautions, we sometimes have to

practice what we call Beaning By Braille, going out late at night with a flashlight and picking the last of the beans and whatever else we can find as the temperature gets down around freezing.

Pests and Problems

Mary: Cabbage butterfly, onion maggot, root maggot, aphids, cutworm, army worm, earwig, slugs, potato beetle, HOPPERS!

Clara: To get rid of insects: malathion and diazinon (but I don't like to use any at all). Plant cabbage early to beat the cabbage butterfly.

Elaine: Pick by hand (yuck); bait traps; take off their heads! Seven; Lily Miller Grasshopper Bait; pay the kids to bring in as many bugs as they can find; prayer, if all else fails.

Bill: The best way to deal with grasshoppers is to keep the area around the garden clean and free of weeds where they can hide.

Other persistent problems include the pollution from drifting commercial sprays, an occasional stray dog or cat, moles, voles or gophers, rabbits, ground squirrels and crows. Deer are also a nuisance for some of us who live on the outskirts of town.

Mary: You can lay chicken wire on the ground around the garden to discourage the deer. They don't like to walk on it.

Recommendations

All: **Tomatoes:** Oregon Spring, Golden Nugget, Sweet 100, Santiam, Super Marminade, Lemon Boy — which is a sweet, less acid tomato — you'd be surprised how many people can't eat the more acidic types — Outdoor Girl, Super Sue, and Bonnie Best.

We make a lot of trials — you must try them at least two years before you can recommend them, because one year might be a fluke.

Corn: Canadian Pride from Earl May Seed Company seems to do well here, producing a couple of weeks earlier than other standard varieties.

A big, ripe tomato doesn't have to be red. Joe and Edythe Collinson grow a yellow variety—less acidic than the red, and some unfortunate people can't tolerate the acid.

Potatoes: Homestead — it is an early potato — Explorer and Netted Gem.

Cabbage: Golden Acre

Herbs: mint, sage, chives, garlic, parsley, basil, lemon balm, peppermint, sage, chives, shallots, borage, rosemary, sweet marjoram.

MERIDIAN: Ross Hadfield

Ross Hadfield is a retired control analyst for Wyeth Labs and is devoting a lot of his time to gardening these days. Besides the daily fare from his vegetable garden, he produces raisins from his own grapes. In fact, he is perhaps best known around the Boise area for this activity. A gardener since he was twelve, he has turned his Meridian lot to the production of food, with two 30x60-foot plots — one for vegetables and one for grapes.

Site and Soil Conditioning

My house and yard here were part of a subdivision made out of alfalfa fields. The soil is alluvial, quite silty, underlain with hardpan, and runs toward alkalinity. The pH is about 7.8 to 8.0 if left to itself.

I have used grass clippings and leaves to make compost, and since 1980 I've been able to get mint hay. That is the plant material left after the mint oil has been extracted — we have quite a production of mint in this valley. I also use mint hay for mulch after the garden is established.

When I started here, I added gypsum for consistency, but I don't need it anymore after years of improving my soil. Ammonium sulfate is a regular addition to the gardens each year, and I keep some all-purpose variety of fertilizer, with a balanced content of nitrogen, phosphorus and potassium, on hand too.

I begin the gardening year by rototilling the garden area — I go over it several times before it is ready to be planted. After planting, I hand-hoe.

I flood irrigate my garden once a week when it doesn't rain, and use the mint hay mulch to keep the moisture in. We are lucky here as there is plenty of irrigation water. This is especially good for growing many varieties of fruits.

Planting, Climate Modification

I am particular about keeping a plan. I make a chart each year showing the variety planted, the time planted, and how I planted it. I use a mixture of methods: row, wide row, block, raised bed. Although I don't use an interplanting method, I use a succession plan so early crops are followed by a second late crop of cole vegetables or carrots and the like.

I don't have a greenhouse, but I do have a coldframe I made from old glass windows. I start plants in it for early transplanting: cabbage, cauliflower, broccoli and onions can be started in February in the coldframe and will go out in the garden in March.

I like to start other seed inside in March and April. Those varieties that don't do well in cold weather will go out in May. I plant potatoes, the seed of peas and the other cole crops right

Retired chemist Ross Hadfield has 3,600 square feet of growing space, half devoted to garden produce, half to grapes. He turns out raisins, not wines.

in the garden in March; carrots, beets and chard in April; and corn and beans in May, along with tomato and pepper plants. I do not put in late crops for a fall harvest. When the frosts have finished my garden, I rototill and leave the ground rough. My rototiller is the ideal tool for this kind of garden management.

We have to be careful in this area that we aren't over-eager and plant too early. It takes patience. There are always late frosts after nice, warm weather that makes everyone want to get all the plants outside.

Pests and Problems

I try to plant the tomatoes and potatoes, in particular, in different spots each year. It seems to keep the pests down. I think the worst insect I have to deal with is the cabbage butterfly.

We have some slugs and snails here that cause us difficulties, and I find the robins, starlings and finches are particularly hard on the grapes.

Recommendations

I think the most important thing to get right is the soil. Plenty of organic matter worked in over the years can make a lot of difference, no matter what your soil problems are.

Varieties:

Tomato	Celebrity
Onion	Walla Walla Sweet
Cucumber	Pot Luck
Corn	How Sweet It Is
Popcorn	Peppy
Green bean	Slenderette
Chard	Rhubarb

From: Vermont Seed Co., Park Seed So., and Burpee.

Tomato varieties recommended by University of Idaho College of Agriculture:

Sub-Arctic series: developed for west-central Alberta, Canada,

these small tomato plants will produce a lot of cherry-size fruit all at the same time:

Sub-Arctic Delight
Early Sub-Arctic
Sub-Arctic Midi
Sub-Arctic Plenty
Sub-Arctic Cherry
Sub-Arctic Maxi

Recommended University of Idaho-developed tomatoes:

Bonner — small (2-2.5″ fruit)
Latah — 1.5-2″ fruit
Shoshone — 1.5-2″ fruit
Kootenai — 2-3″ fruit
Sandpoint — 2-2.5″ fruit
Ida Gold — (a Sub-Arctic Midi cross) very early, small plant, many fruit 1-2″ diameter, gold color. (If not available contact local extension agent.)
Super Star — especially disease-resistant
Payette — dwarf, curly-top, disease-resistant for greenhouse

All these have been developed for early-setting fruit and Idaho growing conditions.

Also recommended:

Immun Prior Beta (IPB) — has unusual, potatolike leaf, 2-2.5″ fruit rather sparsely borne on each plant, not great for eating, best for sauce or canning.
Rocket — a very small vine with few leaves, indeterminate, fruit 2″ diameter.
Farthest North — small, cherry-sized fruit, ripens over short time period.
Pixie Hybird — medium small fruit, very early.

Corn: Plant early, mid and late for continuing crop:
Early varieties (60-69 days): Seneca 60, Early Sun Glow, Golden Beauty, Tokay Sugar, Miniature, Earliking, Spring Gold, North Star, Sundance and Sprite.
Mid-season (70-79 days): Carmelcross, Early X-tra Sweet, Golden Earlipack, Harmony, and Barbecue.
Late varieties (80 to 90 days or more): Seneca Chief, Illini Xtra-Sweet, Golden Cross Bantam, Jubilee, Dominator, Iochief, and Silver Queen.

Prime agricultural land measures by the square mile in the wide valley of the Snake, the thousand-mile-long river that arcs across southern Idaho. Meridian lies between Boise and Nampa, where the sinuous Snake turns northward.

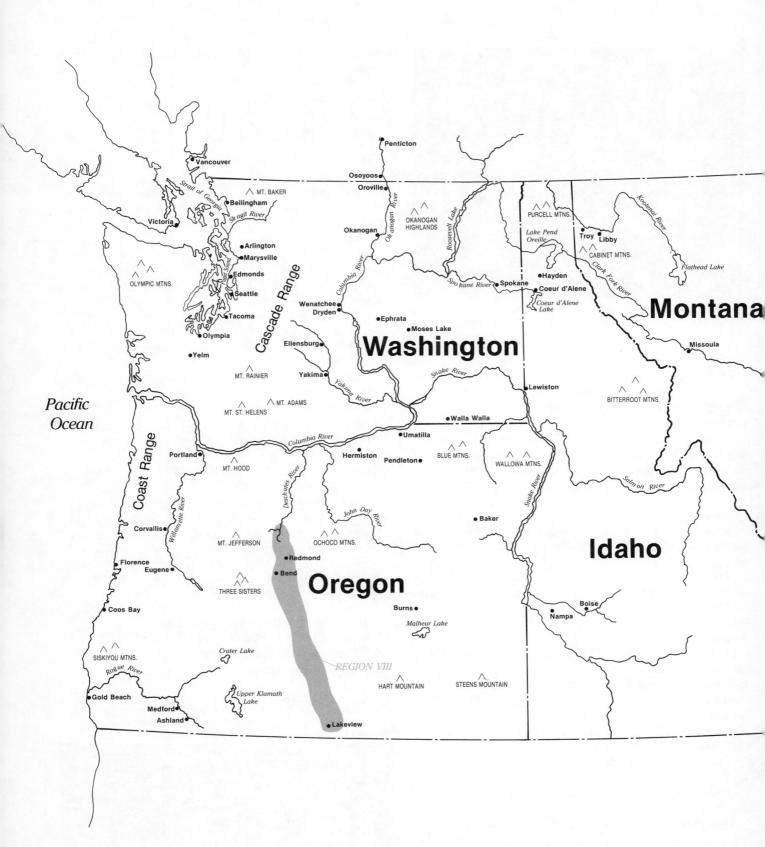

Pacific
Ocean

- Vancouver

MT. BAKER

- Bellingham
- Victoria

Strait of Georgia

Skagit River

OLYMPIC MTNS.

- Arlington
- Marysville
- Edmonds
- Seattle
- Tacoma
- Olympia
- Yelm

MT. RAINIER

MT. ST. HELENS

MT. ADAMS

Cascade Range

Penticton

Osoyoos
Oroville

Okanogan

Okanogan River

Columbia River

Wenatchee
Dryden

Ellensburg

Yakima

Yakima River

- Ephrata
- Moses Lake

OKANOGAN
HIGHLANDS

Roosevelt Lake

Spokane River Spokane

PURCELL MTNS.

Lake Pend
Oreille

Troy Libby

CABINET MTNS.

Kootenai River

Clark Fork River

Flathead Lake

Montana

- Hayden
- Coeur d'Alene

Coeur d'Alene
Lake

Snake River

Lewiston

BITTERROOT MTNS.

Missoula

Washington

Columbia River

Coast Range

Portland

MT. HOOD

Willamette River

Deschutes River

Hermiston

Umatilla

- Walla Walla

- Pendleton

BLUE MTNS.

WALLOWA MTNS.

Snake River

Salmon River

Corvallis

Florence
Eugene

MT. JEFFERSON

THREE SISTERS

Redmond
Bend

John Day River

OCHOCO MTNS.

Oregon

- Baker

Idaho

- Coos Bay

Burns

Malheur Lake

Boise

Nampa

SISKIYOU MTNS.

Rogue River

Crater Lake

REGION VIII

HART MOUNTAIN

STEENS MOUNTAIN

- Gold Beach

Medford
Ashland

Upper Klamath
Lake

Lakeview

120

The Central Plateau of Oregon

INTRODUCTION

Central-southern Oregon is generally high and flat, with some very notable exceptions in the scattered lava buttes, and in ranges such as Hart Mountain and Steens Mountain. Great hollows or basins in the plateau are sometimes filled with alkaline lakes, or sometimes dry. The volcanic rocks, the sparsity of vegetation, the miles and miles of emptiness surrounding the traveler in this land, the winds and the extremes of temperatures, all make the place seem raw and new — somehow just created. There is no coziness in nature here.

Bend lies just at the western edge of this high plateau, and is perhaps most influenced by the weather and terrain to its west — the high Oregon Cascades. The towns of Burns and Lakeview contain most of the population living in the middle of this region.

Altitudes are high: usually well above 3,000 feet for the lower areas, climbing into 5,000- and 6,000-foot ridges, where the traveler can look westward at the 10,350-foot bulk of the Three Sisters.

In some respects this central plateau resembles the Columbia Basin of Washington, but it is higher, has a coarser, volcanic soil, and any trees or shrubs are more likely to be juniper and bitter brush than pine and bitter cherry. Species of *Artemisia,* the ubiquitous "sage brush," will be found in both areas, however.

A look at weather records for Burns gives a picture of the harshness of the climate:

Highest recorded temperature — 103 degrees F. in August
Lowest recorded temperature — −26 degrees F. in Jan.
Mean number of days with minimum temperature 32 degrees F. or less — 187

Mean number of days with precipitation — 90
Average mean temperature — 46 degrees F.; 68.4 in July and 25.2 in January
Precipitation — 11.83 inches; 1.76 inches in January and .32 in July

In Bend the residents claim that it can frost any time of year and usually does, and bring up the July freeze to prove it. But hardships separate the real gardener from the dilettante. Vegetables and flowers are produced in profusion by dedicated growers who have their ways of getting through the unseasonal little touches of weather that sometimes come along.

BEND: Patsy and Clay Vincent, Doris Warren
REDMOND: Jim Powell

These four gardeners have gained a lot of expertise from work with the local Master Gardeners. They have gardens of varying design and purpose, but they all generally agree on the basic aspects of gardening in the Bend and Redmond area.

The Vincents have been residents of Bend for thirty-five years and built their present home on the outskirts of town in 1972. Jim Powell moved into his Redmond home only recently and has had about two years to work on the garden. Doris Warren started her garden in 1974, even before her house was finished, so eager was she to get started.

Site and Soil Conditioning

Patsy: There's a difference between Bend and Redmond, though they are only 15 miles apart. Bend is at an altitude of 3,600

121

A gardener's beginning chore on the central Oregon plateau is to get out the rock. Clay and Patsy Vincent of Bend used some of theirs to create a rock garden, an oasis of coziness where there is none in nature. A holding pond (below) helps them solve the problem of water. Rights to irrigation water six months of the year came with their property—"a very important right," says Clay, "and hard to get, but land is useless here without water."

feet, and Redmond sits about four hundred feet lower. That means that Redmond has temperatures two to four degrees warmer during the day and seven to eight degrees at night — year around. Sometimes you'll see leaves out in Redmond as much as a month earlier than in Bend. Corn ripens at least a couple of weeks earlier. But there are higher places, such as Sisters, which are even colder. And La Pine — well that is almost hopeless for growing anything but native vegetation.

In this country we display green tomatoes at the fair.

Jim: I had the best stand of quack grass in the state when I moved in. It was a neglected flower garden. I had to take each shovelful of soil as I dug it and sift it through hardware cloth with a quarter-inch mesh to get all the roots out. I had only recently had heart surgery, but I knew that gardening was going to be one of the best therapies for me. The soil is a kind of pumice sand,

grainy and very well drained. My son rototilled the garden spot for me first so it was loose and easy to dig up.

We don't use the techniques of raised bed gardening here very much; they tend to dry out too fast. We have a high amount of solar radiation in the summer — watering problems enough without making them worse.

The Vincents: We had all juniper trees and native grasses here, and a lot of rock. Since we had so much rock, we put in a rock garden first thing. Every year our garden got bigger, like the lawn. We were determined never to have more than a fifteen-minute lawn, meaning it would not take more than fifteen minutes to mow, but it's become a one-hour lawn. One year we won a local Sears garden award. Our vegetable garden is about fifty by one hundred feet, and about twenty-five feet of that is in raspberries, strawberries and asparagus.

Our soil is also very grainy and porous — considered to be sandy. Some of it is particularly shallow with basalt ledges that we have had to literally break out by hand to get rid of them. On the other hand, there are deep, rockless pockets where soil has blown and collected over many years. It is neutral soil, mainly needing humus and nitrogen.

Doris: I have four little plots of garden. I like to grow vegetables mixed with flowers. One plot is fifteen by thirty, where I grow all my favorite squashes. Two plots are twenty by thirty feet and two others are ten by twelve feet. I think we have less than the usual six or eight inches of soil. I have cleared out a lot of rock. We have put in grass clippings, straw, compost and manure to build up the soil.

Jim: I hurry my compost pile along by turning it every four days or so. That way I can have it ready in thirty days. I start out fresh each spring with garden waste and lots of lawn clippings I get from neighbors who don't spray their lawns. I leave my own clippings on my lawn and let them go right back into the soil. I put garden dirt into the compost to help in decomposition, and I use all my vegetable kitchen waste. All of this is done in one bin about two feet high. New material is added along the side.

Doris: I have a strip pit with wooden partitions which divide it into three sections. I start a new pile with six or eight inches of grass clippings, straw, manure, dirt and some nitrogen. After I've turned it and let it work for awhile I move it to pit number 2. My final, usable, compost comes from the last pit.

Vincents: We have one five-by-ten-by-three-foot bin. We pitch everything into it starting in the spring. We add some nitrogen and manure, turn it often during the summer up to November, then top it off with three or four inches of manure and let it compost all winter. The next spring it's ready to shovel out of the bin onto the garden and I start a new batch. We keep a pile of manure on hand next to the compost bin for convenience.

Jim: Our average rainfall is twelve inches, with much of it falling as snow. We need to make effective use of mulch once the ground is warmed up, to preserve the soil moisture. I use city water in Redmond, and consider the rates rather stiff but still worth paying. Anyway, it's "pasturized" — it's gone through pasture after pasture after pasture. Seriously, we do have severe water limitations in the summer so I can water only about once

a week in each garden area. It's enough, since I have put a lot of rotten manure and other humus in the soil, but it wouldn't be if I hadn't.

Vincents: We use ditch irrigation water because we have a water right for it that goes with the property. We can use it from April 15 to October 15. It is a very important right to have in this country, and not easy to get, yet land is useless without it — at least for gardening. We usually water on a demand basis, averaging two to four days between waterings in each place. If the wind is fierce, we have to take extra care because the soil dries out even faster. The top of our rock garden is a good place to watch — if the soil is dry there, we water everywhere.

We have dug a large basin at the side of the lot to act as a holding pond for the water. We pump from that onto the gardens.

Planting

Doris: I make a detailed plan each year for my garden, using graph paper and colored pencils. I draw in each variety with a different color — yellow for lettuce, green for peas, etcetera, and keep my plans in a notebook over three or four years so I know how I have been rotating. Also, I usually take a snapshot of each area in production. This helps in planning the next year's garden.

Jim: It makes a difference, too, if you remember not to put corn in the same place twice. Beans or peas usually follow corn in my garden. Another strategy I use in planning is to start my earliest vegetable nearest the house, so I don't have to walk over the rest of the garden to get them.

Vincents: We believe it is important to buy seed from companies that specialize in supplying gardeners who live in areas of similar latitude. We like Burpee, Park and Johnny's in particular.

Jim: I buy my seed from Burpee, Thompson and Morgan, Park, and sometimes from Nichols for a special seed. I always like to start my seed myself, you don't really know what you are getting when you buy starts at the supermarket.

Doris: I gather seed from my garden when I can, especially leek, peas, garlic, and occasionally tomato seed.

Patsy Vincent: Something I've found out is that recent tests made by the Washington State Extension Service have shown that soaking seed before planting may not be as useful after all. It seems if you presoak the seed it softens the hull, and allows in disease and other damage before the seedling has a chance to develop properly. Without prior soaking, the seed absorbs just enough moisture to sprout and develop without getting soggy or soft.

Climate Modification

Vincents: We are generally impressed with the Walls-o-Water here and use them extensively. We are using them in our Master Gardener trial garden in Redmond as well, and making tests on them. We have put tomatoes, peppers and cantaloupe out in May in these Walls-o-Water, had the night temperature go to nineteen degrees, so cold that the walls froze solid. But the plants were all alive and well except for that part of them that was sticking out above the top. That is a good test of their capabilities. Other

Plastic and ingenuity combined to produce Walls-o-Water, a new sort of cloche said to add weeks to the growing season. Clay tells of a night when water in his Walls froze solid, but plants inside them didn't freeze.

gardeners think they get the best results with black plastic mulch. A combination might be a good choice. Without these Walls, we would not be able to plant the nonhardy varieties of vegetables outside before June 10.

One thing we disagree with the Walls manufacturer about is

their use for the whole growing season. We find that the foliage gets crowded and tends to turn yellow and moldy. Nevertheless, when it is 44 degrees outside the Walls, it is 64 degrees inside.

In this part of the country it is extremely difficult to grow a garden. There are many, many microclimates. A new gardener would be wise to check the microclimate in his or her own yard before taking anyone's word about it. Some places are warmer than others — sometimes an underground stream will give soil temperature a boost.

Doris: Placement of trees sometimes creates a draft effect and keeps air moving so frost doesn't settle during those colder nights in the growing season. You want to create a funnel effect to direct moving air across the garden, but not a dam effect to stop it altogether.

Jim: Once in Prineville I tried growing tomatoes in tires, but you might say I was less than successful. Tires definitely do not give the protection plants get from Walls-o-Water or cloches and other methods closer to the plant.

Vincents: Our seedlings are started in the basement. We have a window seat we can convert to a growing bench for the season. Also we have tried building a temporary greenhouse on the workshop with plastic and pvc pipe. We set plastic jugs of water painted black on one side on the inside of this greenhouse to store some of the day's heat, and release it on the cold nights. It worked well, but we would make better venting arrangements next time, as it could get extremely hot inside during the day — hot enough to wilt the plants.

Jim: I have a greenhouse which has a very well-insulated section. I can use this — mostly unheated — for starting my seed.

Doris: I use my sun porch and grow-lights for getting my transplants going. I also use it for germination tests on leftover seeds to see whether they are still viable.

Vincents: We usually can count on a ninety-day growing season, June 1 to September 10, but that isn't necessarily a frost-free season. If you want to put something out because the weather seems too fine to ignore, go ahead, but keep a few plants on reserve just in case you misjudge the weather.

Doris: Another thing — our nights are quite cold, so what is printed on the vegetable seed packet as being the average time to maturity should be extended twenty more days, just because the plants are retarded in their growth by every cold night. I have seen climate charts that lump us together with Rocky Mountain areas, as far as growing conditions, but I have lived and gardened in Boulder, Colorado, and know that I had a warmer season there than I do here.

I use my greenhouse for growing, right in the ground, all summer long. I plant about mid-February, putting in lettuce, chard, spinach, beets, parsley and cabbage — things that will do well in cool temperatures. I keep the soil built up with the addition of compost. At the height of the summer I may have to turn on the sprinkler to lower the temperature in the greenhouse. It's also important to make sure there is four-way cross ventilation.

Jim: I think a valuable tool for successful gardening is choosing varieties carefully for their growing time and their resistance to disease. With care, many kinds of vegetables can be raised here.

Gardeners in Redmond, altitude 3,200 feet, have it better than those in Bend, only 15 miles away but 400 feet higher. Even so, Master Gardeners in Redmond gladly extend their season with Walls-o-Water, as shown here.

Some of them can stay in the ground if you cover them after the first frost or two. Soil raked right up over the tops of such vegetables as carrots, beets, rutabagas and parsnips, and left very loose, not packed down, will insulate them and allow you to chip down into the ground later to get some of them out.

For an early crop, try fava beans — I can sometimes start them in April here and they do well in cool weather.

Clay: Even if it does freeze very late and the whole garden looks done for, don't have a fit and pull everything out. It may be that some of the plants will survive — even just at the bottom, where they will begin to grow again. I take a wait-and-see attitude now.

Pests and Problems

Vincents: Our biggest problem seems to be cutworms. We make collars from the tubes of toilet tissue rolls, or waxed Dixie cups with the bottoms taken out. These can be set an inch below the surface of the soil to keep the cutworms out. Powdered diazinon is our last-ditch stand and we don't use it as long as there's anything else. The new bonded row covers will keep out the cabbage butterflies and root maggot fly. Sevin is the choice for dealing with the potato beetle, if we can't get it off by hand-picking, and for aphids too. On the hazardous pesticide scale, where 1 is the most hazardous and 4 is the least, Sevin rates 4 and diazinon 3. We aren't one hundred percent organic, but we won't spray unless everything else fails.

Clay: We had a call from the Game Department at the Master Gardener clinic one day. They said someone had brought in a "big-game" specimen they couldn't identify and needed help. Turned out it was a tomato hornworm. They *are* big, but . . . !

Patsy: We have a lot of deer here, and like to see them, but they are murder on the garden. We have found that Irish Spring deodorant soap discourages them from coming into the yard. It's the perfume, not the deodorant, that keeps them out. We tie bars of it in net bags around the edges of our yard, on poles or on the fence.

Jim: Along that line, I discovered by accident that gophers don't

From posts around the Vincents' yard there dangle bars of Irish Spring soap in net bags. Deer don't like the perfume. The Vincents do like the deer, but not in their garden.

Recommendations

All: Get out the rock.

Use all the humus you can get, and put it in the garden a month or so before you plant.

Pick your absolute best location for getting sun.

Doris: Don't be discouraged if something doesn't turn out. There will always be splendid successes to make up for the failures.

Tomatoes: Santiam, Oregon Spring, Golden Nugget, Patio, and possibly Rutgers. Big Boy, Earliana, and Early Girl are likely to be too late here.

Cabbage: Early Flat Dutch — grows huge in the experimental garden in Redmond.

Corn: How Sweet It Is, or Kandy Korn

Pepper: Golden Whopper banana

Beans: Blue Mountain bush — developed in Prosser, Washington, and available from extension service. Yellow wax.

Cucumber: (no variety given) — they do well in Walls-o-Water, but will have to be hand-pollinated. According to Patsy Vincent, male flowers are ripe for use in pollination only about two days, females for three days; pollination should be done before noon, and preferably with a small paintbrush.

Cantaloupe: (no variety given) — does best in Walls-o-Water also, and again may need hand-pollinating.

Patsy Vincent's herb-garden: Thymes (assorted), marjoram, spearmint, peppermint, tarragon, chamomile and borage (an annual). The rest do fine with minimal protection. Some herbs need greenhouse protection during the winter. The Bend-Redmond area has some quite extensive herb gardens.

like Hai Karate perfume and will attempt to cover it over if they find the scent on something. If you put it by the gopher trap, the gopher will spring it trying to get rid of the smell.

Patsy: We have tried sardines on gophers, and that didn't seem to work. Juicy Fruit gum doesn't work on moles either, as far as we can tell. Both of those remedies have been recommended to us. They must have worked somewhere.

Here is Patsy's recipe for "Mint-o-Mile Tea:"

9 parts dried mint leaves, preferably two or more kinds
3 parts dried chamomile flowers
1 part dried lemon thyme leaves
1 part dried lemon balm leaves
½ part coriander seeds
½ part dried orange peel
½ part whole cloves
Combine and store in closed container. Use 1 tsp. per cup of boiling water. Drink either hot or cold.

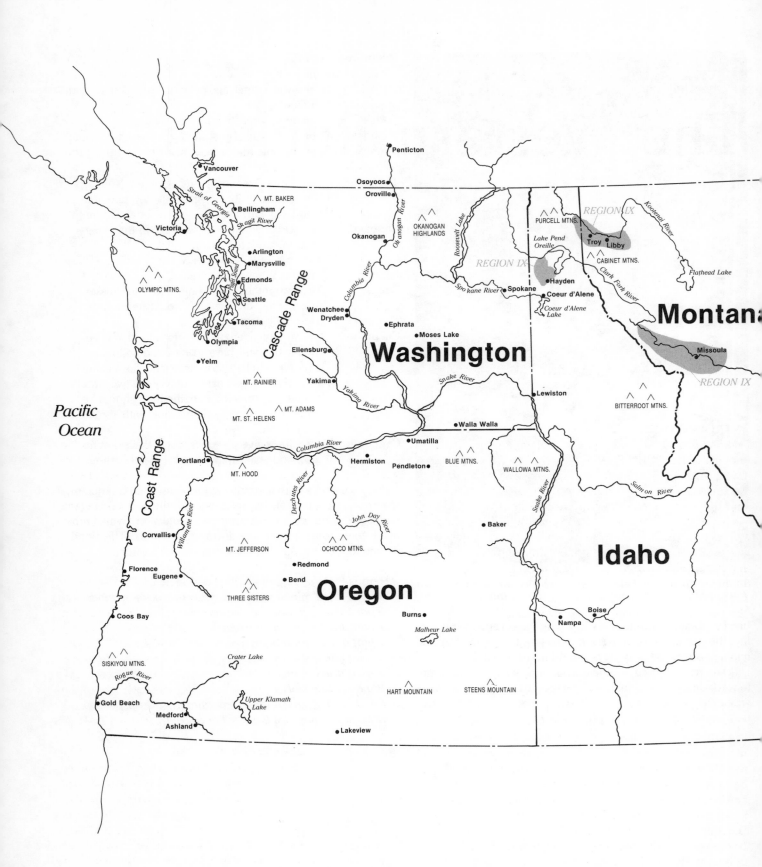

Penticton

Vancouver

Osoyoos
Oroville

∧ MT. BAKER

Bellingham

Strait of Georgia

Sk agit River

Victoria

Okanogan

Ok anogan River

OKANOGAN
HIGHLANDS

Roosevelt Lake

PURCELL MTNS.

REGION IX

Arlington
Marysville

Edmonds

∧∧∧
OLYMPIC MTNS.

Seattle

Puget Sound

Tacoma

Olympia

Yelm

Cascade Range

Wenatchee
Dryden

Ephrata

∧
MT. RAINIER

Yakima

Ellensburg

Moses Lake

Yakima River

∧
MT. ST. HELENS

∧ MT. ADAMS

Columbia River

Washington

Spo kane River

Spokane

*Lake Pend
Oreille*

REGION IX

Hayden

*Coeur d'Alene
Lake*

Coeur d'Alene

CABINET MTNS.

Troy ● Libby

Kootenai River

Flathead Lake

REGION IX

Montana

Clark Fork River

Missoula

REGION IX

∧∧
BITTERROOT MTNS.

Lewiston

Snake River

Walla Walla

Umatilla

Pacific
Ocean

Coast Range

Portland

∧
MT. HOOD

Hermiston
Pendleton

∧∧
BLUE MTNS.

∧∧
WALLOWA MTNS.

Salm on River

Columbia River

Deschutes River

Willamette River

Corvallis

∧
MT. JEFFERSON

John Day River

∧∧
OCHOCO MTNS.

Baker

Idaho

Florence
Eugene

Redmond

Bend

∧∧∧
THREE SISTERS

Oregon

Boise

Nampa

Coos Bay

Burns

Malheur Lake

∧∧
SISKIYOU MTNS.

Crater Lake

Rogue River

*Upper Klamath
Lake*

∧
HART MOUNTAIN

∧
STEENS MOUNTAIN

Gold Beach

Medford
Ashland

Lakeview

126

The Western Rockies

INTRODUCTION

Beyond the Snake and the Columbia and their tributaries, the first ranges of the Rockies begin to rise. The big lakes of Coeur d'Alene, Pend Oreille, Flathead and, to the north, Kootenay, lie between timber-covered ridges. The Clark Fork and the Kootenai Rivers drain great sections of the western slopes of the Rockies, and flow eventually to the Columbia.

This is mountain country, even when you live in the valleys and basins between. Weather is more unpredictable, and in the northern valleys rainfall is higher, than in the regions to the immediate west. The clouds that scud across the desert scrublands without leaving a drop catch again on the first ranges to the east, and drop some of their moisture.

The climate is continental, but as in Boise, it is modified by the Pacific air masses traveling east from the West Coast. Drainage of cold air from the ridge tops into the valleys is a definite factor influencing local temperatures. Often gardeners on a small slope above a valley will have less trouble with unexpected frosts than those lower down.

Average annual precipitation for both Missoula and Lewiston is about thirteen inches. In days of freezing, the two areas are not comparable: Lewiston has a month longer growing season than Missoula. Winters in Missoula are less sunny than might be expected — more like coastal than inland skies, with fog and clouds collecting in the basin. Winter temperatures can go to an average low of 20 degrees F. in Missoula, and 31 in Lewiston, to a summer high of 65 for Missoula and 73 for Lewiston — averaging day and night temperatures for a July or August. Highest temperature to be expected (from the records of these two cities) is 115 degrees in Lewiston; lowest to be expected is −33 in Missoula.

Generalities are of even less value in this region than in the rest. It is well known that mountains make their own weather, and which side of a mountain you are on makes a lot of difference to your backyard climate. Close watch on the weather, comparing possible sites, keeping records — these will help the gardener know what conditions he is facing when preparing to dig into a particular spot of soil in the western Rockies.

HAYDEN: Barbara Arnold

Barbara Arnold has gardened in several western states, and is now, she says, making the adjustment from a one-acre farm garden to a town garden in Hayden, Idaho. She grows the family vegetables and some everlasting flowers for wreaths, besides every kind of herb that will grow there. The town of Hayden is still rural — Barbara has cows for neighbors. The third-acre she has for yard, garden and house isn't quite large enough, so she borrows a bit of land from a friend. Although her husband does the rototilling, Barbara is the one who cares for the garden.

Site and Soil Conditioning

Barbara: My garden is about 1,400 square feet. It was an old garden site that had not been used for several years when I took it in hand and started improving it for my own garden. This property is in a generally rocky area, but the garden soil I'd call on the clay-loamy side. Of course I do as much as I can every year to improve it, with sheep and rabbit manures. I'm a spinner, and I keep angora rabbits. They provide me with a bonus of manure, and I garner sheep and goat manure from friends' barns when I can.

I believe in easy compost — I just dump what I have into a big pile, deal with it when I remember, and use it when I need it. I put grass clippings, plant materials and rabbit manure into it.

We rototill with the Troy-Bilt several times in the spring to get the winter mulches of maple leaves, wood ash and other materials well mixed in. After that we work by hand, using a hoe. In the fall, before putting the garden to bed, we rototill again.

Planting

I make a garden plan, but usually find it necessary to make some changes as I go. I draw my garden plan on graph paper, with the generic names of the crops. Then in a separate binder I keep a list of the varieties grown, their germination, hardiness, yield, and recommendations for future use. I do another plan in the fall because by then I have transplanted, or bought new perennials, and I tend to forget where I put things by the time spring comes again.

I find that keeping good records will help me remember where things were each year, and I won't put the same crop in the same place for at least three years as long as I know where it has been before.

I use a wide-row method of planting and try to interplant various kinds of vegetables. I like that method for pest control as well as general companion planting principles — and for aesthetics too. I like to see flowers and herbs growing alongside the vegetables. I also keep flowers for cutting in the garden because they are often too gangly for flower beds and they brighten up the vegetables.

The one thing I don't interplant is corn — it goes in a block by itself so it will be thoroughly pollinated and produce well.

After the plants begin to grow I use a mulch of maple leaves from our trees to discourage weeds in the garden. I also put leaves on in the winter for insulation against freezing.

Climate Modification

I don't use any kind of row covers or hot caps in the garden, but we have a greenhouse. It's free-standing, eight by twelve feet, located right next to the garden for convenience. We heat it with electricity if we have to. I start seeds in it from March on until June. Later I use it as my potting shed and then to dry flowers, garlic and onions, and seed pods and other things I may use to make my wreaths.

I find that I can plant most of my starts after the middle of May. By June 1 I have everything in the garden. For the earliest direct-seeding, I can put in the peas just about Easter time, and onions and spinach go in about April 15.

I don't put in any late plantings or try to use the garden in the fall. By then I am too tired and find I'm ready for a little rest from the work. Spinach does manage to overwinter with my help. I let some of it go to seed, then shake some of the seed over newly rototilled ground in the fall.

Pests and Problems

The worst pest I have is the larvae of the cabbage moth. I use *Baccillus thuringiensis (Bt)* to get rid of it. We also have grass-hoppers, which I try to ignore, and aphids, which can be washed off with soapy water.

Recommendations

I raise statice, strawflowers, star everlasting, money plant, Chinese lanterns and others for drying. As for herbs, they are my pride and joy. The only herb I have tried with no luck at all is cumin. Mints, winter savory, lovage, tarragon, oregano, sage, thyme and chives are among the most reliable perennials in our climate here. I grow rosemary as a potherb and bring it indoors in the fall. All my other culinary herbs are grown as annuals. Basil is my favorite: I grow five or six varieties for drying, for fragrance and for making pestos. I also grow some herbs for dyeing.

Varieties:

Tomatoes	Northern Cascade
Cucumbers	Northern Pickling
Broccoli	Pak Man
Snap Pea	Sugar Daddy

(and Park's Fragrant Giant nasturtium for planting all around flowers.

Seed is ordered from Nichols, Stokes and Richters; Park is for flowers.

TROY: Cecil and Ruth Rogge

The Rogge family has a house on one side of the Kootenai River, but they are living on the other — caretaking a large spread for an absentee owner. Both places have gardens — the one on the town side of the river is mostly raspberries right now. The garden that is the subject of this investigation is a part of a great flat deposit of fine alluvial soil, the kind any gardener would be glad to have. It was pastureland until Cecil put a plow to it.

Cecil Rogge's competition squash weighed 72 pounds! He and Ruth have his-and-hers gardens, and together grow enough produce to last them the year around.

Ruth plants marigolds to lure insects from her food crops. She plants by the phases of the moon. "It does make a difference," she says, and "You have to pay attention to your plants." She does, two back-bending hours a day.

Site and Soil Conditioning

Cecil: I estimate that we have a good four feet of sandy-silty soil here, with a streak of rocks through it that is easily avoided. We have about a third of an acre in garden. Ruth has hers and I have mine, and they are pretty far apart. I won't let her in mine and she won't let me in hers, but we cooperate in putting vegetables on the table.

I figure the soil is a little acid — it generally is around here. Once in awhile I put some lime on to sweeten it. I also put sawdust on when I can get it — anything but cedar chips, which are toxic — compost after it is well plowed up in the spring, chicken manure with straw from the chicken house. Then we use a commercial 5-10-5 fertilizer to round it all off.

Climate in this country changes from one mile to the next. Libby, eighteen miles east of here on the river, is definitely colder than we are. I worked there in the mill for awhile once and would sometimes be surprised to come home to temperatures as much as twenty degrees warmer. The extension agent in Libby says that Troy's growing season is a month longer than Libby's. But we have our weather difficulties. We even have microclimates right here on the property. Once we had a frost strip right down the middle of the garden — with no frost on either side of it. If we suspect a late frost is on the way we will go out and put boxes over the tomatoes and peppers, and plastic over the boxes if it looks particularly bad.

Planting

I don't plan my garden, I just go out and put it in. I know that some things don't grow very well with others. If I plant beans with tomatoes I won't get many beans. Mostly we both use the row method, but I plant corn, onions and potatoes in hills.

Ruth: I follow the Farmer's Almanac, try to plant by the phases of the moon. I really think there is a difference. If I don't follow it, the plants don't grow so fast. I don't even transplant until I've looked at the almanac.

Another important thing: people ask me how to get a garden that looks like ours, and my answer is: "Two hours a day." That is really the answer. You can't expect to have a good-looking and productive garden without a little back-bending, no matter what anyone says. And simply paying attention to the plants is important. They need tender, loving care. The more time you spend in your garden, the better your vegetables will grow. Not just because they love your company, but because you will understand what they need better and notice what makes them happiest.

Cecil: I built a greenhouse right onto the big garage and workshop here. I have a large wood stove right near the wall of the greenhouse, and I plan to put in a pipe and blower to bring some of the heat into the greenhouse so we can use it longer in spring and fall. I have double-glazed the roof and walls of the greenhouse, which is good insulation.

I have a lot of tools I like. One is the small rototiller with the outside blades off for cultivating during the growing season. I have three of the do-it-yourself push-plows with different kinds of attachments — one is a regular plow, one is a blade, and one is slanted so it pushes the soil up to the side as you go along.

Climate Modification

We start as much as we can in the greenhouse — cabbage, cauliflower, broccoli, tomatoes, peppers of various kinds (pimiento, jalapeno and green bell), even corn, zucchini, pumpkins and squash. We plant a lot of marigolds for bug protection, too, and put them in right along with the vegetables. We study the catalogs and like to try the very earliest varieties. We have bought a lot of seed from Gurney's in the past, but now we order a lot from Jung's.

Cecil doesn't plan his garden, he just goes out and plants. But things that don't grow well together, he doesn't plant together. Beans, for one, wouldn't do so well near tomatoes.

We can start at least as early as March to plant greenhouse flats. Outside, we can start the first of May to plant onions, cabbage, broccoli, carrot, beet and spinach seed.

Ruth: I figure we had over four hundred plants in the greenhouse this year, some of them repotted because they were getting too big for their original pots. We give them Miracle-Gro liquid fertilizer while they are inside, to keep them growing at top rate. We had far too many, of course, and sold a lot of the extras to people around here. One man came over from Kalispell to get some of our tomatoes. We like the variety Cold Set. It does well in this country.

We can pick from the garden until mid-October. Then we bring in the last of the squash, dig the potatoes, rutabagas, beets and carrots, and shut it down for the winter.

Cecil: I like to leave some of the potatoes in the ground. They usually do better in the spring garden than the new seed potatoes I put in, and I can get an earlier picking from the older ones.

We also like to grow some things in containers along the driveway and walkway to the house. We have peppers, tomatoes, melons and even peas on trellises in pots. We use Miracle-Gro in the suggested dilution, and water them thoroughly a couple of times a week with that.

Pests and Problems

Cecil: Our worst problems are the cabbage moth, black leaf hoppers (flea beetles) and grasshoppers. If we can, we use tobacco juice, cayenne pepper or black pepper to discourage them. Sometimes we use malathion if things get bad, but we don't really like to use it. We also have deer that wander into the garden when they feel like it, even though we have a couple of dogs that ought to be able to keep them out.

Recommendations

Corn:	Sugar and Cream, and Golden Bantam: We plant the seed thick, then thin out by snipping off the tops of the ones we don't want.
Tomatoes:	Cold Set, Early Girl: I carry a pair of scissors around and snip off all the nonflowering branches so the plant doesn't waste time and energy growing those. I plant the new starts with the stem laid out almost horizontally and a cushion of soil up at the top next to the leaves to keep them from breaking off.
Potatoes:	Red Norland — I never cut and dry out the new seed potatoes in spring — it seems to me a waste of moisture when we need all we can get. I've raised these in beds with very old, well-rotted manure (never new manure) and had potato vines up to my shirt pockets.
Beans:	Royal Purple Pod pole beans, and regular bush and wax beans.
Cucumbers:	Any pickling type; Ruth does a lot of canning and pickling.
Rhubarb:	I take the chicken-house scrapings and put them right around the rhubarb — not quite

touching the stems — 3-4" thick.

Carrots:	Danvers Half-long
Onions:	Walla Walla Sweet in sets
Cabbage:	Early Jersey Wakefield
Cauliflower:	The self-blanching type
Peppers:	Jalapeno, pimiento, green bell
Mangels:	They are a whole lot better as greens than beet tops. I always put in two or three rows. In the winter I store the roots in straw and give them to the chickens a little at a time for extra feed.
Sunflowers:	I have grown them a couple of feet across, so heavy the heads had to be held up with pitchforks. They take a lot of water during a summer, though. I reseed them by throwing out a whole head into the garden in the fall. When I plow it spreads the seed around — I take up the best new seedlings sometime in spring and put them where I want and get rid of the rest.
Squash:	One time a buddy of mine challenged me to a squash-growing contest, which I won, and here's how: I made a sugar-water solution for the plant and fed it drip method through a hypodermic needle in the main stalk about 3 or 4 inches above the squash. It was 72 pounds.
Marigold:	Cracker Jack

Ruth: We raise enough to have our vegetables year around. I can and freeze. Usually I can the first of a crop, then freeze what comes later. I even can potatoes. And we store such things as cabbage and onions. I just put thirty bags of cauliflower into the freezer.

LIBBY: Lila Campbell

The Campbells live outside the town of Libby on land that was essentially pine and fir forest before they built seventeen years ago. It still is forest around the edges of their land. Lila claims that the conditions are totally different from anything she has experienced in her gardening years in Nebraska, California, Oregon and Montana. But she has been gardening since she was six, and difficult conditions are certainly not going to make her give up now.

Site and Soil

Lila: The soil is a silty clay that doesn't drain well. But it is full of forest duff and organic matter. There are occurrences of moss and fungi that tell me it is quite sour or acid. The first year we grew exceptional rhubarb. Period. I have had to lime it, but I don't do it every year. I could use another one hundred pounds of lime on there right now, I believe.

We started out small — about twenty by twenty feet, but the

"People who come here to garden shouldn't," says Lila Campbell, who nonetheless does it successfully on a quarter acre of their forest-fringed land. Deer are a bigger problem to her than the short growing season. The structure in the trees beyond the garden is the children's playhouse.

years have passed and the garden has grown to a quarter acre. I sell a lot of produce at the local Farmer's Market and supply family and friends.

Conditioning

For organic matter, I get a load of cow or horse manure at least once a year, keep it in a pile for use where I want it — in my compost, for instance. I also use it to make manure tea to water with.

It depends on what kind of year it is how soon we can rototill. It has been workable as early as March and as late as May. We start out with a newly plowed field, with all last year's mulch and manure turned in, tilled three times — the last time very shallowly to avoid bringing up any more weed seed. I recommend leaving a rough texture on the garden in the fall by digging it up once and leaving it in lumps. It seems to encourage faster snow melt.

I make pigwire bins, three of them, for my compost by taking circles of the wire and fastening it together. In the first one goes all the vegetable matter. I turn it every three days. In the second one goes the part-rotted stuff, with a layer of green material for nitrogen. Again, turn every three days. When it is about finished, it goes in the third bin, where I can dig it out for use. I make sure there are green materials in it and kitchen scraps, but never anything greasy. Some manure goes in too. If it is turned regularly, it should be ready for use in a month. I use it for potting house plants and for filling holes in the garden when I take something out.

For fertilizing, I fill a 50-gallon drum of water half-full of the fresh manure and add water to the top. It sits outside in the sun and warms up and composts a little. When I need to water, especially new seedlings, I do it by hand from this drum. As it is used up, I add more water. After about six weeks of use, I dump the manure out onto the compost and start over. It gives the fast-growing new plants a wonderful start, and the activity does me good too. After all, the garden is *my* therapy as much as it is the plants'.

Besides my manure-tea barrel, I have 150 feet of black pipe laid out around the garden for warming the irrigation water — which comes from our well — before I use it on the plants. I never do any overhead watering, all of it is by hand.

I don't use black plastic for mulch — it is expensive. Nor do I use hay — it usually has a lot of seeds in it. Instead, I use torn-up cardboard boxes laid flat on the ground. I don't use mulch early in spring — I wait until the soil is warm. The cardboard material keeps the moisture in and the weeds down, and in the fall I can have it dug right in with the compost and manure to add organic matter.

Planting

I write out my plan on gridded paper each year, and make sure that my potatoes, in particular, are rotated to a different spot over a three-year period. I like to try new varieties and will buy as many as five kinds of carrots, then pick the three I like the best for the following year, adding two new varieties from new catalogs. My style of gardening might be called raised wide-row. For small seed, like lettuce and carrots, I fill a spice shaker and shake it evenly over the wide row.

I have no particular system for companion planting, but I do it just the same. I like to put dill in with the tomatoes — the dill seems to draw away the bugs. I learn from experience rather than taking someone else's word. I ask questions if I need to know; if I don't need to know, no one can tell me anything. I have learned that beets and broccoli don't mix well. I have also found out that deer don't like marigolds — and that if I plant a wide row of them, the deer won't cross into the garden at that point. For that purpose, I save a gallon or more of seed from my non-hybrid marigolds and sow it very thickly every year. If I have other spots where I need marigolds, there's always more than enough to transplant.

I start all the seed right in the garden; I don't use a greenhouse or any other device. Since we plant only a few of the smallest

"Gardening should be fun," says Lila, who's been doing it since she was six, "and for sharing. What's the point of growing a five-pound cabbage for two people?"

cherry-type tomatoes, I buy what we need. When I want to move some of the seedlings from one place in the garden to another, I use one or two vitamin B-12 capsules — the kind you can get from the drugstore — in a gallon of water as a transplanting solution. Incidentally, while I'm there I may stock up on Geritol tablets for my house plants.

My favorite tools are my hands. There are no such things as green thumbs, only dirty fingernails — and callouses. Well, actually I do use a hoe or a shovel sometimes — but I don't have any hand tools.

Climate Modification

We get adequate rain here, but not during the growing season. Sometimes there will be too much rain early and that can cause as much damage as frost can, in heavy soils like mine. The difficulty is to get the soil to warm up. But at least I have no trouble with wind. In Nebraska I used to think that tomato plants just naturally grew a shingle on one side for wind protection.

People use different strategies for soil warming. Using rocks and spray-painting them a dark color is one. Or dark-colored shale can be spread as a mulch to help warm the soil. The difficulty is in getting it up again. One device that is not recommended is the old-tire planter. We who live right at the edge of the forest have far too many deer mice to willingly provide them with more places to hide, and an old tire is a perfect place for a deer mouse.

We don't use any season-extending strategies. We simply wait until the weather is "right," and put the seed in the ground. Of course, I am very careful about what I order for seed — I want only the fastest-growing, earliest-maturing varieties. That is why I am always looking for new ones to try.

It seems to me that seed left in the ground over the winter sometimes does better and grows faster than seed put in from packages in the spring. I sometimes plant pea seed in the fall.

It comes up as a super-early crop in spring. Lettuce which seeds itself in fall will be very hardy and early, and volunteer tomatoes have a tremendous start over others.

We have our troubles with early and late frosts, as everyone does. If snow should happen to come before a heavy freeze, it insulates the ground and you may be able to keep a lot of root crops right in the ground. In the spring it is often helpful to keep the sun off plants after a surprise frost, until they have had a chance to get dried off. It is surprising how many young seedlings you can save that way. I have all these trees around me, so I don't get the first rays of sun anyway. You could probably cover plants for the same effect.

Pests and Problems

For us, the worst problem we have is deer. They will eat anything, even the carrots and beets left in the ground and heavily mulched. I've looked out and seen them feeding on beets — red juice dripping out of their mouths as though they were bleeding to death. But no, they were just feeding off my garden and having a great time. It is difficult to see what kind of roses I have sometimes — they eat them off so fast. I used to have an Afghan hound that kept them away, but somebody shot it. Where there are deer there are a lot of people who have few principles about what they shoot.

People who come here to garden shouldn't.

But if you have to garden, then the best thing is to look over the neighbor's fence and see what is doing well there. If you don't have any neighbors with gardens, you may have to reshape your plans. Actually, such a short season makes gardening fun. It never has time to get to be a chore.

Other problems are the usual soil insects, the root maggots. Slug eggs seem to winter over so we will always have some small ones in the garden. I combat them by letting the soil between the rows get as dry as possible and by spreading sand, which they don't like crawling on.

The only insecticide I use is Sevin. Sevin, I am told, is safe enough that birds can eat the bugs that eat the Sevin. I use it when there are so many holes in my cabbage leaves I have to do something about the cabbage moth.

Recommendations

I think gardening should be fun. When my children were little we used to think up unusual things to do, like growing pumpkins in small boxes so, as they developed, they spread out over the top like mushrooms and had square bottoms to sit on. Sometimes we tied flannel rags around a long squash so it grew in lumps. We tried cross-pollination of different squashes to see what we'd get. Once we got one that was green on one end and yellow on the other!

Gardening is a good way to get acquainted in your neighborhood. Like walking babies and dogs. One time when we were living in California, I took my English bulldog for a walk down the alley to look at the gardens of the neighborhood. By the time I had gone one block I had three new rose bushes. In Tacoma, I gave a gardening class for young mothers. It was the first time

I found I had something to teach that others didn't know.

The garden is a lesson in resurrection every spring. Every year we can start all over, correct the mistakes we made the year before.

A garden is for sharing, too. What point is there in growing a five-pound cabbage for only two people? I enjoy working at the Farmer's Market because I get to know many young people — and if I can help them with their gardens, I am glad to do it.

Varieties

I order all my seed from Burpee or Stokes, and buy the two or three tomato plants I grow each year.

Beans	Bush beans — I don't grow pole beans, and I pre-sprout my seed for the bush beans, to make sure they will grow after I plant them.
Beets	Formanova — don't seem to get pithy rings in them.
Broccoli	Any large-headed variety
Carrot	Orange Sherbet
Cabbage	Earliana — a three-lb. cabbage in July. Sometimes a cold July rain will split the cabbages, but if you stagger plantings — or transplant some of your starts to slow them down, you can beat the problem.
Cauliflower	Snow Crown
Corn	Polar Vee, Early Gold and Silver
Cucumber	Victory or Straight 8; and Patio Pick or Double Yield for pickling
Eggplant	The nights are too cold for this plant.
Kale	A good plant here because bugs don't touch it.
Lettuce	Great Lakes or Buttercrunch
Muskmelon	Much too difficult, don't recommend.
Onion	Any seed for green onion, sets for Walla Walla Sweets.
Parsnips	Hollow Crown best — they grow well in deep soil. Don't dig until after a frost or two.
Peas	Sugar Snap. Lincoln is long and straight and has lots of peas, lasts well into July, disease tolerant.
Pepper	California Wonder and some hot peppers.
Pumpkin	The earliest is too slow for this country.
Radish	Easter Egg mix, very successful and can be planted early enough to beat root maggot.
Spinach	Bloomstanding, and for later — New Zealand which can be clipped back for another crop.
Swiss Chard	Another good green, like kale.
Squash	Scallopini, Crookneck, Early Golden Summer, Patty Pan, and Vegetable Spaghetti Golden Nugget winter. My neighbors can grow the big ones like Hubbards, Hungarians, and the like, because they have a south-sloping bank in full sun — but I don't try.
Tomatoes	A neighbor can grow these easily by starting them in her greenhouse. Though I don't grow them now, I like Ultra Girl VFN, Sub Arctic Maxi,

	Cold Set, Campbell 1327 VF, San Marzano and Nova paste types.
Zucchini	Black Jack

MISSOULA: Bill Ballard, with Lee

Rattlesnake Canyon runs north from Missoula, leading up toward the hills out of town. Homes with acreage attached have been built out this way, and the Ballards' is one of them. It isn't a new place — they have been there twenty-eight years. When they first moved here, pasture surrounded them and they had to have fences to keep the cows out. As the area has developed, the pasturing of cattle has become a thing of the past. Fences have been removed, and white-tailed deer are thriving instead. Recently the Ballards added another lot and now care for about three acres of very slightly sloping land at the bottom of a steep ridge covered with ponderosa pine, aspen and a few cottonwoods.

Site and Soil

Bill: We have about four thousand square feet here and there, between the perennial beds, the fruit trees, the ornamentals and all the rest of it. Although our soil is shallow and rocky, we do have a deeper strip of fine soil at the back where part of our garden is now. I think it eroded from the slopes above, a little bit at a time. The portion in front, devoted to the principal vegetable garden, formerly served as the winter feeding ground of the cattle, resulting in dark, fertile soil. Even with rocks, it provides us with a rich, loamy garden bed.

Conditioning

We dug most of the beds by hand to start with. When we bought the newest addition, however, we had it disked. We have hauled

Ballard's tomatoes, started inside, grow unpruned, on stakes, in a polyethelene hut, which extends the season three weeks. Rocks in the foreground are part of the tons hauled off his three acres of one-time cow pasture.

Outside planting starts April 15, or a good deal later if the weather isn't cooperative, and the growing season ends before time to get back to the classroom.

My favorite tools include a Cape Cod weeder, a trowel that is rounded on the end, and a "tobacco" hoe, or one that is sharp on three edges.

Planting

I like to get the garden organized before I plant. A friend and I have similar tastes in gardening so we order our seed together. We get together when the seed catalogs arrive and decide what we want to try of the new varieties and the old standbys. We also compare our notes from the last year, to see what did well and what didn't turn out the way we'd hoped.

I have found that different seedsmen have different ideas of what is early. The same variety will differ in the time indicated for maturing according to the company it comes from. There is nothing like trying out for yourself the many varieties offered.

We start tomato, pepper and eggplant seed inside during the spring break at the University of Montana, where I teach math. That is usually sometime late in March. We start the seeds in potting soil in the basement, using a soil-heating cable and grow lights. Before we set them out, we harden off the seedlings on the front porch. About the tenth of April we start the cole crops, and then the cucumbers and squash about the first of May. Outside planting starts no earlier than the fifteenth of April and a good deal later if the weather is not cooperative.

By the first of September the season is over for us. We can expect a frost any time after that — even though we will still have our underground crops such as parsnips and carrots. Winter squashes will survive those first frosts, too, though the vines die. Once in awhile we are lucky and don't get an early frost, but we can't plan on it.

Climate Modification

People who live up on the hillside have a little longer growing season than we do, and so do the people right in town. But those

tons of rock out of it, and I believe the rocks grow, because there seems to be just as many as ever.

Of course we have our compost pile. We haul in manure from a nearby feedlot, a pickup load at a time. It does have a wealth of seeds in it. We learn to identify new weeds that way — it broadens our education. We add the manure to the compost along with a lot of other things — shredded corn cobs, all the healthy garden refuse, and a 16-20-0 commercial fertilizer. We aren't terribly organized about our compost, but keep several piles going at one time, retiring one and starting another one somewhere else.

We plant most vegetables in double rows, with about three feet between them. In the corn, cabbage and squash patches we use plastic mulch to keep down the weeds and warm up the soil. In other areas we use newspaper, grass clippings or pine needles — which we have an abundance of — for mulch. I think the pine needles add a bit of acidity to the soil, which we need — especially in the strawberry and blueberry beds.

At the end of the season we take up the plastic and the rocks that hold it down, clear out the stalks and old plants as we get around to it, and just leave the garden until the following spring. Then I borrow a tiller and get everything — old mulches, especially — worked into the soil very well and cultivate thoroughly for the next planting. We don't grow anything over the winter. It has happened that spinach seed has remained in the ground and sprouted the next spring, but that was totally unplanned.

All our watering is done from overhead sprinklers. We pump water for irrigation from a ditch which diverts water from Rattlesnake Creek about a mile up the valley. In the dry part of the summer, we keep sprinklers going all the daylight hours. Any one part of the yard or garden is watered every four to seven days. There are no restrictions on the use of this irrigation water, except that we and the neighbors have to look after the diversion line, and tear out beaver dams from time to time.

Ballard keeps notes, re-orders things that did well, and tries out new varieties in the seed catalogues. Lacy Lady, a leafless (almost) pea, doesn't need support if it's planted in double rows.

who live up the canyon from us have an even shorter season than ours. A lot depends on where your garden is, what the cold air drainage patterns are, which way your garden slopes and so on. The point is to know what your own immediate areas will do.

We grow our tomatoes on stakes, but unpruned, in a tomato house. The house is a Quonset-shaped frame covered with polyethylene sheeting. Our main crop grows there all summer, and the tomatoes do very well. Occasionally a big wind whips the plastic around a little, but it is replaceable. The house keeps the plants warmer at night, and we're convinced that most years it extends our growing season by three weeks.

We put our peppers and eggplant in a box planter framed with conduit pipe. We will put 6-mil plastic over this framework at the first hint of a cold night, to keep them alive and growing as long as possible.

With the steep slope right at the back of the property, we have an ideal situation for a root cellar. I have dug into the hillside there and constructed a storage room with outer and inner doors for insulation. We can keep a lot of our root crops, carrots and potatoes in particular, and other long-lasting foods there safely through the winter. The temperature stays at just about 41 degrees F. all winter.

Pests and Problems

We use rotenone or diazinon on the small pests here, if necessary. It isn't so easy to know what to do with the big four-footed kind. Deer are probably the worst problem. Potatoes, parsnips, carrots, spinach, kohlrabi, cauliflower and cabbage all must be planted within a high deer fence.

Recommendations

Tomatoes	Sweet 100, New Yorker, Early Girl, Park's Extra Early (superb), Burpee's Longkeeper. We have stored the Longkeepers into February and though they are yellow outside and pink inside rather than red, they have a flavor far superior to that of store tomatoes. We take unblemished green tomatoes at the end of the season, wash them with a chlorine solution, and lay them out on a piece of corrugated plastic so we can see any that begin to rot. The very green ones we pack in boxes and put them out as they begin to show a little yellow. We can have homegrown tomatoes at Thanksgiving this way.
Summer squash	Crookneck, Zucchini, Sunburst, Patty Pan, which we like to grow for its shape.
Winter squash	Sweetmeat, Buttercup
Cucumbers	Burpless, Market More, Sweet Slicer, Straight 8, but no pickling types.
Eggplant	Dusky is an early good one. The neighbor up the hill grows Japanese eggplant but we've had no luck with it. A new one from Harris, Little Fingers, may do well here.
Pepper	Ace green bell, Cubanelle, Gypsy — a sweet

	yellow, Burpee's Fordhook, Stokes' Early Hybrid.
Potatoes	Red Norland and Russet — which we grow for the new potatoes especially.
Beans	Blue Lake pole
Greens	Tyfon is a good mustard green, does not go to seed, and is mild tasting. Corn salad and amaranth have not done well for us.
Spinach	Melody, Bloomsdale Longstanding and Missouri spinach, which has big leaves, seeds itself, and is a lot like lamb's quarters. We have seedlings from friends and don't know what the general availability of this plant is.
Cantaloupe	Hopeless for us — even with black plastic.
Radishes	Champion — grow some for the pods; they are very good in salads.
Lettuce	Assorted leaf lettuce — Bibb, Cos, Great Lakes
Corn	Sugar and Gold, from Farmer's Seed; Sun Glow is excellent. Get different varieties for staggered maturing times. Also like Seneca Horizon from Stokes, and Park's Butterfruit or Stokes' Northern Supersweet for the ultra-sweet kind. We like a lot of corn — give much of it away.
Pea	Maestro from Burpee is a good dwarf with long pods; Alderman is a good big one, but somewhat susceptible to mildew; Lacy Lady is one of the "leafless" types, self-supporting if grown in double row; Laxton Progress is good, and so is Lincoln for a late pea.
Sugar Snap Pea	Sugar Ann, Sugar Daddy
Snow Pea	Blizzard is prolific and early.
Cabbage	Stonehead, Copenhagen Market
Broccoli	Premium Crop and Green Comet are good oldies and Bonanza and Green Goliath are newer ones with very large heads. Watch early heat on these — it is easy to lose them. Our neighbor thinks such plants as broccoli and cauliflower need a lot of fertilizer at the start to get a lot of leafy growth, thus being able to manufacture energy for the production of large heads.
Seed sources	Stokes, Burpee, Harris, Farmer's, Vermont Bean Seed, and Johnny's.

MISSOULA: Barbara Hauf

The Haufs moved recently from Boise to Missoula, but to look at the garden you'd think they had brought it full-blown along with the dining room table and the living room sofa. There is nothing new or tentative in the size or looks of the huge garden that takes up more than a fourth of their one-and-a-quarter acres.

In this section of Missoula there are many gardens and some very sizable truck gardens as well. The soil is good, valley-bottom

We keep a compost pile going all the time and put our grass clippings, pine needles, coffee grounds and kitchen vegetable waste in it. When decayed, the pine needles and coffee grounds should acidify the soil just a bit, which is helpful for us. In one spot we seem to have a streak of very alkaline soil, so we have been using iron sulfate on it to raise the pH.

We are just learning our way around this garden now. We will try out various ideas as we go. This year we are planting in rows, and Jake tills with a twenty-four-inch blade to cultivate. Later he takes off the outer tines when the plants start growing together and filling in the rows.

Planting

I practiced intensive gardening in Boise before I knew what it was. Among other things, I had melons trained up a fence and squash growing right in the corn rows. Here we haven't felt the need to do that, since there is room for everything and then some.

We have kept our written plan for this garden and will evaluate it at the end of the year to see what we did right or wrong, what we will repeat, what we won't, and how we will rotate the types of vegetables next year. It is useful to have a plan to know what seeds you want to order the next year. I don't trust to memory — it's too likely to trick me.

Having so much space, we like to plant rows of flowers in between the vegetables. I put marigolds in amongst the vegetables too, with the idea that they may keep out some pests. I get them started there, then when I want a bunch for out in the front or for a planter, I dig them out and put them where I want them. The ones I leave in the rows give a decorative effect to the vegetables.

Climate Modification

We find that along with soil differences between Boise and Missoula there are very definite temperature differences.

I would say that the days are about the same, but the nights

In Missoula, Barbara has space for everything and for her everything expands to fill the space. She likes the decorative effect of flowers among the food plants.

Sweet potatoes, bought at the store and sprouted under the wood stove, looked pretty in the Haufs' garden, but they got a better food yield from yams.

alluvial loam. The Haufs chose well when they selected their home in this part of town, for the success of their future gardens there.

Barbara: We haven't been here long, but I've learned a lot working with the Master Gardeners here in Missoula. I tend the office once a week during the summer and hear a lot of questions from local gardeners, so I've had to brush up on local conditions.

Site and Soil Conditioning

The soils right around the river are reported to be more alkaline, while the soils in the higher areas around the fringes of Missoula are on the acid side. In the alluvial soils there are deposits of rock in some places, clay in others, so gardeners take their chances.

The way we make a new bed is to first kill the quack grass with Roundup, then add rotted horse manure — lots of it — before tilling. In a year this is ready to use.

136

are much cooler here. The cool nights have a tendency to slow down the growth of plants. Boise's growing season is a bit longer, probably a result of several factors, cooler nights here being one of them.

We have been surprised a couple of times by mighty gusts of wind out of a clear blue sky. They did a lot of damage — snapping bean plants off right at their bases. If this turns out to be a common occurrence here we will do something permanent about it, like building a wind screen. A row of bushes or trees will help break its force.

I tried rutabagas, radishes, lettuce and beets as a late planting of vegetables for the fall, or at least until October. I planted them about the third week of July. Radishes did fine; we had a couple of pickings of lettuce; the beets and rutabagas, with a few exceptions, were very small. Also the deer ate off the tops and pulled them out.

Jake dug a root cellar in the woodshed and it seems to keep a temperature of from 38-42 degrees F. That will be perfect if we can keep it at that.

Onions and potatoes go as well together in the Haufs' garden as they do in the cooking pot. Jake dug a root cellar in the woodshed for storage of root crops.

Pests and Problems

We like to be as organic as possible, but we have been known to use diazinon and malathion on occasion — when we see that we are about to lose something to the bugs and the situation seems pretty desperate. If I can, I will use wood ashes to discourage root maggots, and it is somewhat successful if the infestation isn't too severe.

Out at the far end of the garden, by the irrigation stream at the back of the property, where we aren't so likely to be, the deer come wandering in to see what's for lunch. Our solution to this is a small, inexpensive, battery-operated radio playing rock music. Not loudly, but enough to annoy the deer. It seems that they definitely are not rock fans. Of course we couldn't do this if we had very near neighbors, but where it is, it doesn't bother anyone but the deer.

Variety recommendations:

Cabbage	Early Flat Dutch — huge, solid heads
Tomatoes	Heinz Italian-type, Sweet 100, Heartland and Better Bush — the latter two started from seed in March, planted in flats then transplanted to Styrofoam cups in late April; went out the third week in May; beautiful bushes and lots of tomatoes.
Spinach	New Zealand. Will try another variety instead of mustard greens next year.
Cauliflower	Snowking; we want to try a late variety for a fall crop next year and will choose a self-blanching type — it's tough getting the curds covered up when the leaves aren't large enough.
Onions	Multipliers and Walla Walla Sweet; late reds and yellows — we and our relatives use *lots* of onions!
Potatoes	Washington White, N.D. red, Red Pontiac. Would you believe some of them were four-pounders, and many were not much less? We harvested about 1,200 pounds. Again, we had plenty to give away and plenty to keep.
Sweet potatoes (and yams)	We got some at the store, put them in some soil in a box and kept them under the wood stove inside to keep them warm, covering them at night with newspapers. Once we got some sprouts on them, we planted the sprouts out in May. The plants were very pretty. The yams grew large, but the sweet potatoes turned out rather small. We will concentrate on yams next year.
Peas	Sugar Bon snowpeas — these need a fence to climb on but are dwarf, compact and easily trained. They are very early. The same variety in a bush type is good, and productive. They are mildew resistant. Peas are another vegetable that can be planted in late summer for a fall crop to extend the stir-fry season.
Lettuce	Romaine, Black-seeded Simpson, Redleaf (planted in July)
Asparagus	Mary Washington — both plants and seed.
Beets	Detroit Dark Red — what the deer didn't get were delicious.
Beans	Kentucky Wonder pole and bush; Blue Lake bush.
Cucumber	Park's Burpless bush — excellent fruit on a small plant.
Broccoli	Early Emerald — I was still cutting the small, lateral heads in November. Relatives and friends received some of the bounty.

137

SELECTED WEATHER INFORMATION FOR NORTHWEST CITIES

WEATHER DATA
AVERAGE PERCENTAGE POSSIBLE SUN

Area	Yrs. of record	Year Average (%)	December (%)	July (%)
Boise	37	67	40	88
Missoula	35	54	29	79
Portland	30	49	21	69
Seattle	31	45	21	63
Spokane	31	57	21	80
Walla Walla	62	59	19	85

HIGHEST/LOWEST RECORD TEMPERATURES
(degrees Fahrenheit)

Area	Yrs. of record	High (summer)	Low (winter)
Boise	40	111	−23
Burns	29	103	−26
Eugene	37	106	−12
Lewiston	33	115	−22
Medford	50	115	−6
Missoula	115	115	−22
Portland	39	107	−3
Seattle	46	100	10
Sea-Tac Airport	35	99	0
Spokane	32	108	−25
Walla Walla	65	113	−16
Yakima	33	110	−25

NORMAL DAILY MEAN HIGH/LOW TEMPERATURES, WINTER/SUMMER
30-year record — Degrees Fahrenheit

Area	Yr. Average	Low Jan.	High July/Aug.
Boise	59.90	29.00	74.50
Burns	46.00	25.20	68.40
Eugene	52.60	39.40	66.90
Lewiston	51.70	31.20	73.40
Medford	53.00	36.60	71.70
Missoula	43.70	20.80	65.00
Pendleton	52.40	32.00	73.50
Portland	52.60	38.10	67.10
Salem	52.30	38.80	66.60
Seattle	52.50	39.70	65.70
Sea-Tac Airport	51.10	38.20	64.50
Spokane	47.30	25.40	69.70
Walla Walla	54.10	33.40	75.60
Yakima	49.80	27.50	70.70

MEAN NO. DAYS FREEZING OR BELOW

Area	Yrs. record	No. Days	from (date)	to (date)
Boise	40	124	Oct. 5	May 2
Burns	29	187	Sept. 4	May 2
Eugene	37	55	Oct. 2	Apr. 3
Lewiston	33	94	Oct. 3	Apr. 4
Medford	18	91	Oct. 5	May 1
Missoula	19	187	Sept. 4	May 2
Portland	39	44	Oct. 1	Apr. 1
Salem	17	68	Oct. 1	May 1
Seattle	29	16	Nov. 1	Mar. 1
Sea-Tac Airport	20	31	Nov. 4	Mar. 4
Spokane	20	141	Sept. 1	May 2
Walla Walla	65	64	Oct. 1	Apr. 1
Yakima	33	149	Sept. 1	May 3

(more weather information on page 140)

MEAN NO. DAYS WITH .01 IN. OR MORE OF PRECIPITATION

Area	Yrs. of record	Days Precip.	Dec./Jan.
Boise	40	90	13
Burns	29	90	12
Eugene	37	136	19
Lewiston	33	103	12
Medford	50	100	14
Missoula	35	122	15
Pendleton	44	99	13
Portland	39	153	19
Salem	42	152	20
Seattle	29	158	20
Sea-Tac Airport	35	158	20
Spokane	32	115	16
Walla Walla	65	105	14
Yakima	33	67	10

NORMAL PRECIPITATION, 30 YRS. RECORD, FOR SELECTED CITIES

Area	Yr. Average	Jan.	July
Boise	11.50	1.47	0.15
Burns	11.83	1.76	0.32
Eugene	42.56	7.64	0.26
Lewiston	13.21	1.27	0.53
Medford	20.64	3.69	0.25
Missoula	13.34	1.17	0.92
Pendleton	12.31	1.60	0.26
Portland	37.61	6.04	0.47
Salem	41.08	6.90	0.57
Seattle	35.65	5.35	0.87
Sea-Tac Airport	38.79	5.94	0.71
Spokane	17.42	2.47	0.40
Walla Walla	16.01	2.07	0.33
Yakima	8.00	1.33	0.16

RECOMMENDED VEGETABLE VARIETIES BY REGION

Following is information on the most popular vegetables, including short descriptions, cultural needs, pests and a little about what to do with them (for more, see Chapter V), and recommendations as to varieties and sources of seed. The recommendations are taken from the gardeners interviewed for this book and from other sources, such as state/county extension service lists for local areas. The varietal lists are not necessarily complete, nor are the source lists comprehensive — they are suggestions only. You may find other varieties and other catalogs and seed stores that suit your needs as well as those mentioned here. In some cases you won't find a vegetable listed at all (okra, for example) because it is not recommended by the gardeners featured here; this is not to say you can't grow it — only that it is not a common nor easy vegetable for the Northwest.

Remember that seed companies and agricultural experiment stations bring out new varieties and new versions of old varieties regularly. Take the advice of experienced gardeners: stick with the tried and true varieties for your basic crops, then add a couple of new ones each year. If a new vegetable does exceptionally well, try it another year before making up your mind to replace your old variety with the new one.

Seed company names have been abbreviated as follows:

Abundant Life Seed Foundation	AL
Alberta Nurseries and Seeds, Ltd.	Alb
Burpee, W. Atlee, Co.	Brp
Earl May Seed Co.	EM
Good Seed	Gd
Harris, Joseph, Co.	Har
Island Seed Co., Ltd.	Is
Japonica Seeds, Inc.	Jap
Johnny's Selected Seeds	Jo
Jung, J.W., Seed Co.	Jng
Kitizawa Seed Co.	Kit
Nichols Garden Nursery	Nic
Park Seed Co.	Pk
Sanctuary Seeds	Snc
Stokes Seeds Inc.	Stk
Suttons Seeds Ltd.	Sut
Territorial Seed Co.	Ter
Thompson and Morgan, Inc.	TM
Tillinghast Seed Co.	Til
Twilley Seed Co.	Twl
Vermont Bean Seed Co.	Vt
Vesey's Seeds Ltd.	Ves

ARTICHOKE, Globe
Compositae: *Cynara scolymus*
Description
Perennial (5-6 years), thistlelike, with large cone-shaped heads; native of Mediterranean climate, grows 3-6 feet tall. Unopened flower buds are eaten.
Culture
Likes humidity. Needs starting and growing inside for 2 months, another 100 days outside. Plants started from seed may not all produce. Starts may be purchased at some nurseries, set out after last frost date. Needs full sun; allow 3 feet all around in good, fertile soil. Soil temp. for germination: 70-75°F. Small, lateral buds will develop after main bud is cut. Survives light fall frost. Cut it to ground in fall, mulch. Will survive winter in mild climates (if it doesn't rot). Suckers may be used to propagate. For cold areas, dig up and plant indoors in cool, dampish spot for winter, set out again in spring.
Pests
Very few: aphids on new shoots; slugs.
Other
Good large ornamental; flower heads can be dried.
Recommendations

VARIETY	REGION	SOURCE
Green Globe	I, II	TM, Is, Brp, Sut — for seed; Til for starts.

ARTICHOKE, Jerusalem
Compositae: *Helianthus tuberosus*
Description
Large perennial (to 12 feet) grown for tubers; one of our few native vegetables, used by Indians. Its Italian name, girasole, meaning "turns toward sun," probably is origin of Jerusalem in name. Can be a troublesome weed if not contained.
Cultivation
Usually planted by tubers; these dry out — plant immediately and use after digging. Plant in fall or spring about 4 inches deep, 12-14 inches apart.
Other
Excellent substitute for potatoes for people who need starch-free diet.
Pests
None to speak of.
Recommendations

VARIETY	REGION	SOURCE
Dwarf Sunray	All	TM
Silver Skinned	"	TM
(none given)	"	AL, Nic

ASPARAGUS
Liliaceae: *Asparagus officinalis*
Description
Perennial native of Europe and N. Africa, fernlike foliage; early unopened stalks are cut to eat. Dioecious — the female plants have red berries.
Culture
Plant from seed or 1-2-year-old roots or crowns. Needs permanent well-drained, fertile soil with (ideal) pH 6.6. May be started inside and left in pots the first year. Beds should be treated with well-rotted manure or fertilized with N and P. Plant crowns in trenches 12 inches deep, at least 2 feet apart, with roots well spread. Fill in as plants mature, mulch to keep out weeds. Also can mulch part of a bed in spring to slow down part of the crop, getting a longer season. Beds need frequent deep watering during dry months.
In very cold areas, mulch for winter. Don't pick first two years from seed, (or the first year from transplants). Pick very sparingly the third (second) year, then pick about 6-8 weeks thereafter, cutting just below soil level. Allow very thin ones to grow and "ferns" to develop, cut in fall and add N or manure to bed. In Regions I and II may need protection from winter rain.
Pests
Black and white asparagus beetle and larvae: use rotenone, and keep area clean. Rust: caused by wet conditions, shows up as orangish powder; destroy volunteers, do not water late in day.
Fusarium wilt: plants turn yellowish and wilt; buy resistant or treated plants (Mary Washington), pick off dead ferns.
Recommendations

VARIETY	REGION	SOURCE
Mary Washington	I, II, IV, IX	Brp, Is, Jng, Til, TM
Martha Wash.	IV, IX	
California 500	I, II	
Faribo Hybrid	IX	

BEAN, broad (English, fava, Windsor, horse, etc.)
Leguminosae: *Vicia faba*
Description
The "Jack-in-the-Beanstalk" bean; a Eurasian native, hardier and larger than other beans, pod usually not eaten, but is tender when young. Plants grow upright 4-6 feet. More like pea than bean, light frost doesn't harm young plants but will damage pods. Takes 2-3 months to mature, likes cool, moist temperatures.

Culture

Plant 1 inch deep at 4-6-inch intervals. May need support. Immature beans may be bitter; don't pick until beans inside are slightly visible as bumps on pod. Mature beans can be used dry, cooked fresh, or preserved like peas by freezing or canning. Follow with nitrogen-loving crop for summer. Do not try to grow in hot, dry summers; plant as early as possible in Regions III through IX. In Regions I and II, plant November 1 for late spring harvest; mulch in colder areas. Soil should have well-composted manure; likes slightly alkaline soil.

Pests

Aphids — use an insecticidal soap; or pinch off plant tops as soon as pods have formed (don't bear long anyway). Thompson & Morgan suggests growing summer savory with the beans to keep these pests away. Chocolate spot — on leaves and stems; prevalent in cold, wet weather, or with potash-deficient soil; add potassium.

Recommendations

VARIETY	REGION	SOURCE
(Various choices available)	All	AL, Alb, Brp, Gd, Is, Jo, Nic, Snc, Stk, Sut, Ter, TM, Til

BEAN, Green (snap, string, wax, kidney, Italian, French, etc.)
Leguminosae: *Phaseolus vulgaris*
Description

Includes a group of beans, all of which can be eaten young in the pod, as young shelled fresh beans, or shelled and dried. Available as tall climbers or in bush form.

Culture

Plant in rich soil, without an overabundance of nitrogen (esp. in short-season areas), after ground is warm (above 50°F.), or germinate seeds before planting to insure good crop. Germination poor and blossoms may drop off in temperatures about 90°. A good choice for late plantings after lettuce, radishes, or other early, quick-growing types have been harvested. Plant bush beans 2 inches apart, 1 inch deep, thin to 4 inches apart. Pole beans need fence or poles for support, and can be clustered, with several to a pole. Black plastic may help keep soil warm in cold areas. Mature in about 60 days, pick quite small for tenderest beans. Can also be left to mature, dried and used as shell beans. Horticultural, kidney and navy beans are cultivars meant to be grown to full maturity and dried. Planting both bush and pole types can give a long season for snap beans. Pick the beans regularly to keep them coming. Cutting plants back slightly and giving a boost of manure and cultivation may induce them to produce another crop.

Pests

Anthracnose — dark brown, sunken spots on pods, promoted by damp, humid conditions. Do not water leaves, do not touch plants when they are wet. Mexican bean beetle, looks like ladybug — check it out before you use an insecticide. Deformed or curled pods may be caused by lack of sufficient moisture, or by insect damage at blossoming time.

Aphids — soap and water sprays, rotenone.

Recommendations

VARIETY	REGION	SOURCE
GREEN		
Blue Lake, pole/bush	All	Most seed cos.
Blue Mountain, bush	V, VI, VIII	W.S.U. Ext. (local seed cos.)
Canyon, bush	VII	U.I. Ext.
Contender, bush	IV, IX	Gd, Pk, Snc
Harvester, bush	IX	Is
Kentucky Wonder, pole/bush	All	Most seed cos.
Oregon Giant	I, II	Alb, Is
Provider	IV, IX	Jo, Til, Vt
Rainier	IX	Jo
Romano, Roma (It.), pole/bush	I, II, IX	Most seed cos., TM
Slenderette	VII	Pk, Vt
Tendercrop, bush	II, V, VI, VII, IX	Har, Nic, Pk, Snc, Vt
Tenderpod, bush	V, VI, VII, IX	Brp
Tendergreen imprvd. pole/bush	I, II	AL, Brp, Is, Jng, Sut, Til, TM
Topcrop, bush	V, VI	Alb, Brp, Jng, Pk, Vt
WAX		
Cherokee	IX	Snc
Eastern Butterwax, bush	IX	Jng
Earliwax, bush	I, II, IX	Vt
Golden Butterwax	IX	Terr, Vt
Goldenrod, bush	I, II, IV	
Goldenwax, pole	I, II	Alb, Is, Pk, Snc
Kentucky Wonder wax, pole	IX	Is, Jng
Kinghorn	IX	Sut
Pencil Pod, bush	I, II	Brp, Vt
Puregold, bush	I, II, IX	
DRY, SHELL		
Pinto, Red Kidney, French Flageolet,	All	Most seed cos.
Cranberry, Horticultural, etc.		
PURPLE-PODDED		
Royal Purple Pod,	I, II,	Most seed
Royal Burgundy	V, VI, IX	cos.

BEAN, Lima
Leguminosae, *Phaseolus limensis*
Description

A more difficult-to-grow bean in most Northwest climates, as it needs more heat than most areas have. Not recommended for immediate coastal areas and higher elevations. Name comes from Lima, Peru, where specimens were found in ancient graves. Flattish beans are eaten fresh from pod. Available in pole and bush varieties.

Culture

Choose the earliest variety, possibly germinating inside and setting out after soil warms. Plant two weeks after last spring frost; seeds need warm soil to germinate and take two weeks or more even then, if the soil temp. isn't about 68°F. Do not give extra nitrogen. Pod should be green and succulent when you pick the beans, with swelling showing where beans are growing inside.

Pests

Subject to snap bean pests.

Recommendations

VARIETY	REGION	SOURCE
Burpee's Imprvd. bush	V	Brp, Jng, Stk, Vt
Christmas	V	Nic, Pk, Vt
Fordhook 242	V	Brp, Har, Jo, Jng, Pk
Henderson, baby bush		Alb, Brp, Is, Gd, Pk
King of the Garden		Brp, Jng, Pk

BEAN, Runner, or Scarlet Runner
Leguminosae: *Phaseolus coccineus*
Description

Pole bean grown for clusters of red blossoms and large leaves as well as for its edible pods and beans inside which may be dried or eaten fresh. Takes about 70 days from planting. Flavor is stronger and more distinctive than snap bean. Tall; needs support. Also has a white-flowering cultivar, *P. coccineus albus*.

Culture

Grow as you would a snap bean.

Pests

Subject to pole snap bean pests.

Recommendations

VARIETY	REGION	SOURCE
Best of All		Sut
Butler		Gd, Sut, TM
Enorma		Sut, TM
Prizewinner		Nic

MISCELLANEOUS BEANS

Adzuki, Azuki Bean, *Vigna angularis*
Native of Asia. Erect, twining bushes to 2 or more feet. Very high in protein, good for sprouting. Use fresh bean very young or as dry bean — like lentil. Also used as cover crop or green manure. Likes cool nights, hot days — tender and not suited to cold areas.

VARIETY	REGION	SOURCE
(None given)	I, II, III, VI	Gd, Jo, TM, Vt

Asparagus Bean (cow pea, yard-long bean, etc.), *Vigna unguiculata*
Needs at least 3 full months after last frost date. Pods up to 1.5-2 feet long. Give plenty of fertilizer and water; use supports.

VARIETY	REGION	SOURCE
(None given)	I, II, VI	Kit

Mung Bean (Green or Golden Gram) *Vigna radiata*
Annual growing to 3 feet, but generally grown as a sprouting bean for nutritious seeds. Has clusters of hairy pods turning black as bean matures.

VARIETY	REGION	SOURCE
(None given)	All regions	Brp, Sut

Princess Bean (Goa bean, Winged bean, Asparagus pea, etc.), *Psophocarpus tetragonolobus*
Pods are square, toothed. Whole plant is edible, high in protein. Usually used when mature, but very young are tender enough to eat pod and pea together. Sow before last frost date, as it will do well in cool weather — neither tender nor difficult. Needs a long growing season, however. Fertilize several times during the season.

VARIETY	REGION	SOURCE
(None given)	I, II, III, VI, VII	TM

Soy Bean (Chinese: Mao du), *Glycine max*
Cultivated in East for centuries. Can now be raised in colder climates because there are varieties that mature faster. Plants grow to about 14 inches. Sow in garden 2 weeks after last frost date (the seeds germinate best at 86°) or start inside. Do not tend when wet. Harvest at about 70-120 days; can be used fresh by picking just as they begin to change from green to yellow, boiling, then cooling and squeezing out the beans; or dry them on the plants or in the oven and store. Has highest protein content of any vegetable. Can be grown as cover, green manure or forage crop. Problems include too-cool soil for germination and in some eastern areas, the bean-leaf beetle. Not recommended for Regions I and II.

VARIETY	REGION	SOURCE
(None given)	III, IV, V, VI, VII	Brp, Jap, Jo, Nic, Snc

Tepary Bean, *Phaseolus acutifolius*
This form of *Phaseolus* requires hot temperatures, including warm nights. Not suitable for coastal areas. Vigorous plant with shell-type bean. Letting them dry out after flowers bloom is recommended by Good Seed, to encourage pods to dry.

VARIETY	REGION	SOURCE
Blue Speckles	IV, V, VI, VII	Gd
Brown Speckles	V, VI	Gd

BEET (Beetroot, Mangel, Mangel-Worzel, Mangold, Sugar Beet)
Chenopodiaceae, *Beta vulgaris*
Description
Now grown for its purple, white or gold root; but originally grown for its greens. A variation is the sugar beet, and another the mangel, a forage crop, though either can be used as table vegetable if dug early. Good in cool, moist climates. The seed is not a seed but a dried fruit of several seeds. Some varieties for late sowing may be grown most of year in some places.
Culture
Plant in loose soil; it will germinate at 45 degrees, though it is faster in warmer soil. Plant thickly, then thin, using the thinnings whole. Plants need plenty of water, will tolerate light frost; plant a quick maturing, small-rooted variety in very northerly spots, as it may bolt in long-day climates. Keep weeded or mulched. Until the beet root is an inch or two you can use some of the outer leaves for greens. They are high in iron and vitamins. Most roots are best at about 3 inches, but for winter storage, larger ones are better. Cut off tops, dry and put in moist sand or peat in cool place to store. In many areas they can be left in the ground, with mulch to increase protection.
Pests
Whitish rings in the beetroot mean they haven't grown steadily.
Internal browning of the root is caused by soil low in boron (happens in alkaline soil after a long hot period).
Scab is also common in alkaline soils. Use high proportion of organic matter in the soil. Bugs or caterpillars can be taken off by hand.

VARIETY	REGION	SOURCE
Burpee Golden	I, II	Alb, Brp, Jng, Sut, TM
Cylindra	I, II	AL, Brp, Pk, Snc, Ter, Vt
Detroit Dark Red	I, II, V, VI	Most seed cos., Til
Early Wonder	I, II	AL, Brp, Pk, Snc, Pk, Vt
Forono (Formanova, Formona)	I, II, IX	Alb, Is, Jo, Nic, Snc, Stk, Ter
Long Season	I, II	
Mobile	II	Jo
Ruby Queen	I, II	Alb, Is, Jng, Pk, Snc, Ter, Vt
Mangel, or Forage Beet	IX	Nic, Jng

BROCCOLI
Cruciferae, *Brassica oleracea italica*
Description
A cabbage mutant, known in the 12th century. The immature florets are eaten, along with parts of stems and leaves. The word broccoli means tender stalks in Italian. A European strain, broccoli raab or sprouting broccoli, is eaten for its stalks, as it does not have a large central head. Same for Chinese broccoli or kale (guy lon).
Culture
Grow in very fertile soil, giving 18 inches around at least; keep mulched for weeds and moisture. Needs couple of months without hard frosts to mature. Start seeds indoors about 6-7 weeks before last spring frost, though they may be started outside 2 weeks before last frost, or later, well into summer. Young plants are more frost hardy than mature ones. Mature in 60-70 days from transplant or 80-90 days from seed. Sow every 2 inches in rows and thin, using the whole plant that has been thinned. Water with a manure tea or fish fertilizer every 2 weeks. Cut large central head before buds open; same for the smaller lateral heads that develop.
Pests & Problems
Root maggots are the worst problem, and diazinon is usually justified here; spread along the root zone when planting. Reemay or other row cover will keep out the root maggot fly if no openings are left. Collars of tarpaper or cardboard are sometimes recommended but haven't been found to be much consistent help. Sometimes wood ashes on or in the soil discourage maggots. Cabbage moth larvae can be found in the little stems — hiding very cleverly. Hand-pick or use a little rotenone or *Bacillus thuringiensis*.
Like cabbage, may be susceptible to club-root, a fungus disease. Rotate your crops, use resistant cultivars, keep the soil clean of debris, keep a neutral pH. Destroy infected plants.
Small heads — keep young plants growing vigorously to form large, mature plants; choose largest headed cultivars.

VARIETY	REGION	SOURCE
Gem	I, II	Brp
Green Comet	I, II, III, IX	Alb, Pk, TM, Sut, Vt

Variety	Region	Source
Green Duke	I, II, IX	Pk
Green Goliath	I, II, V, VI	Brp, Str
Italian Green Sprouting (or Purple Sprouting)	I, II, VI, VIII, IX	Most seed cos.
Mercedes	II	Sut
Packman	I, IX	Jo, Nic, Stk
Premium Crop	I, IV, V, VI, VII, VIII, IX	Brp, Jo, Nic, Str
Waltham 29	All regions	AL, Ter, Til
Broccoli Raab (Brassica Rapa, or B. campestris)	I, II	Brp, TM

BRUSSELS SPROUTS

Cruciferae: *Brassica oleracea gemmifera*

Description

Brussels sprouts, or spruyten, were grown in Belgium for many years before they got out to France and England in the 18th century. The sprouts are tiny cabbages that grow in leaf axils in place of branches. A late fall crop — the second year produces flowers and seeds. Very hardy; thrives in very fertile soil in moist, cool conditions. There are purple varieties.

Culture

Sprouts take a little longer than broccoli, but are enhanced by the first fall frosts. Give plenty of fertilizer and water. Take off the leaves on lower part of stem as they begin to yellow. To encourage sprout growth, pinch off the growing tip of the plant about 2 weeks before first frost date or when sprouts at bottom are about 1 inch. Pull the plant in the fall and hang upside down to get a few more sprouts.

Pests

Brussels sprouts have less trouble with pests than broccoli because it matures later, after the worst of the pest infestations have got your other cole crops. Early plants may be troubled by the same insects that attack other cabbage family plants: root maggot, cutworm. Since you may leave this in the garden late in the season, it is more likely to be attacked by rots and molds. Keep the garden area clean, pick leaves off the lower stalk, and rotate plants from year to year. In regions I and II, plant in mid-July for a midwinter harvest of sprouts.

VARIETY	REGION	SOURCE
Catskill	VII, IX	AL, Alb, Snc
Green Gem	I, II	
Jade Cross (E or F)	All	Most seed cos.
Long Island Impr. (Catskill)	All	Most seed cos.
Lunet (also Lanet)	II, IV	Ter
Fortress	IV	Ter

CABBAGE

Cruciferae: *Brassica oleracea capitata*

Description

Another cole that thrives in cool, moist places. General categories include savoy (with crinkled leaves), smooth-green, and purple. The greens and purples come in early, midseason and late varieties, the later being the most dense and easiest to store. There are varieties to produce "mini" sizes, or the opposite.

Culture

Should be encouraged with plenty of watering and manure to grow quickly. Cabbage is very frost hardy, once it is hardened off. Earlies mature about 70 days from transplanting, or 10 days longer from seeding. It is possible to delay maturity by transplanting some at an early age, or twisting them somewhat or cutting away some of the roots later. If the main head is removed and leaves left, small heads should develop on the central stem. One way to store is to harvest entire plant with roots and hang upside down in cool place.

Pests & Problems

Splitting of heads usually caused by overwatering or rain.

Root maggot: grow under Reemay; use diazinon in soil when transplanting or along root zone.

Cabbage butterfly (worm): grow under Reemay; use Bt.

Club root: raise pH of soil with lime; only real remedy is to keep *Brassicas* out of the area for 5 or more years.

Aphids: spray with insecticidal soap or rotenone.

Cutworms: use sections of paper cups or other collar-type devices around bases of plants; rotenone, diazinon.

Rots: keep areas clean, pick off old leaves, water root zone only, not leaves.

Slugs: sand, sawdust or ashes on soil; container of sourdough or beer; slug bait.

VARIETY	REGION	SOURCE
April Green	V, VI	Stk
Baby Head	VI	
Charleston Wakefield	V, VI	Vt
Copenhagen Market	V, VI, VII, IX	Alb, Brp, Stk, Til
Danish Ballhead	I, II, V, VI, VII, IX	Most seed cos.
Drumhead Savoy	VII	
Earliana	I, II, III, IX	Alb, Brp
Early Flat Dutch	I	
Early Jersey Wakefield	I, V, VI, IX	Most seed cos.

Variety	Region	Source
Early Marvel	IV	
Early Round Red Dutch	VII, IX	
Early Wonder #1	IV	
Emerald Cross	V, IV, IX	Alb, Brp, Stk
First Early Market	I, II, IV	Ter
Golden Acre	I, II, VII, IX	Most seed cos.
Green Winter (Winter Green)	I, II	Is
Harvest Queen	IX	
Houston Evergreen	IV	
January King	I, II	AL, Nic, Sut, Ter, TM
Little Leaguer	I	
Marion Market	VII	
Market Prize	I, II, V	Har
Market Topper	II, IV	
Market Victor	V, IX	
Penn State Ballhead	IV, IX	Snc, Stk
Red Acre	I, IX	Alb, Brp, Is, Til
Red Head	II	Stk
Resistant Danish	V, VI, IX	Har
Rio Verde	II	
Salarite Savoy	I, II, IV	Stk, Ter
Savoy Ace hybr.	V, VI, IX	Brp, Har, Jng, Pk
Savoy King	V, VI, IX	Brp, Nic, Pk, Stk, Ter, TM
Stonehead	I, II, V	Har, Jng, Nic, Pk, Stk, TM
Spivoy	I, II, IV	TM, Pk
Tastie	II, III	

CARROTS

Umbelliferae: *Daucus carota*

Description

A horticultural version of Queen Anne's lace; originated in the Middle East. A root vegetable with various forms: short, medium ("half-long") and long, with ferny tops.

Culture

All varieties do best in deep, loose soil. For shallow or rocky soil, try raised beds, or use the mini or shorter varieties. Will do best in soil that is about 70°F. Carrot seed may be slow to germinate. One way to mark the planted row is with quick-sprouting radishes, which can be eaten before the carrots are very large. Be sure the soil does not dry out. Thin to at least one inch apart as they grow, using the tiny ones to eat. Keep the shoulder or crown of carrot covered with soil to prevent bitterness. Second-plant mid-July and leave in garden until ready to use in fall and winter. Mulch in colder areas. Or pull and store in moist sand or peat in cool place.

Other

Carrot tops can be used fresh or dry as a potherb.

Pests & Problems

Wireworms, carrot rust fly: can be controlled partially by good crop rotation; also, rotenone, diazinon; use of spun-bonded cover is possible in some areas, but cuts down light.

Hairiness: too much nitrogen, or an uneven weather pattern during their development. Splitting: will occur if heavy rains come when they are maturing.

Forked carrots: the result of heavy soil or stones in the soil.

VARIETY	REGION	SOURCE
A-Plus	I, II	Jng, Pk, Stk
Baby Orange	I	Stk
Caramba	II, III, VI, VII	Ter
Danvers	I, II	AL, Gd
Danvers Half-long	I, II, V, VI, IX	Alb, Brp, Is, Pk, Snc, Stk, Til
Gold Pak (Pac)	IV, V, VI, VII, IX	Alb, Brp, Jng, Snc, Stk, Twl
Imperator (58)	All regions	AL, Brp, Gd, Is, Snc, Stk, Til, Vt
Kinko	I	Jo
Minicor (Amsterdam Minicor)	II, III, VI, VIII	Jng, Jo, Stk
Mokum	I	TM
Nantes (coreless)	All regions	Brp, Gd, Is, Snc, Stk, Sut
Orange Sherbet	IX	Stk
Pioneer	I, II, III, V, VI, VII, VIII, IX	Har
Red-cored Chantenay	II, III, V, VI, VII, VIII, IX	Alb, Is, Jng, Nic, Ter, Til
Rondino	I	Jo
Royal Chantenay	I, II, IV, V, VI, IX	Brp, Har, Pk, Snc, Ter, Twl
Scarlet Nantes	IV, V, IX	Jng, Jo, Stk, Til, Vt

CAULIFLOWER

Cruciferae: *Brassica oleracea botrytis*

Description

Cauliflower means "stem" flower. It is hardest of all *Brassicas* to grow because it is more tender and choosy about its growing conditions. Purple types are easier than white, but have less flavor. Use the dwarf types for fastest results, though they aren't truly dwarf.

Culture

Prefers cool, damp weather with few fluctuations, and fertile soil with lots of organic matter. Start plants later than broccoli for somewhat warmer temperatures. In transplanting from nursery-grown starts, do not choose the biggest ones as they are most likely to bolt or be stunted. When heads (or "curds") of cauliflower are three inches or so, blanch by tying leaves over the top to keep sun out, but leave room for air to get through or they may rot. Purples do not need blanching; unblanched white plants have more vitamins, even though they are less tasty. Give plenty of water at root zone; remove rotting leaves or parts; harvest before flowers begin to open. Plants produce only one head each. Purple types turn light green when cooked. May be planted July 1 for a late crop in warmer, late-fall areas.

Pests & Problems: similar to broccoli, cabbage.

Leafy "curds" are caused by high or fluctuating temperatures, or too much nitrogen. Browning of heads *may* be a boron deficiency.

VARIETY	REGION	SOURCE
Celesta	II, III, VII, VIII	
Burpeeana	IX	Brp
Delira	V, VI	Stk
(Early) Purple Head	VII, IX	Alb, Brp, Jng
Early Snowball	VII, IX	AL, Gd, Is, Snc, Stk, Vt
Igloo	IV	
Imperial	IV	
Jura	I	Ter
Self-Blanching	I	Jng
Silver Star	II, III, VII, VIII	
Snow Crown Hybr.	All regions	Most seed cos.
Snow King Hybr.	I, V, VI, VII, IX	Alb, Jng, Pk, TM
Snowball (X,Y, or M)	I, II, III, IV, VII, VIII, IX	Alb, Jng, Jo, Sut
Snowball Imperial	V, VI	

CELERY

Umbelliferae: *Apium graveolens dulce*

Description

Grown for stalks. Name comes from Greek *selinon* or parsley. It is slow to germinate and grow; must have a very fertile soil and plenty of moisture.

Culture

This is difficult to grow in short-season areas. Best started indoors, at 70°F+, and moved to cooler spot after they have emerged. Set outside about one week *after* the last frost date, six inches apart in well-manured soil. May be set in double rows. Plenty of water and nutrients are needed to get the plants growing fast. To blanch, pile dirt up around stalks as they grow. To harvest, cut entire plant just below surface of soil, or pull a stalk or two from the outside of the plant as it grows. In warmer regions it will last into fall or winter.

Pests & Problems

Celery or parsley worm, the larva of butterfly: can be handpicked, or use rotenone or Sevin.

Stem cracking may be caused by boron deficiency.

Early, late blight — rotate.

Aphids — use insecticidal soap, rotenone or Sevin.

VARIETY	REGION	SOURCE
Clean Cut	IV	
(French) Dinant	II	AL, Nic, TM
Florida	IV	Stk
Giant Pascal	V, VI	Har, Pk
Golden Self-Blanching	VII, IX	Alb, Brp, Jng, Sut, TM, Ter, Til, Vt
Golden Plume	VII	Stk, Til
Surepak	IX	Stk
Tendercrisp	V, VI	Brp, Stk
Utah Improvd. (15B, 52)	I, II, IV, V, VI, IX	Most seed cos.

CELERIAC

Umbelliferae: *Apium graveolens rapaceum*

Description

A type of celery; has thick crown with flavor of celery. Can be used like celery, sliced, or in soups and stews for flavor.

Culture

Grown for its root, or crown, which matures in about 4 months. Grow as for celery, but blanching is not necessary. Roots may be stored if fairly large.

Pests & Problems

Same as for celery.

Recommendations

Although few recommendations were made for this vegetable, it is desirable and useful for those who have room. It will grow in any region where celery will grow. Many seed companies carry at least one variety.

CHICORY

Compositae, *Cichorium intybus*

Description

(Witloof, Magdeburgh, Italian dandelion.) A hardy plant with bitter taste unless blanched; various kinds grown for greens, stalks, or roots (coffee substitute). Witloof is grown usually inside in sand for the second, forced crop of blanched leaves. Magdeburgh, or large-rooted chicory, is the escaped roadside weed seen widely around the country. Asparagus chicory is grown for thick, asparaguslike shoots. *C. endivia*, radicchio or radichetta, is a looseleaf type of chicory with tender foliage, popular with gourmet salad-makers.

Culture

Plant after last spring frost, sowing 1 inch apart, ½ inch deep and thin to 1 foot. All summer greens can be eaten, but taste better if grown under a pot so they are pale. For the Magdeburgh type, dig the roots in fall, trim, wash and grind roots, roast in oven until brown and use for coffee. For witloof, cut stems and foliage back to within 1 inch of soil, dig and replant in box of wet sand, place in dark, cool spot (60-65 °F). When white shoots are 4-5 inches long, cut at soil level. One root will produce more than one crop, each smaller than the one before. Roots may be stored until needed by placing horizontally in sand, like beets. Radicchio is used as a leaf vegetable; in near-freezing temperatures it will produce tender salad greens (or reds). In most areas radicchio will overwinter in the garden under a mulch of straw.

Pests & Problems

Has few serious cultural problems.

VARIETY	REGION	SOURCE
Witloof	IV	Alb, Brp, Is, Jo, Nic, Snc, Stk, Sut
Radicchio	I, II	Brp, Jo, Nic, Stk, TM, Vt
Magdeburgh	All	Is, Til, Stk
Asparagus chicory	I, II	Nic

CHINESE CABBAGE (Celery cabbage, michihli, wong bok, suey choy, pe tsai)

Cruciferae: *Brassica pekinensis*

Description

There are more than one of these, but the most common is a wrinkly-leaved lettuce-type bundle of crisp green leaves.

Culture

Will stand a light frost, but definitely will bolt in hot weather or long days. Sow in early spring and do not transplant unless absolutely necessary — again, it may bolt. Plant will grow in temperatures as low as 40 °F. A late variety can be planted for fall crop. Harvest by taking a few leaves or the entire head; stores well. A good greenhouse or coldframe crop.

Pests & Problems

Bolting: caused by slow growing, long days or too much heat. Plant only in early spring or start seeds for fall growth, if you live in long-season area. Keep plants growing vigorously with lots of water and nutrients. Root maggot: grow under row cover; use diazinon. Flea beetle: ashes on leaves may help; rotenone, diazinon.

VARIETY	REGION	SOURCE
(no particular variety recommended)	I	Most seed cos.

Burpee Hybrid (Two Seasons, Dynasty)	All regions	Brp
Jade Pagoda	V, VI	Har, Pk, Twl
Michihli	V, VI	AL, Jng, Har, Pk, Stk, Twl
Monument	II	Stk, Twl

COLLARD (collards, collard greens)

Cruciferae: *Brassica oleracea acephala*

Description

A hardy cabbage green that can stand hot weather better than most others and so is popular in the South. Forms loose head of thick leaves.

Culture

Plant in early summer for a fall harvest. Not a choosy plant; will grow in rather poor soil, but responds to reasonable care. Greens are actually better if frosted, and are hardy in cold weather. Outer leaves may be harvested a few at a time.

Pests

Very few; treat as for cabbage.

Recommendations

Although I came across recommendations for this green in Regions I, II and III only, there is no reason collards could not be a very good fall crop for hot-summer areas.

VARIETY	REGION	SOURCE
(none given)	I, III	Jo (Champion) TM (Hycrop F,)
Blue Max	II	Twl
Georgia	I, II	Brp, Is, Pk
Vates	I, II	AL, Brp, Ter, Til

CORN (maize, sugar maize)

Graminae: *Zea mays rugosa*

Description

Even when the Indians grew it, there were many varieties — now there are even more. Several rows must be planted to make sure the flowers (silks) are pollinated from the tassels by air movement. Each strand of silk on the female receptacle means one kernel pollinated. Comes in various colors and styles and many hybrid strains, early, middle and late. The earliest varieties are not necessarily the best tasting.

Culture

Start inside or use a plastic mulch to warm soil early and plant outside, around the last frost date. Do not plant in cold, wet soil. Sow in rows at 2-inch intervals or in hills. For a long season, plant early, midseason and late hybrids, or (less effective) make several plantings of the same variety over a several-week period. Different varieties that mature at the same time will cross-pollinate: to avoid this, keep varieties as far apart as you are able. Corn is a heavy nitrogen user. Keep

well weeded; mulch helps to keep weeds down; as the stalks grow they shade out many weeds. When silks are brown and kernels at top are full, ears may be picked. The ultra-sweet hybrids may be best grown by starting inside. They retain their sweetness longer but are often poor germinators with low seedling vitality; the seed coatings are thinner and more susceptible to damage than those of other corn. All corn will retain sweetness longer after picking if kept cool.

Pests & Problems

Poor germination: cold, wet soil; type of hybrid used — try more than one variety; don't rush the planting season. Incomplete filling of ears can be caused by too-small patch of corn, poor weather during pollination, or from lack of phosphorus (ear doesn't fill out at tip).
Corn smut: causes swelling of kernels, distorted ears, black spores. Diseased plants should be eradicated before spores can spread; use resistant variety if smut is a problem in your area.
Corn borers: can overwinter in old corn stalks — get rid of stalks at end of season and keep garden clean; use Sevin or rotenone.
Cutworm: can chop off the young plants; use paper collars; dig around roots to find and eradicate cutworms.
Corn ear worms: can be combated by squirting mineral oil down the silks 4-5 days after they begin to wilt; Sevin.
Earwigs: eat cornsilk and kernels, may cause low kernel development by feeding on silks; can be eliminated by hand if you have the patience — make a trap of rolled newspaper or cloth and set it between plant leaves; check every so often for earwig presence. For larger predators (crows, jays, raccoons, etc.), try a paper bag over ears after pollination, electric fence, cayenne pepper applied to ears after each rain, or planting squash around the corn.
Ornamental corn, *Indian* corn, *dry* corn, are longer-season corns of over 100 days, and are treated as other corn. Isolate plantings from other types. *Popcorn* (var. *praecox*) is like sweet corn but harvested after the stalks and ears are dry. Dry ears inside after picking and test for readiness by popping a few kernels every now and then.

VARIETY	REGION	SOURCE
Beacon	I	Ves
Bi-color Harmony	I	Har, Ves
Bi-color Sugar Dots	II	Ter
Butterfruit	IX	Pk
Canadian Pride	VII	
Earliking	IV, V, VII, VIII, IX	Jng
Earlivee	IX	Jo, Til
Early Extra (Super) Sweet	IV, V	Brp, Jng, Stk, TM, Vt

VARIETY	REGION	SOURCE
Early Giant	IX	
Early Gold and Silver	IX	Stk
Early Sunglow	All regions	Brp, Nic, Pk, Til
Garden Treat	IV	
Golden Bantam (imprvd.)	IX	AL, Gd, Jo, Jng, Snc, Ter, Til
Golden Beauty	IV	
Golden Cross Bantam	All regions	Brp, Is, Vt
Golden Hybrid popcorn	V, VI	Grn, Har, Twl
(Golden) Jubilee	All regions	Gd, Is, Jo, Nic, Stk, Ter, Til, Vt
Honey and Cream	V, VI	Brp
Honeymoon	II, V	Ter
How Sweet It Is	I, II, IV, VI, VII	Most seed cos.
Illini Extra Sweet	V, VI, VII, IX	Brp, Jng, Pk, Til, Vt
Kandy Korn	All regions	Brp, Is, Jng, Nic, Stk
Miniature	VII, IX	
Morning Sun	IV	
NK 199	IV	Jng
Northern Super (Extra) Sweet	VIII	Jo, Stk, Vt
Peppy (Popcorn)	VII	Brp
Polar Vee	IX	Stk, TM
Quicksilver	IV	
Royal Burgundy, Burgundy Delight	II	Jo
Seneca	I, VII, IX	
Seneca Chief	IV, VII, VIII, IX	Is, Nic, Pk, Stk
Seneca Horizon	IX	Har, Stk, Ter
Silver Queen	All regions	Brp, Har, Pk, Til, Vt
Spring Gold	I, II, IX	Har
Style Pak	All	Stk
Sugar Loaf	II	Har
Sunburst	IV	Stk
Sundance	All	Har, Til
Sunnyvee	IV	AL, Is
Supersweet	I, II	
Sweetie	I	Jng
Tendertreat	I, II, III, VI, VII, VIII	
Three-Way Mix	V	
Tokay Sugar	I, II, III, VI, VII, VIII, IX	
White Cloud popcorn	V, VI	Har, Stk, Vt

CUCUMBER

Cucurbitaceae: *Cucumis sativus*

Description

Vines with tendrils, or bushes; male and female flower parts separate on same plant; male flowers open first. Various cultivars are available, some specifically for pickles, others "burpless," or for slicing, or "lemon." Japanese cucumber is same species, different cultivars. Disease-resistant cucumbers are used where scab or mosaic virus is a problem (look for SMR label). Seedless (or small-seeded) cucumbers are generally popular for greenhouse use, do not need pollinating and are not bitter. Some varieties have primarily female flowers for high yield. Pickling cukes tend to produce all at once; the slicing kind produce over a period of time, as long as they are picked when ready.

Culture

Very frost-sensitive; should be protected if there's danger of frost. Vining types can be grown along a wall, fence, or other support. Train when vines are warm, not cold and brittle; bush varieties take less space; some can be grown in containers. Roots very delicate; transplant with care or seed where you want them to grow. Excessive winds damage plants. Grow about 6 inches apart. Covering plants or using a plastic mulch under them will help get them started. If you live where bees are scarce or you grow your cukes under cover, hand-pollinate the female flowers of regular varieties or use the new, all-female types. Cucumbers are about 96% water. They need a lot of it.

Pests & Problems

Squash bugs: place boards around plant where the bugs congregate, then collect and kill; look for and rub off the yellowish eggs between the veins of the underside of the leaf.

Cucumber beetle: spread a wilt, see Chapter V for description.

Mildews, other fungus diseases: keep area clean, plant in airy (not windy) spot, do not grow any *Cucurbitaceae* species in same place two years in a row.

VARIETY	REGION	SOURCE
Amira, Amira II	I, V	Nic, Pk, Ter
Burpee Hybr.	All	Alb, Brp
Burpless Hybr.	All regions	Brp, Har, Nic, Pk, Stk, Til
Chicago Pickling	VII, IX	Alb
Earlipik 14 Hybr.	VII, IX	Alb, Brp
Euro-American	I	Pk
Gemini	V, VI, VII, IX	
Lemon	I, II, VII, IX	Brp, Gd, Is, Har, Jng, Nic, Ter, Til
Liberty Hybr.	V, VI, IX	Brp, Jng, Nic, Pk
Long Green (Improvd.)	I	Alb, Gd, Sut
Marketmore	All regions	Most seed cos.
Marketer	IV, V, VI, VII, IX	
Northern Pickling	IX	Jo
Pacer	I	Har
Patio Pik	IX	Alb, Pk, TM
Pickle-dilly	IX	Pk
Pioneer Hybr.	II, III, V, VI, VIII	Pk, Stk, Til
Poinsett	II, III, VI, VIII	Brp, Jng, Pk
Pot Luck	VII, IX	Jng, Nic, Til, Vt
Raider	II	Har
SMR 58	I, II, III, VI, VIII	Jng, Nic, Ter
Spacemaster (bush)	V, VI	Brp, Jo, Stk
Straight Eight	I, VII, IX	AL, Brp, Is, Vt
Sweet Slice	I, II, IX	Brp, Har, Jng, Pk, Stk
Sweet Success	I, II, V, VI	Most seed cos.
White Lightning	II, III, VI, VIII	
Wisconsin SMR 18	V, VI, VII, IX	

EGGPLANT (aubergine)

Solanaceae: *Solanum melongena esculentum*

Description

This plant loves heat; only since special, short-season varieties were developed has it been possible to grow here. The elongated varieties tend to be the short-season ones, maturing in 60 days or so. There is a white form. The oriental eggplant produces more fruits than the regular, but they are quite small.

Culture

Must be started indoors 10 weeks or more before last frost; will not germinate below 60°F. Don't put outside until the nights are consistently above 45°. Choose a warm, sunny spot — soil may be warmed with black plastic mulch. Hot-caps can be used for a couple of weeks to get plants started. Fruit does not store well. For largest fruit, remove all but 5-6 blossoms. Fertilize more than once early in the growing season. Keep the fruit picked as it matures. For cool coastal and high inland areas, it may be better to grow under cover all summer.

Pests & Problems

Flea beetles: spray with rotenone.

Wilts: do not plant where wilted tomato plants have been a problem.

Cutworms: eradicate by hand by scratching a bit around plant roots to find; use paper collars.

VARIETY	REGION	SOURCE
Black Beauty	IV, VII, IX	Brp, Is, Jng, Pk, Snc, Vt

Black Magic	All	Har
Burpee Hybrid	IX	Brp
Dusky Hybr.	All regions	Most seed cos.
Early Beauty	VII, IX	Brp, Pk
Early Black Egg	I, II	Ter
Ichiban	I, V, VI, IX	Vt
Moneymaker	I	Sut
Short Tom	I	TM, Ter

ENDIVE (escarole)
Compositae: *Cichorium endiva*
Description
Very closely related to chicory, more sensitive to cold. Goes to seed in hot weather, but more frost-hardy than lettuce and is used like lettuce in fall after frosts. Long spell of hot weather will increase its bitter taste; cool weather is best. Green endive has deeply serrated, curly leaves. Escarole, or Batavian endive, has upright, broad leaves and a self-blanched heart.
Culture
Sow thickly and thin to 12 inches; can sow in midsummer for fall and winter. Tie up the outer leaves to get tender inside leaves, but leave loose for air circulation or the inside leaves will rot. Mulch for protection in cold weather.
Pests & Problems
Very few; possibly slugs, flea beetles.

VARIETY	REGION	SOURCE
Broad-leaved Batavian	All regions	Is, Nic, Snc, Stk, Sut, Ter, Til, Vt
Deep Heart	All	Har
Green Curled (Ruffec)	All regions	AL, Alb, Is, Har, Jng, Nic, Pk, Stk, Vt

GARLIC
Liliaceae: *Allium sativum*
Description
An onion-type of plant; has flat leaves, bulb divided into cloves; used for flavoring in many dishes. Elephant garlic is just larger-cloved garlic, but may be milder.
Culture
Takes three or more months to mature; plant either very early in the spring, or in the fall. Needs cool temperatures (below 64°F) to make bulbs. Plant only the fattest cloves, pointed end up, 3 or more inches apart. Can be interplanted; repels some insects. Shallow-rooted; mulch heavily in cold areas. Harvest when tops have died.
Pests & Problems
No problems of note.

Recommendations
Garlic may be grown anywhere in the Northwest. Most seed companies carry at least one variety; it may be planted as purchased from a grocery, produce market or seed store.

SHALLOT
Liliaceae: *Allium cepa*
Description
A small, mild garlic- or bunching onion-type bulb, prized in gourmet kitchens.
Culture
Propagate from bulbs only; save a few for next year's seed or leave in ground over winter. Plant with top of bulb just above soil surface. Treat as with onion sets, harvest when leaves turn brown. May be dried and stored like onions.
Recommendations
As with onions and garlic, shallots may be planted in any Northwest garden. Available locally or from: No, Nic, TM.

KALE (borecole)
Cruciferae: *Brassica oleracea acephala*
Description
A perfect short-season crop; will not grow well in hot weather. Siberian kale has smoothish leaves; Scotch kale has very curly leaves. Ornamental kale is variously colored pinks, purple and white, and can be eaten. Chinese kale or broccoli (gai lohn or gai lan) has smooth leaves and broccolilike, edible buds.
Culture
Grow from seed, thin to 1-foot spacing (eat the thinnings); take outside leaves as needed. Should have about two months before fall frost. May be best in shade in hot-summer areas; keep well watered. Fertilize about once a month for large, tender leaves.
Pests & Problems
See broccoli.

VARIETY	REGION	SOURCE
Dwarf Blue (Green) Curled Scotch	All regions	Most seed cos.
Siberian	All regions	AL, Alb, Brp, Snc, Ter, Til, Vt
Vates	All regions	AL, Har, Jng, Vt

KOHLRABI (stem turnip)
Cruciferae: *Brassica oleracea caulorapa*
Description
Grown for its turniplike swelled stem about half-way up the plant. It is easy to grow, good when young. Green and purple varieties. Grows well in cool temperatures and withstands light frost. In Regions I and II, leave late crops in garden for storage until needed.

Culture
Needs fertile, loose soil about 8 inches of space all around, and very rapid growth. When the swelled stem is 2-3 inches across, pull the plant and cut it off. Peel and use fresh or cooked. In cooler areas, even the larger kohlrabis may be used, grated as a cabbage substitute. May be stored for awhile in cool, dark place.
Pests & Problems
Very few of any consequence; see cabbage.

VARIETY	REGION	SOURCE
Grand Duke	I, II, V, VI, IX	Brp, Har, Jng, Pk, Stk, Sut
Purple Vienna	All regions	AL, Alb, Is, Jng, Pk, Stk, Sut, Til
White Vienna	All regions	AL, Alb, Is, Har, Jng, Nic, Stk, Sut, Vt

LEEK
Liliaceae: *Allium ampeloprasum porrum*
Description
Thickened sweet onion with flat leaves, mild flavor; best when blanched by piling soil around base. Does well in fertile, fine soil — does not like weed competition. Frost-tolerant and hardy, but needs a 3-month growing season.
Culture
Sow indoors in January or February, or start in the fall in milder regions and plant out overwinter. Can plant in spring as early as a month before last frost. Set in trench and fill in as they grow. Mulch in cold areas in fall. Leave in garden as long as you can — some places until it goes to seed in spring; small bulblets that form around larger bulbs can be transplanted for new crop. Can be used fresh or cooked, dried or frozen.
Pests & Problems
Root maggots in some areas: use diazinon, rotenone, or grow under cover.

VARIETY	REGION	SOURCE
American Flag (Broad London)	All regions	Alb, Brp, Is, Pk
Carentan	I	AL
Titan	IX	Brp
Giant Mussleburg	All regions	AL, Nic, Snc, Stk, Sut, TM, Til

LETTUCE
Compositae: *Lactuca sativa*
Description
A salad leaf vegetable of many forms, generally leaf and head. Head lettuce is more difficult to grow, more demanding. Leaf comes in curly, broad, narrow, crinkled, red,

green, etc. types. *Cos* lettuce is upright and thick-leaved (Romaine); *bibb* is intermediate between head and leaf. Generally, lettuce grows best in cool weather (but some are not frost-hardy) and bolts in hot weather, but slow-bolting varieties are available.

Culture
Will germinate and grow at 40° or more, but germination is fastest at 75°; growth best at 60-65°. Sow seed very shallowly, transplant or thin to one foot apart, keep plants well watered and fertilized. Eat thinnings, outside leaves. Make several plantings over the season. Some varieties are available for late fall crop.

Pests & Problems
Poor germination: seed too deep, soil too thick and heavy; plant and cover thinly with fine soil.

Slugs: dust with diatomaceous earth; use bait.

Fungal diseases: wilting and discoloration; common in wet gardens — space plants, water roots only, remove all rotted plant material.

Tipburn: may be caused by wide temperature variations between day and night.

VARIETY	REGION	SOURCE
LEAF		
All the Year Round	I	AL, TM
Black-seeded Simpson	All regions	Most seed cos.
Continuity	II	Nic, Sut
Grand Rapids	All regions	Most seed cos.
Oakleaf	All regions	Most seed cos.
Prizehead	All regions	Most seed cos.
Red Head	II	
Red Sails	I, II, V	Brp, Jng, Jo, Pk, Stk, Ter
Rose Red	II	
Ruby Red	VII, IX	Alb, Brp, Jng, Nic
Salad Bowl	All regions	Most seed cos.
Slobolt	IX	Ter
HEAD		
Calmar	I, II, III, VI, VIII	
Golden Gem	I	
Great Lakes (659)	All regions	Brp, Har, Stk, Twl, Til
Iceberg	All regions	Alb, Brp, Vt
Ithaca	All regions	Har, Til
Kwiek	I	AL, Sut
Merveille de Quatre Saisons	I, II	Ter
Pennlake	I, II, III, IV	Stk
Premier Great Lakes	IX	Stk
Salinas	II	Ter
BIBB		
Burpee Bibb	IV, V, VII	Brp
Butter King	IV	Snc
Buttercrunch	All regions	Most seed cos.
Dark Green Boston	IV	Brp, Har
Green Ice	IX	Brp, Pk
Summer Bibb	VII, IX	Har
Tom Thumb	I, II, IX	Gd, Is, Nic, Pk, TM, Vt, Sut
COS		
Dark Green	I, IV	Snc
Little Gem	I	Sut, Ter, Gd, TM
Paris, Parris White	V, VII	Brp, Gd, Jo, Nic, TM, Til
Valmaine	I, II, IX	Jng, Pk, Vt, TM, Stk, Ter
Winter Density	I, II	AL, Jo, Sut

MELONS
Cantaloupe (muskmelon)
Cucurbitaceae: *Cucumis melo*
Description
Name cantaloupe comes from Italian Canta Lupo, a papal villa where first melon in Europe was grown. A heat-loving, sweet, juicy orange-meated melon. Some quick-maturing varieties have been developed for colder climates.

Culture
Grow only fastest-maturing varieties, best on black plastic mulch and/or under cover. Cold weather causes wilting. In Regions I and II, ocean coastal regions, and cold-night areas, will probably not ripen most years without special attention. Start indoors 4-5 weeks before last frost date, about 72°F, 3-4 to a large container and thin to 1, transplant well after last frost date. If covered, remember to hand-pollinate flowers, or leave open during hottest part of day and cover at night. Give plenty of water and manure or fertilizer. When ripe, the fruit will slip easily off the stem.

Pests
Basically those of the cucumber. Keep fruits off the ground by vining the plant on supports or growing over plastic.

VARIETY	REGION	SOURCE
Alaska Hybr.	IV, V, IX	Alb, Nic, Vt
Ambrosia	I, II, III, IV, V, VI	Brp, Stk
Burpee Hybr.	I, II, III, IV, V, VI	Brp, Stk
Charantais	IX	Nic, Stk, Sut
Classic	II, III, VI	Jng, Vt
Delicious	VII	Alb, Jng, Stk
Early Sweet (Earlisweet)	II, III, VI, VII	Nic, Stk, Sut
Edisto	II, III, VI	Pk
Far North	IV, IX	Alb, Snc, Vt
Gold Star	II, III, IV, V, VI	Jng
Hale's Best (#36)	V, VI, VII	Jng, Vt
Harper Hybr.	I, II, III, IV, V, VI, VII, VIII	Stk, Til
Hearts of Gold	V, VI	Gd
Minnesota Midget	IV, V, VII, VIII, IX	Pk
Musketeer	I	Northrup-King, Stk
Roadside	I, II, III, VI	Jng, Vt
Supermarket	I, II, III	Jng
Sweet and Early	I, II	Brp
Yakima Sweet	V, VI, VII, VIII	

WATERMELON
Cucurbitaceae: *Citrullus lanatus*
Description
In some areas, especially where cantaloupes may be easily grown, the small watermelons may be expected to ripen. Flesh may be yellow or red. Since watermelon will not grow in cold weather, planting under row covers on black mulch may give it the extra edge needed for ripening. Not a recommended crop for coastal areas, Regions I and II. Only in Region VI and the warmest parts of Region VII are larger, market-type watermelons recommended in home gardens.

Culture
Plant in hills, giving about 4 feet all around for space. Vines may be trained up trellis but they must have support for fruit. One way to tell ripeness is to check the tendril on the stem closest to the melon to see whether it is dried. Some melons have whitish "ripe" spots on belly; some do not. The only use for an unripe melon is for pickles or candying like citron (a melon grown exclusively for candying).

Pests & Problems
Has the diseases and pests of other melons and cukes.

VARIETY	REGION	SOURCE
Charleston Gray	III, VI, VII, VIII	Brp, Pk, Stk, Vt
Crimson Sweet	III, V, VI, VII, VIII, IX	Brp, Har, Jng, Stk
Green Klondike	V	Is
Klondike No. 11	III, VI, VII, VIII	
New Hampshire Midget	III, IV, V, VI, VII, VIII, IX	Vt
Striped Klondike	V, VI	Vt
Sugar Baby	V, VI, VII, IX	Alb, Brp, Har, Is, Jo, Snc, Stk
Triple Sweet (seedless)	VII, IX	Brp
Tri-X 313 (seedless)	V, VI, VII, IX	Brp, Har, Pk
Yellow Baby	V, VI	Brp, Har, Stk, Pk
Other Melons:		
Early Hybr. Crenshaw	II, III, VI, VII	Brp
Venus honeydew	VI	Brp

ONIONS

Liliaceae: *Allium cepa* (and other spp.)

Description

Biennial, setting seed second year. Globe onions — red, yellow and white, the harder ones good for storage; Egyptian — tree, top or walking onions, hardy plants for overwintering, forming bulbets at top of stalks; spring onions — scallions, bunching onions — grown from seeds or sets; the true spring onion produces clusters of greens but no bulbs: pickling or pearl onions mature when very small; shallots, garliclike bulbs (not so frost hardy as garlic), planted in early spring and harvested in fall. All are quite frost-hardy and pest- and disease-resistant.

Culture

May be interplanted with other crops; do well in light, well-drained, fertile soil with plenty of organic matter. Shallow-rooted: mulch and water regularly, keep weeds out; if onions are interrupted in growth they can be too strong and hot. Globe onions are usually started indoors 2 months or more before last frost, or from sets. Plant sets either in fall or very early spring, with pointed tips at soil level. Sow bunching-onion seed thickly; cover them well, as they won't germinate in light. For green, eating onions in fall and/or winter, seed in August in the garden. Any onion can be harvested young and used as a scallion. For globe onions, dig when the stalks are dead. If

onions stay in ground overwinter they will set flower stalks, and are not so tasty. Use of too-large sets (use only ½-inch or less) or prolonged cold weather early in season may cause the same problem. Dig and use immediately. If tops are not down 2 weeks before expected frost, bend them down. Best to pull the onions on a sunny day; leave them outside on newspaper to cure in the sun, if you have it, for several days. When thoroughly dry, bring in and store in cool, dark place.

Pests & Problems

Onions serve as an insect repellent and should have little problem themselves.

Onion root maggot: may cause some difficulty; rotate crops, use rotenone, diazinon or malathion.

White rot: watery, rotten spots on onions; rotate, destroy any onions with the symptoms.

VARIETY	REGION	SOURCE
DRY, GLOBE		
Ailsa Craig	I,	Dom, Is, Sut, TM
Autumn Spice	II, III, IV, VII, VIII, IX	Alb, Is, Stk
Buccaneer	I	Har
Ebenezer	VII, IX	Nic, Pk
Fiesta	All	Har, Pk
Red Hamburger	V, VI, IX	Pk, Brp
Southport Red Globe	II, III, VII, VIII, IX	AL, Gd, Is, Jng, Jo, Vt
Southport White Globe	II, III, VII, VIII	Jng
Spartan Banner	I, II, III, VII, VIII	Stk
Spartan Sleeper	I, II, III, VII, VIII	Jng, Stk
Stokes Exporter	IV	Stk
Sweet Sandwich	I	Brp, Dom, Jng, Jo, TM
Sweet Spanish (type)	All regions	Most seed cos.
Walla Walla Sweet	V, VI, VII, VIII	AL, Is, Jo, Nic, Til
Yellow Globe Danvers	I, II, III, IV, VII, VIII	Gd, Is, Snc
GREEN		
Evergreen Bunching	IX	AL, Brp, Har
Green Bunching	II, III, VII, VIII, IX	
Japanese Bunching	II, III, IV, VII, VIII	Har, Snc, TM

Silver Queen	IV	
White Bunching	II, III, VII, VIII	Har, Pk
White Portugal (multipurpose)	IV, VII, IX	Alb, Gd, Har, Is, Stk, Til
Egyptian Walking (multipliers)	All regions	AL, Alb, Gd, TM

PARSNIP

Umbelliferae: *Pastinaca sativa*

Description

Pastinaca refers to the fact that this vegetable is dug from the ground. The flavor of the root improves with fall frost. Easy- but slow-growing.

Culture

Since this is a long root, it is best grown in light, loose soil. If it is allowed to go to seed in spring it may self-sow. Sow whenever soil can be worked (germination temperature is anything above 36°). Doesn't like hot temperatures. May not appear for several weeks; might grow radishes as a marker crop, using the radishes before the parsnips are very large. Thin to 4 inches. Roots are mature (can be eaten earlier, though) in late fall, becoming sweeter with each frost. In most areas will overwinter even without mulch. To harvest all winter or save until spring in the colder areas, mulch heavily.

Pests & Problems

Usually not bothered by many pests.

Cabbage root maggot: start and grow for first part of season under cover; use diazinon, rotenone.

Flea beetle: ignore unless very heavy infestation; use diazinon, etc.

VARIETY	REGION	SOURCE
All America	All	Har
Model	All regions	Alb, Har, Jng, Jo, Ter
Hollow Crown (Imprvd.)	All regions	AL, Alb, Brp, Is, Pk, Stk, Sut, Vt

PEA

Leguminosae: *Pisum sativum*

Description

The Northwest grows a great many peas: snow peas, snap peas, sugar snap peas, and dry peas, as well as seed. This is an annual vining or tendril-bearing plant which has the advantage of producing extra nitrogen (with nitrogen-fixing bacteria in the soil), thus enriching the garden. It is usually grown early in the season, removed after harvest, and replaced by a later crop (e.g., lettuce), but may be planted in fall for an overwintering crop in some areas. Wando peas are more heat-resistant than others.

Culture

Peas grow best in cool temperatures (below 81°F); can be planted in 40-60° soil. Pods tender, though plants will have some frost-hardiness. A commercial inoculant will help growth, especially in new soil. Pre-germinate in damp paper towels and sow in shade if you want a late crop. Plant in double row about 1 inch apart near trellis or support, or plant bush variety 2 inches apart. Can use some twigs or prunings from fruit trees for supports. Even bush varieties can use a little help. Pick shell and snap peas when peas inside are visibly swelled; sugar snaps when peas are formed but not large, and snow peas when swellings just begin to show. Pick carefully, weed carefully.

Pests & Problems

Aphids: can spread a fungus fatal to the pea plants; spray with water, insecticidal soap.
Root rot: causes stunted plants; leaves may lose color and dry; keep area clean, rotate pea crops, do not overwater.
Wilt: remove and destroy wilted and stunted plants.
Cutworms: cultivate soil, search for cutworms around roots.
Powdery mildew: remove all dead plant material, allow plenty of air between plants.
Virus: (carried by aphids) fight aphids, use resistant varieties: in Regions I and II use Enation-virus resistant varieties, especially for late spring plantings; take out affected plants.

VARIETY	REGION	SOURCE
Alaska	VI, VII, VIII, IX	AL, Brp, Jo, Pk, Vt
Blizzard Snow Pea	VIII	Pk
Burpeeana	VI, IX	Brp
Corvallis (EV-resistant)	I, II, III, VI, VIII	Nic
Dark Green Perfection	All regions	Ter
Dwarf Gray Sugar	IV, VII, IX	AL, Alb, Gd, Pk, Vt
Dwarf Telephone	IV	Gd, Vt
Freezonian	VII, IX	Brp, Har, Til
Frosty	VII, IX	Har, Til
Green Arrow	All regions	Most seed cos.
Knight (EV-resistant)	I, II, III, VI, VIII	Har, Jo, Pk
Lacy Ladies (Lady)	IX	Is, Vt
Laxton('s) Progress	All regions	Is, Pk, Snc, Stk
Laxton('s) Superb	IV	
Lincoln (Homestead)	IX	AL, Alb, Har, Is, Stk, Vt
Little Marvel	All regions	Most seed cos.
Little Sweetie	IV	
Maestro	IX	Brp, Jng, Jo, Til
Mammoth Melting	IV, IX	AL, Brp, Har, Snc, Vt
Oregon Sugar Pod	All regions	Most seed cos.
Onward	IV	Sut, TM
Progress #9	IV, IX	Alb, Brp, Jng, Sut, Vt
Rembrandt	II	Ter
Sparkle	IX	Har, Jo, Ter
Sugar Ann	II, IX	Most seed cos.
Sugar Bon	II, IX	Brp, Pk, Sut
Sugar Daddy	IX	Brp, Jng, Nic, Pk, Stk, Vt
Sugar Snap	I, II, III, VI, VIII, IX	Most seed cos.
Tall Telephone (Alderman)	All regions	Most seed cos.
Wando	VII, IX	Most seed cos.

LENTILS

Leguminosae: *Lens culinaris*

Description

Attractive, bushy plant about a foot tall, small white or pale blue flowers, hardy, easy to grow, but on small scale not practical as each pod has only 2-3 lentils, and shelling is very time-consuming.

Culture

Plant early spring, 4 inches apart, in loose, cool, moist soil, like peas. Leave pods on until they dry; a couple of months after planting, harvest and store in pod or shelled.

Pests & Problems

No serious pests.

PEPPER (Sweet, bell, hot, pimiento, chili, banana, etc.)

Solanaceae: *Capsicum annuum*

Description

Tropical species — used by the Aztecs of Mexico. Like their cousins, the eggplant and tomato, they need hot weather, slightly less than eggplant and slightly more than tomatoes. The red bell pepper is the ripened green bell in most varieties. Red color develops at between 65-75°F, but not at 55° or less. Best to choose an early variety; grow in light, porous soil; will take about 3 months to produce properly.

Culture

Start indoors about 2 months before last frost, maintain 80°F soil temperature for germination. Transplant to 4-inch pots and keep growing well, with plenty of light, until time to set out. Set roots and stems lower in soil when transplanted. Plant with a foot or more of space all around, preferably in black plastic mulch. For cooler areas, row covers or hot-caps will be of benefit, but ventilate or uncover on sunny days.

Pests & Problems

Aphids: especially under cover; use insecticidal soap, spray with water; rotenone.
Surface pitting: cold temperatures.
Cutworms: use paper collars; dig up and remove by hand.
Flea beetles: use Tanglefoot-painted boards (also good for white fly); dust with rotenone, diazinon.
Leaf roll: leaves roll downward, do not yellow or otherwise look affected; do nothing — it isn't a big problem.
Curly and yellowed new growth: curly top; destroy infected plants.
Mosaic virus: various yellow spots and blotches on plants; destroy.
Verticillium wilt: wilted plants; browning of leaves, streaks; rotate pepper, tomato, potato, and cucumber/squash crops with other families; cold, wet weather exacerbates the problem — use black plastic, row covers, etc.
Corn earworm, and other worms: remove by hand or use Bt.

VARIETY	REGION	SOURCE
Ace Bell (New Ace)	IV, V, IX	Alb, Brp, Jo, Stk, Vt
Anaheim Chili	IV, V, IX	AL, Brp, Gd, Har, Nic, Pk, Ter, Vt
Belaire	II, III, VII, VIII	
Bell Boy	II, III, VII, VIII, IX	Brp, Jng, Pk, Stk, Vt
California (Cal) Wonder	All regions	Most seed cos.
Canape	I, IV, V, VII, IX	Har, Nic, Vt
Cayenne	V, VI, VII, IX	Most seed cos.
Cherry Sweet	IX	Gd, Har, Pk, Ter
Cubanelle	V, IX	Pk, Stk, Ter
Early Bountiful	II, IX	Nic
Early Calwonder 300	All regions	Jng, Snc
Early Pimiento	VII, IX	Brp, Nic
Early Thickset	II	Pk
Emerald Giant	V, VI	Til
Gedeon	II	Brp
Golden Bell	I	Alb, Har, Ter, Pk, Vt

151

Golden Whopper Banana	VII	Pk
Gypsy	V, VI, IX	Most seed cos.
Hot Portugal	V, IX	Stk, Ter
Hungarian Wax	I, V, VI, VII, IX	Most seed cos.
Idabelle	VII, IX	ID Ext. Svc.
Jalapeno	V, VI, IX	Most seed cos.
Keystone Giant	VII, IX	Ter
Merrimack	V, IX	Brp
Red Cherry	VII, IX	Is, Stk, Vt
Red Chili	IV, V	Alb, Is, Ter
Staddon's Select	II, V, IX	Jo, Ter
Sweet Banana	II, V, IX	Most seed cos.
Sweet Chocolate	I	Gd, Jo
Thai Hot	II	Pk
Yolo Wonder L	All	Jng, Pk, Stk

POTATOES
Solanaceae: *Solanum tuberosum*
Description
The potato originated in the Andes, was taken to Europe, and returned to the Western Hemisphere with the first settlers. It grows well in cool, somewhat moist climates. True seed is available, but most gardeners use the tuber, cutting it into portions with "eyes," at least one eye, or bud, to a piece (and preferably two). Commercial seed potatoes are usually treated to prevent development of various diseases. Early, midseason and late strains are available; they come in several colors (even blue), and some are better for storing than others. Dry potatoes, those with less moisture content, are best for baking; those with higher moisture content are best for frying and boiling.

Culture
Does best in well-drained, slightly acidic, sandy soil, where a legume grew previously. In higher altitudes, plastic mulch should be used to heat ground. When soil has warmed to over 40°F in spring, cut potato pieces and plant about 18 inches apart, covering with a couple of inches of soil. As the plant grows, fill soil in around it but do not bury foliage. The tubers develop above the eye or new shoot, but will green and become less desirable if exposed to light. They can also be planted under a thick layer of mulch. Early potatoes can be dug a month or so after planting. The tubers are fully mature when the tops die. Dig carefully to avoid injuring the tubers. Lay them out and brush off dirt, let them cure over one dry day, then store in cool (45-50°), dark spot. Treat the storage tubers very gently; injury to the skins will allow soft rot bacteria to enter and potatoes will spoil.

Pests & Problems
Colorado potato beetle: eats foliage; watch for bright orange eggs early in season on underside of leaves; orange larvae and adults (orange and black striped) can be removed by hand.
Wireworm: makes tunnels in tubers; rotate; make several plantings to see when is best time to avoid these.
Scab: corky looking scabs on surface of potato which aren't pretty but don't hurt the insides; may be caused by alkaline soil or use of wood ashes; some varieties (e.g. Nooksack) are resistant.
Verticillium wilt: like peppers, the vines die early, show browning and streaking; rotate and avoid spots where other *Solanaceae* vegetables have been grown.
Flea beetle: small holes in leaves; use rotenone, Sevin, or Tanglefoot.
Various viruses: cause leaf discoloration, stunting of plant; use only certified seed, control insects and destroy infected plants.

Recommendations
Each potato has distinct characteristics: earlies such as Norgold and White Rose are not often good for storing and are used as boiling or "new" potatoes; Fingerling is good for salads; Burbank Russet is an excellent late storage potato; Yellow Finn is only a moderate producer but has high-quality flavor and texture; Kennebec and Nooksack are blight-resistant; Red Pontiac stores well. Potato seed is generally purchased from seed stores and nurseries; Burpee, Jung, Park carry a few; Tillinghast carries both Yellow Finn and Norway Blue; Jung has Fingerling.

VARIETY	REGION	Early, Mid, or Late
Acadian Russet	I	
Bliss Triumph red	VII, IX	E
Burbank Russet (Netted Gem)	All regions except IV	L
Butte	I	
Chippewa	VII, VIII, IX	M
Early Epicure	IV	E
Early Rose	I	E
Explorer	VII	Seed: Alb
Finnish, Yellow Meat	I, II, V	L
Fundy	IV	E
Irish Cobbler	V	E
Katahdin	VII, VIII, IX	M
Kennebec	I, IV, V, VI	M, L
LaRouge	IX	M
Nooksack	IV, V, VI	M
Norgold Russet	All regions	E, M
Peruvian Blue	I, II	
Red Lasot(d)a	All regions	M, L
Red Norland	All regions	M
Red Pontiac	All regions	M
Superior	IX	E
Viking	IX	M
Warba	IV	E
White Rose	I, II, V, IX	E

SWEET POTATO (Yam, but not a true, tropical yam)
Convolvulaceae: *Ipomoea batatas*
Description
A long-season, warm-weather crop, refusing to grow in temperatures below 50°F. Not an easy vegetable to grow in the Northwest, but some gardeners do manage it — especially in warmer, inland areas; not recommended for Regions I, II or VIII. A few early varieties will mature in 100 days.

Culture
Start from seed potatoes by planting in 2-3 inches of sand inside, in 70-80° temperatures. Remove slips and plant individually in black plastic mulch, cover with Reemay or other row cover until weather is dependably warm. Reserve caps for covering if cool weather threatens again. Give plenty of room for growth — 2 feet or more all around. Roots must be cured before eating, by storing 2 weeks in high humidity at about 75°. The main thing is to keep the soil warm while growing.

Pests & Problems
With this vegetable, almost any problem will be associated with temperatures that are too low, which will weaken or destroy the plant. Be sure soil is not too high in organic matter, as it causes a rough skin.

VARIETY	REGION	SOURCE
Centennial	rec. for	Brp, Pk
New Jewel	VI, VII,	Pk
Porto Rico bush	IX in	Brp, Vt
Vardaman	warmest	Pk, Vt
Vineless Puerto Rico	areas only	Pk

RADISH
Cruciferae: *Raphanus sativus*
Description
Daikon and other oriental radishes are winter radishes which store well. The radish is the fastest-maturing root crop, the regular type taking less than a month. Winter radishes can grow to more than a pound and take a couple of months to reach maturity, but may be eaten at any stage. All radishes

like cool, moist soil, short day lengths. In long-day areas or seasons, choose a rapidly maturing species. Mild radishes come from speedy growth in cool weather. Good fall crop in Regions I and II especially.

Culture

Sow early spring and late summer ½ inch deep and ½ inch apart, and thin to 1 inch. Can be interplanted. Can be used to mark slow-to-emerge crops such as parsnips, asparagus, carrots and beets. For large roots, mulching and regular watering help ensure good root quality, but too-wet soil causes cracks. Large-rooted or oriental type radishes can be kept in storage as beets are; greens are used as well as roots.

Pests & Problems

Flea beetles: dust with diazinon, rotenone; or trap.

Cabbage root maggot: worst problem; rotate; grow under cover; dust or treat soil with diazinon, malathion.

VARIETY	REGION	SOURCE
Black Spanish winter	All regions	Most seed cos.
Burpee White	All regions	Alb, Brp, Jng
Champion	All regions	Alb, Har, Is, Pk, Stk, Ter, Vt
Cherry Belle	All regions	Most seed cos.
Comet	All regions	Alb, Stk, Til
Daikon (various names)	Most regions	Most seed cos.
Easter Egg Mix	IX	Brp, Jo, Jng, Nic, Til, Vt
French Breakfast	II, III, VII, VIII	Most seed cos.
Inca	II, III, VII, VIII	Jo, Pk
Red Boy	II, III, VII, VIII	Alb, Stk
(Early) Scarlet Globe	V, VI, VII, IX	Most seed cos.
Scarlet Knight	IX	Ter
Sparkler	V, VI	Brp, Is, Jng, Nic, Sut, Vt
White Icicle	V, VI, VII, IX	Most seed cos.

HORSERADISH
Cruciferae: *Armoracia rusticana*

A perennial with light green, crinkly leaves and grayish white roots usable in sauces and cooking where a strong, tangy flavor is wanted.

Propagated by roots only, the horseradish plant can turn into a weedy nuisance if not confined. Any loose, rich soil will suit it; put in permanent part of garden. Clean and grate the root, mix with a little vinegar, other condiments, for use with meat.

VARIETY	REGION	SOURCE
Maliner-Kreb	All regions	Brp, Nic

RHUBARB (pie plant)
Polygonaceae: *Rheum rhabarbarum*

Large, stalked vegetable with big, ornamental leaves, used as a fruit. Red-stalked varieties are sweeter and more flavorful but somewhat less vigorous than green. Plants are best from purchased roots, set out late fall or very early spring, but may be started from seed. Does best in cool climates.

Culture

Set even with soil surface in a sunny location; sandy loam is the best soil, with a mix of compost or manure. Rhubarb is a heavy feeder; needs plenty of fertilizer. Do not harvest first year, harvest for two weeks the second year, then use the stalks in spring and fall but leave in summer to build up plant roots. Pull the stalks rather than cutting them off the plant. Leaves have high concentration of oxalic acid, do not eat — but they can go on the compost pile. For those with little space, rhubarb can be interplanted in the flower garden to add color and greenery.

Pests & Problems

Pests in rhubarb are rare.

Flower stalks: occasionally your rhubarb plants may send up a flower stalk or two; remove immediately if you are more interested in harvesting stalks than in the decorative flowers, as they draw on the energy of the roots.

Spindly stalks: divide plants, cut apart and replant; be sure to give plants plenty of fertilizer in form of manure, compost, or 5-10-5 fertilizer.

VARIETY	REGION	SOURCE
Canada Red	All regions	(rhubarb roots are
Cherry	I, III, VII, VIII, IX	generally available
Crimson Wine	All regions	at local seed stores
German Wine	II, III, VII, VIII, IX	and nurseries)
MacDonald	IV, VII, IX	Brp
Ruby	VII, IX	
Valentine	VII, IX	Brp
Victoria	I, VII, IX	Alb, Brp, Gd, Sut, Vt

RUTABAGA
Cruciferae: *Brassica napus*
Description

Sometimes called Swede or turnip, though it is not the common turnip, *B. rapa*. Name comes from Scandinavian word *rotabagge* or "round-root." Hardier than a turnip and has different leaf, which is edible; takes longer to grow. Generally seeded in early summer and used as a fall crop. May be left in the ground, mulched, in all but coldest regions.

Culture

Should have a soil pH above 6, plenty of water. Plant in June or July in generally fertile, light soil. Wait until after frost to harvest. May be stored.

Pests & Problems

Soft brown interior: symptomatic of boron deficiency; apply borax.

Flea beetle: control with rotenone and pyrethrum.

Clubroot: acidic soil, too much moisture.

Turnip mosaic virus: prevent by crop rotation, disposal of infected plants.

Root maggot: grow under cover; use diazinon or rotenone.

VARIETY	REGION	SOURCE
American Purple Top	All regions	Har, Jng, Pk, Til
Best of All	II	Ter
Laurentian	IX	AL, Jo, Jng, Stk, Snc

SALAD GREENS, MISCELLANEOUS

ARUGULA (roquette, ruchetta, or rocket)
Cruciferae: *Eruca vesicaria sativa*

This is a favorite European green with a strong, horseradish flavor; grows well in cool weather but bolts in warm weather. Needs plenty of water for tender leaves. Cut often and keep growing rapidly. Use in salads and sandwiches.

Sources: Alb, Gd, Nic, TM, Ter

CORN SALAD (lamb's lettuce, mache, feldsalat, doucette, fetticus)
Valerianaceae: *Valerianella locusta*

An easy-to-grow cool-weather crop, frost-hardy. Plant in September for fall or winter, and in October for early spring in Regions I and II. In other regions, plant in August to have a later fall crop, or in late September for an early spring crop. Harvest outer leaves as they grow; use as you would lettuce.

Sources: Har, Is, Jo, Pk, Sut, Ter, Vt

CRESS (peppergrass, garden cress, etc.)
Cruciferae: *Lepidium sativum*

Takes only 10 days to 2 weeks to have a crop of this fast-growing green and it can be grown indoors as well as outdoors. Do not pull but cut off with scissors and let it continue to grow; use in sandwiches or salads like watercress.

Sources: Alb, Har, Is, Jo, Snc, Sut, TM

PARSLEY
Umbelliferae: *Petroselinum crispum* and *P. crispum neapolitanum*

A slow-germinating green. Leaf segments are variously curled or mosslike, or flattish (in the *neopolitanum*, or Italian). Plants are quite hardy; may survive over winter, and if left in garden to go to seed, may perpetuate themselves indefinitely. Give plenty of nitrogen. Another variety, *P. tuberosum*, has a thick, edible root.

Sources: Most Seed Companies.

SORREL (sourgrass, French sorrel, garden sorrel)
Polygonaceae: *Rumex* sp.

This is a hardy annual, easily grown, and is used for its distinctive acid flavor in soups, salads and other dishes. Grows well in moist soil and cool weather. A wild variety grows as a garden weed and can be used in the same way.

Sources: Brp, Jo

TYFON
Cruciferae: *Brassica hybrid* (cross between turnip and Chinese cabbage)

Recommended as a good cold-weather, very hardy green. Can be cut back for several harvests. Quick to germinate; plant late in season for winter use; use fresh or cooked.

Sources: Nic, Vt

WATERCRESS
Cruciferae: *Nasturtium officinale*

Very often found in ditches and streams, growing wild, but better to grow your own, away from roadsides and their various pollutants. It is a good plant to grow in a soggy place where nothing else will grow, as long as it gets some sun. Start from either seed or cuttings made from fresh watercress bought at the store.

Sources: Brp, Sut

DANDELION
Compositae: *Taraxacum officinale*

A horticultural variety may be purchased from some nurseries and seed companies. It is slightly milder than the wild kind. The leaves are rich in iron and vitamin A, and can be used like endive. Blanching will render them even milder in flavor.

Sources: Brp, Nic, Sut

LAMB'S QUARTERS
Chenopodiaceae: *Chenopodia album, C. bonus-henricus,* and *C. capitatum*

Members of a weedy, widely distributed genus; used early in spring as a spinachlike green. Classified under herbs in some catalogs. A similar spring green, known as giant lamb's quarter or orach *(Atriplex hortensis)* is also available. A member of this genus is a prolific volunteer (weed) in most lately turned soil. Though it is usually pulled and discarded, it can be cut and used raw or cooked.

Source: Ter

MUSTARD GREENS
Cruciferae: *Brassica juncea*

B. juncea includes Chinese mustard or gai choy and mizuna or potherb mustard. Both are primarily potherbs rather than salad greens, but may be used either way. Mustard bolts easily and must be sown very early or grown in fall. May be cut as needed; give plenty of water and fertilizer for tenderest growth. The youngest leaves are the best.

Sources: Most Seed Companies.

SALSIFY (oyster plant, vegetable oyster)
Compositae: *Tragopogon porrifolius*
Description

Has a long white root, longer than a parsnip, which it somewhat resembles. Its flavor is definitely reminiscent of oyster and may be used (peeled) baked, fried, or in soups. The plant may be found naturally growing as a weed in many parts of the country; has purple flowers.

Culture

Treat as you would a parsnip; needs very deep, light soil for best growth; biennial, frost-hardy: takes about 4 months to mature. Mulch and leave in the ground until needed.

Pests & Problems

No pests of note.

VARIETY	REGION	SOURCE
Mammoth	All	Most seed
Sandwich Island	regions	cos.

SPINACH
Chenopodiaceae: *Spinacia oleracea*
Description

An attractive, thick-leaved green for cooking or eating raw. Grows best in cool weather; bolts in hot weather, long days and crowded conditions. There are bolt-resistant cultivars.

Culture

Grows best in spring and fall with a 6-6.8 pH, very fertile soil and water. Sow spinach outdoors 6 weeks before last spring frost and until frost, or seed a late crop in latter part of summer. In mild areas, seed can be sown in fall and mulched to provide early spring greens. Or start inside. Seeds will germinate and plants will grow in soil 36°F, though higher is better. Fertilize often, give about 4 inches to each plant. Use single outer leaves after each plant has 6-8 leaves, then pull entire plants.

Pests & Problems

Bolting: (seed stalks begin to grow) grow slow-bolt varieties, plant in late summer or fall; avoid highs and lows of temperatures if possible.

Aphids: cause yellowing and wilting; use sprays, traps, etc.

Leafminers: spots and tunnels between cell layers of leaves; pick infected leaves.

VARIETY	REGION	SOURCE
America	V, VI, VII, IX	Alb, Stk, Til
Bloomsdale Longstanding	All regions	Most seed cos.
Bouquet	II, III, VII, VIII	Til
Hybrid #7	IX	Alb
Iron Duke	II, III, VII, VIII	Vt
King of Denmark	IV	Alb, Is, Snc, TM
Melody Hybrid	All regions	Brp, Har, Is, Jng, Pk, Stk, TM
Nobel	VII, IX	Til
Perpetual	V	Is, Snc

NEW ZEALAND SPINACH
Tetragoniaceae: *Tetragonia tetragonioides*

A nonrelative of regular spinach, originated in South Africa, although apparently came to western countries via Captain Cook and New Zealand.

This is a spreading plant with smaller leaves than regular spinach. It grows rapidly and is especially good in hot weather because it is very slow to bolt. Has thick green, tasty leaves.

Especially recommended in Regions I, IX. Available from: AL, Brp, Har, Is, Jng, Snc, Sut, TM, Vt

MALABAR SPINACH, INDIAN SPINACH
Chenoposiaceae: *Basella alba*

Another spinach substitute. The fleshy, edible green or purplish-green leaves are held on fast-growing vines. It is also a native of the tropics and thus is suited to the warmest part of the Northwest summers. It is long-season, however, and must be started early indoors. It is also very frost-tender.
Available from: Nic, Brp

TAMPALA, VEGETABLE AMARANTH
Chenopodiaceae: *Amaranthus tricolor* (or *gangeticus?*)
Description
A relative of the grain amaranth; used like chard, New Zealand spinach, Malabar spinach, beet greens as producer of greens in hot, dry weather. Tampala is best eaten when young.
Culture
Plant at about last frost and thin to 1 foot, eating the thinnings.
Pests & Problems
Has no pests of note.

VARIETY	REGION	SOURCE
None	I	AL, Brp, Gd, Pk

SQUASH (summer, winter squash; pumpkin; marrow)
Cucurbitaceae: *Cucurbita maxima, mixta, moschata* or *pepo*
Description
Any of a number of variously shaped and colored, tender, vine or bush, annual Cucurbits. Summer squash is eaten while immature, winter squash and pumpkins are thick-skinned and may be stored.
Culture
Summer squash: cultivars are harvested while immature and skin is still edible. Plant and tend as a cucumber, but give more space. All plants have both male and female flowers. Frequent picking will encourage greater fruit set. Most summer squash are best early; use the young whole. Flowers and seeds of all kinds are edible.
Winter: These squash are left to mature or harden, taking longer than summer squash (generally the biggest ones take the longest to mature). Not recommended for immediate coastal areas. A naked-seeded pumpkin has shell-less seeds easily roasted and eaten.

Culture
All squash does best in warm, fertile soil with temperatures of at least 55°F, and will get a better start with cloche or cover, on black plastic mulch. Usually they are started outside (under cover), but in coldest places should be started inside in peat pots, and set out within about two weeks after appearing. Grow at about 3 per hill, with 6 feet all around for vining varieties. They can be grown up a trellis, but may need slings to hold up the fruit. Bush types take much less space. About three weeks before expected frost, pinch off all growing shoots, flowers and new fruits, since they take the energy of the plant and will not develop. Some types change color when mature, or the green ones have orange bottoms. A light frost may not damage, or may enhance the squash, but it won't keep long after if the frost has got inside the shell. Leave stems on squash for storage, dry and store at 50°F, or slightly above, in airy spot.

Pests & Problems
Blossom end rot: may occur in soils deficient in calcium; or after a long rainy period. Squash will improve when these conditions improve.
Cucumber beetle: see cucumbers.
Aphids: spray with water, use insecticidal soap, trap.
Vine borer: use insecticide; if a persistent problem, grow Butternut or other *C. moschata* cultivar, as they are more resistant to the resulting virus introduced by the borer.
Squash bug: in E. Washington especially; leaves turn yellow, then brown; use Sevin, Thiodan, or handpick.
Verticillium wilt: wilting and death of plant; keep ground clean, and rotate; avoid planting with potatoes, tomatoes.
Leafhoppers: transmit a virus called curlytop in E. Washington; the bugs do not like shade; try growing squashes amongst corn to keep it shaded to some extent.

VARIETY	REGION	SOURCE
SUMMER		
Ambassador zucchini	II, III, VII, VIII	Alb, Pk
Aristocrat (bush)	V, IX	Alb, Nic, Pk
Black Jack zucchini	I, II, III, VII, VIII, IX	Stk
Burpee Hybrid zucchini	II, III, VII, VIII	Brp
Butterbar	IX	Pk
Cocozelle	VII, IX	Gd, Jo, Nic, Stk
Early Prolific	II, III, VII, VIII, IX	Brp, Ter, Vt
Early Summer Crookneck	All regions	AL, Brp, Gd, Is, Jo, Pk, Ter, Til
Elite zucchini	II, III, V, VI, VII, VIII	Har
Golden Girl	II, III, VII, VIII	Har
Golden zucchini	IV	Sut
Hybrid zucchini	All regions	Brp, Gd, Sut
Scallopini	All regions	Jng, Stk, Ter
Seneca zucchini	II, III, V, VI, VII, VIII	Jo, Nic
Sweet Banana	II, III, IV, V, VI, VII, VIII	Til
Vegetable Marrow (bush)	IV	Stk
White Bush Scallop	VII, IX	Til
WINTER		
Baby Hubbard	IV	Is, Stk
Banana	II, III, VII, VIII, IX	
Butterbush	I, II, III, VII, VIII	Alb, Brp, Stk
Buttercup	All regions	Most seed cos.
Butternut (Waltham)	All regions	Most seed cos.
Delicata	II, III, VII, VIII	AL, Jo, Jng, Nic, Stk, Ter
Golden Delicious	All regions	Stk, Vt
Gold Nugget	All regions	Alb, Jo
Hubbard (green, gold, blue, warted)	All regions	Most seed cos.
Marblehead	II, III, V, VI, VII, VIII	AL
Perfection	IV	Stk
Ponca Butternut	II	Jo, Ter
Spaghetti (vegetable)	All regions	Most seed cos.
Sweet Meat	I, II, III, VI, VII, VIII	AL, Gd, Ter, Til
Table King	All regions	Brp, Pk, Stk, Vt
Table Queen (Acorn)	All regions	Most seed cos.
Turk's Turban	VII, IX	Brp, Gd, Har
PUMPKIN		
Big Max	II, III, VII, VIII	Brp, Pk
Big Moon	II, III, VII, VIII, IX	Pk, Vt

Cinderella	II, III, VII, VIII	Brp
Connecticut Field	All regions	Alb, Gd, Is, Jo, Pk, Stk
Funny Face	IX	Alb
Howden	II, III, VII, VIII	Ter
Jack O'Lantern	All regions	AL, Alb, Brp, Is, Pk, Stk, Vt
Lady Godiva (hull-less seed)	V, VI	AL
New England Pie	V, VI	Gd, Jo
Small Sugar	All regions	Most seed cos.
Spirit (bush) pumpkin	All regions	Alb, Brp, Nic, Pk, Stk, Ter

SUNFLOWER

Compositae: *Helianthus annuus*

Description

Nutritious seeds from very large, yellow flowerheads. Can grow from 3-10 feet tall, the smaller ones maturing at about 2 months, the larger ones later.

Culture

Needs large, sunny, fertile spot to grow, can be used for bean vine support. Plastic mulch and covers can give them a boost when young — mulch could be left in cold areas. Seeds are mature when they turn brown. Cut entire head and dry in the sun, then rub the seeds off. To hull the seeds, crack them with rolling pin, drop into cold water and stir; kernels will sink and shells will float. Kernels may then be dried and roasted for future use. The seeds may also be germinated inside, in a sunny place, and eaten as sprouts.

Pests & Problems

Birds, squirrels, etc. like them; they must be picked as soon as ripe.

Recommendations

Sunflowers may be grown in all regions, and are available from most seed companies. Dwarf varieties are available, as are dark-red-flowered Purpureus cultivars.

SWISS CHARD (leaf beet)

Chenopodiaceae: *Beta vulgaris cicla*

Description

Easy, frost-resistant, and will not bolt with hot weather; can be grown in pots, even in some shade; comes with white, red or golden leaf ribs, the red being called rhubarb chard. Can be grown as an ornamental as well as a vegetable. Use as you would a spinach green; ribs of the large leaves may be trimmed and used separately, like celery.

Culture

Sow any time soil can be worked, as long as it is still cool (45-70°F), in rows, thin to about 4-6 inches. For most regions, plant mid-July for fall crop; for Region I and II, plant late August for winter and early spring. Will grow best in fertile soil with regular doses of fertilizer. The outer leaves can be pulled as plant gets larger, but taste will not improve with frost and should be harvested before then.

Pests & Problems

See spinach.

VARIETY	REGION	SOURCE
Fordhook Giant	I, VII, IX	Most seed cos.
Lucullus	I, IV, VII, IX	Most seed cos.
Perpetual	II	Brp, TM
Rhubarb (Ruby Red)	I, IV, VII, IX	Most seed cos.
Swiss Chard of Geneva	II	Pk
White King	IX	

TOMATILLOS

Solanaceae: *Physalis ixocarpa*

Description

Used in Mexican cooking, but can be substituted in any dish for whole tomatoes. Grow about 3 feet tall, bushy and spreading.

Culture

Sow like tomatoes, indoors, 4 weeks before last frost. Set out after or on last frost date, about 2 feet apart. Are most weather-resistant and require little care. Fruit is ready in about 10 weeks from transplant. Harvest when fruit is deep-green and husks are tan. Can be eaten raw or cooked, frozen or canned. Can be stored with husks on in cool, well-ventilated spot.

Pests & Problems

Insects: control by handpicking or by rotenone.

VARIETY	REGION	SOURCE
(None)	II	TM, Stk, Vt

GROUND CHERRY, HUSK CHERRY

Solanaceae: *Physalis peruviana* (or *pubescens*)

Description

A close relative of tomatillos; produces small, sweet yellow fruits which may be eaten raw, dried, cooked.

Culture

Grow like a tomato; are slow to germinate. Ripe when the husks are dry and light-colored, fruits are golden yellow.

Pests & Problems

see above

VARIETY	REGION	SOURCE
(None)	II	Jng, Jo, Stk

TOMATOES

Solanaceae: *Lycopersicon lycopersicum*

Description

A South American perennial and close relative of the potato; the most popular fruit (vegetable) in the food garden. Tomatoes come in several shapes and colors, small and large. Many fast-growing varieties have been and are being developed for the Northwest, and there is no place in the area where they cannot be grown in some way or another (albeit with growing aids). Tomatoes are either *determinate* or *indeterminate*. The determinates are the earliest varieties, bushy, and produce for a shorter time than the indeterminates. They need not be staked, and should not be pruned. Indeterminates grow tall, produce over a long period, and are usually staked and pruned. There is an intermediate variety, called semi-determinate, which has qualities of both. There are also small *cherry* tomatoes and *pear* tomatoes, both named for shape, not taste.

Culture

Tomatoes should be grown with plenty of space around them, all the sun available, in a deep and very rich soil of about 6.0 pH. They must be purchased as young plants at the nursery or grown from seed in a sunny indoor location or under lights, preferably in greenhouse. Plastic mulch, row covers, Walls-o-Water, and other such devices will promote ripe fruit production. Seeds should be started 6-8 weeks before last frost date, and will germinate fastest in 70-85°F though they are very persistent, even in much cooler temperatures. They may be started in a dark, warm spot but as soon as they are up they should be put in a warm, sunny place. Transplant one to a pot when they have first true leaves; burying up to the first seedling leaves. It is best to have flower buds set when the plants are put out. Set them about 18 inches or more apart in rows and stake at this time, if they are indeterminates and if you want to grow them this way (there is little effect on the rate of ripening for unstaked tomatoes). If disease is not a problem, tomatoes may be grown in the same place for several years; they actually enjoy a compost of old tomato plants. Give plenty of fertilizer, water. Pinch out suckers in the branch axils but do not prune away leaves, as they are needed to produce energy for the plant. The suckers can be rooted in moist soil, and will produce a later plant. Leaving up to four or five main stems on indeterminates is best. Both the determinates and semi-determinates should be pinched off at shoots toward end of season to concentrate energy into fruit development. Although many seed catalogs offer early, middle and late types of tomatoes (and all kinds are recommended below), it is doubtful that this is useful for the Northwest

gardener who does not have a long-season, sunny garden and consequently needs to use the fastest-maturing varieties. Special varieties have been developed for greenhouse growers, and are so designated in the list following.

Pests & Problems

Cutworms: put a collar around the stem that extends 1-2 inches above and below ground. After first fruit, water with liquid fertilizer every 2 weeks.

Blossom end rot: caused by drought, uneven watering or soil calcium deficiency.

Catface, or oddly shaped fruit: cold weather during pollination.

Nematodes: attack roots; plant marigolds. Verticillium and fusarium wilts, and curly top (E. Washington): choose resistant varieties.

Do not plant within 40-50 feet of a walnut tree, as the juglone, an exudate from the walnut, causes death.

Tomato hornworm; Colorado potato beetle: eradicate by hand; Sevin or Thiodan.

Flea beetle: many tiny holes in leaves; trap or use Sevin.

Aphids: insecticidal soap or traps.

Hollow fruit: poor pollination, low light or bad weather; temperatures too high or low; too much fruit-setting hormone spray.

Cracking: high temperatures, too much water after drying.

Sunscald: white or yellow spots on green fruit; too much sun.

VARIETY	REGION	SOURCE
Ace	All regions	Brp
Ailsa Craig	I	Sut, TM
Beefmaster	V	Har, Vt
Beefsteak (bush)	IV, VI	Most seed cos.
Better Boy	II, III, VII, VIII	Most seed cos.
Better Bush	II, V, IX	Pk
Big Boy	All regions	Most seed cos.
Big Early	All regions	Brp
Bonnie Best	VII	AL, Gd, Jo, Nic
Burpee Delicious	V, VI	Brp
Brp's Sonnybrook Earliana	IX	Brp
Campbell 1327 VF	IX	Stk
Celebrity	I, II, V	Most seed cos.
Chico III, paste	II, III, VII, VIII	Jng, Ter, Til
Coldset	IX	Stk
Columbia (resistant)	V, VI	Locally available
Cougar Red	I, V	Locally available
Earliana	V, VI, VII, IX	Gd, Is
Earlirouge	IV	AL, Jo, Stk
Early Cascade	II, V	Alb, Jo, Nic, Ter
Early Girl	All regions	Most seed cos.
Early Pak 7	II, III, VI, VII, VIII	
Early Palouse	I, V	Locally available
Early Pik (Pick)	V	Brp
Extra Early	VIII	Pk
Fantastic	II, IX	Is, Pk, Stk, Ter
Fireball	IV, V, VII, IX	Is, Stk, Til
Floramerica	All regions	Most seed cos.
French Cross	I	Sut
Glamour	VII, IX	Har, Stk
Golden Boy	II, III, VII, VIII	Is, Jng, Pk, Vt
Golden Jubilee, Jubilee	All regions	Brp, Nic, Til
Golden Nugget	II, VII, VIII	Nic
Greenhouse	II	Pk
Heinz 1350	II, III, VII, VIII	Brp, Har, Stk, Ter
IPB Cherry	I	Locally available
Jet Star	I, II, III, VII, VIII	Har
Jetfire	I	Stk
Kootenai	I	Ter
Lemon Boy	I, VII	Most seed cos.
Longkeeper	II, V, VI, IX	AL, Brp, Jng
Michigan-Ohio (greenhouse)	All regions	
Moreton Hybrid	II, III, VII, VIII	Har
Moscow	II	
New Yorker	All regions	Brp, Har, Stk, Vt
Northern Cascade	IX	
Nova, paste	IX	AL, Gd, Jo, Stk
Orange Queen	I, II, III, VII, VIII	Stk
Oregon 11	II	Ter
Oregon Cherry	II, III, VII, VIII	
Oregon Spring	I, II, VIII	Nic, Ter
Patio	All regions	Nic, Stk, Vt
Payette	VI, VII, IX	
Pik-Red	I, II, III, VII, VIII	Har, Til
Pixie	All regions	Alb, Brp, TM
Presto	IX	Har
Red Pear	V	Nic
Roma VF, paste	I, V, VI, IX	Most seed cos.
Ropreco	II	Ter
Rowpac (resistant)	V, VI	Locally available
Roza (resistant)	V, VI	Locally available
Rushmore	I, V, IX	Stk
Salad Master (resistant)	V, VI	Locally available
San Marzano, paste	VII, IX	Most seed cos.
Santiam	I, II, V, VIII	Nic, Ter
Siberian	VII	AL
Small Fry	All regions	Har, Jng, Pk, Ter
Spring Giant	All regions	Alb, Jng
Springset	All regions	Alb, Har, Stk
Sprinter	II	Ter
Starfire	IV	Alb
Starshot	All regions	Stk
Stokesdale, Super	IV	Stk
Stupice	I	Ter
Subarctic Maxi	IX	Alb, Jo, Stk
Subarctic Plenty	V	Alb, Jo, TM
Sunray	VII, IX	Har, Vt
Super Marmande	VII	Sut, TM
Super Star	VII, IX	Univ. Idaho
Sweet 100	All regions	Most seed cos.
Sweet Chelsea	V	Vt
The Amateur	I	Sut
Tiny Tim cherry	All regions	Most seed cos.
Ultraboy	IV	Stk, TM
Ultragirl	I, IX	Stk
Vendor	IV	Is, Jo
Park's Whopper	VI, IX	Pk
Willamette	I, II, III, VII, VIII	AL, Nic
Yellow Pear	I, V	Most seed cos.
Yellow Plum	V	AL, Har

TURNIP
Cruciferae: *Brassica rapa*
Description
The turnip is much like a large radish; it does its best in cool weather and needs to grow rapidly in fertile soil with plenty of water. It is frost-hardy, but less so than rutabagas or parsnips. Takes about 2 months to mature from seeding.

Culture
Plant as soon as soil can be worked; thin to 4 inches apart, eating thinnings if you want. Will become tough if growth is checked by lack of water, hot weather, etc. Like parsnips, turnips taste better after a light frost. Greens may be eaten raw or cooked, and the roots are ready to be eaten at about 2 inches or more. Harvest only as needed; mulch in cold areas, as they do not store well.

Pests & Problems
Root maggot: grow under row cover; use diazinon, malathion.

Aphids: trap, use insecticidal soap or water spray.

Tough roots: too old, or slow growth; harvest young, be sure to water and fertilize sufficiently.

Small roots, large tops: too much nitrogen.

Cracked roots, rot and water-soaking: lack of boron; use a complete fertilizer with trace elements.

VARIETY	REGION	SOURCE
Just Right	IX	Har, Pk
Purple Top	All	Most seed
White Globe	regions	cos.
Shogoin (for greens)	II, III, VII, VIII	Nic, Stk, Ter
Tokyo Cross	I, IX	Alb, Brp, Jng, Pk, Stk, TM
Tokyo Market	II, III, VII, VIII	Nic

HERBS
Most Northwest gardeners tuck a few herbs into their gardens, the perennials (that are not disturbed) along the edges or amongst the flowers, and the annuals such as dill and basil, which are grown right along with the vegetables. Basil, in fact, is said to have a beneficial effect on tomato plants when interplanted.

I list the major herbs available, but I make no attempt to discuss their virtues and cultivation needs. It would take a separate book, of which there are many available, to investigate the possibilities of the herb garden.

Most of the major seed catalogs have separate herb lists, some more comprehensive than others. Of the Northwest seed companies, Nichols is exceptionally strong in the herb line, and Sanctuary Seeds has a companion organization called Folklore Herb which offers a very large selection, listed in the same catalog as the vegetable seeds.

There should be at least one small nursery in each geographic region that specializes in herbs, and some are very large and well stocked indeed. In the Puget Sound region it is especially rewarding to visit The Herbfarm, off Interstate 90 at Fall City, for an eyeful of what a large subject herb gardening can be. Unfortunately, they do not fill orders by mail. Garland's Nursery, on the Corvallis-Albany highway in Oregon, is another well-stocked supplier, and for ideas on planting, stop by the Marysville Demonstration Garden at Jennings Park in Marysville, Washington (call the Snohomish County Cooperative Extension office for directions). The University of Washington's herb garden is being restored and should be worth a look, as well.

Agrimony
Angelica
Anise
Balsam tea
Basil: sweet, licorice, opal, lemon, cinnamon, etc.
Bee balm, Bergamot
Borage
Caraway
Catnip
Chamomile
Chervil
Chives
Coltsfoot
Comfrey
Coriander, Cilantro
Costmary
Cumin
Dill
Epazote
Fenugreek
Feverfew
Garlic
Germander
Horehound
Hyssop
Lamb's ear

Lavender: French, Spanish, etc.
Lemon balm
Lovage
Marjoram, sweet
Mints (too many to list here)
Moneywort
Mustard
Oregano: common, golden, Greek
Parsley
Pennyroyal
Rosemary
Rue
Saffron, American
Sage: clary, golden, pineapple, tri-color, etc.
Salad burnet
Samphire
Santolina
Savory, winter and summer
Sesame
Shallot
Sorrel, French
Southernwood, wormwood
Sweet bay
Sweet cicely
Sweet woodruff
Tarragon: French, Russian
Thyme: caraway, coconut, common, golden, lemon, orange, oregano, silver, woolly, etc.
Yarrow

Some Varietal Recommendations for Container Gardens

Beet	
Cylindra	Jng
Little Ball	Brp
Miniature	Is
Spinel	TM
Broccoli	
Green Dwarf	Pk
Cabbage	
Spivoy	Pk
Morden Dwarf	Sut
Minicole	Sut
Carrot	
Baby Long	Nic
Early French Fame	Vt
Kundulus	Pk
Little (Lady) Finger	Bp, Is, Pk
Minicor	Jo
Paris Market	Is
Parisienne	Alb
Suko	TM
Sucram	Nic
Cauliflower	
Mini-cauliflowers	TM
Corn	
Golden Midget	Pk
Cucumber	
Bush Champion	Nic
Patio Pik	Alb
Petita	Sut
Pot Luck	Jng, Nic
Lettuce	
Little Gem	Sut, Ter
Tom Thumb	Nic, Pk, TM

Onion
  Purplette   Jo
  Quicksilver   Jo
  (or any small, bunching
  variety)
Squash
  Peter Pan   Nic
Tomato
  Basket King   Brp
  Goldie   Pk
  Minibel   Pk
  Patio   Nic
  Pipo   TM
  Pixie   Brp
  Tiny Tim   Sut
  Toy Boy   Nic

**Some Varietal Recommendations
for Winter Gardens**

Bean
  (Broadbean) Aquadulce   Sut
  The Sutton   Sut
Broccoli
  Broccoli Raab   TM
  Green Sprouting   Is
  Packman   Nic
  Purple Sprouting   Ter

Brussels Sprouts
  Fortress F_1 Ter
  Aries F_1 Ter
  Stabolite F_1 Ter
Cabbage
  First Early Market   Ter
  Green Winter
  January King   Ter
  Savoy Monarch   Ter
  Wivoy   Ter
Carrot
  Winter Scarlet   Jap
  Caramba   Ter
  Tamino F_1 Ter
Cauliflower
  Armado Spring mix   Ter
  All the Year Around   Sut
  Angers, Nos. 1, 2   Sut
  Jura   Ter
Chinese Cabbage
  Nagaoka Spring   Jap
  Other   Kit
Collards
  Vates   Ter
Endive
  Broad-leaf Batavian   Nic
  Green Curled Ruffec   Har
Kale
  Dwarf Blue Curled Scotch   Nic

Kohlrabi
  Any variety   Most seed
                                     cos.
Lettuce
  All Year Around   Ter
  Avondefiance   Sut
  Little Gem   Sut
  Winter Density   Sut
Mizuna, Mustard, Japanese Greens
  Pak Choi (Bok Choy)   Most seed
                                     cos.
Onion
  Ishikura long white   Jap
  Kyoto Market   Jap
  Egyptian Walking   Gd
Parsnip
  Hollow Crown   Most seed
                                     cos.
Pea
  Little Marvel   Pk
  Novella   Pk
Radish
  Oriental   Kit
  Round black Spanish   Most seed
                                     cos.
Swiss Chard
                                     Most seed
                                     cos.
Turnip
  Shogoin   Kit
  Tokyo Cross   Brp

SOURCES OF HELP

- *Seed companies' addresses for catalogs*

- *Governmental agencies and other addresses for Extension Service and Master Gardener information*

WHERE TO GET YOUR CATALOGS:
(Names and addresses of seed companies whose catalogs were used for reference in this book.)

Abundant Life Seed Foundation
P.O. Box 772
Port Townsend, WA 98368

Alberta Nurseries and Seeds, Ltd.
Bowden, Alberta T0M 0K0

Burpee, W. Atlee, Co.
Warminster, PA 18974

Earl May Seed Co.
Shenandoah, IA 51603

Good Seed
P.O. Box 702
Tonasket, WA 98855

Harris, Joseph, Co.
Moreton Farm
Rochester, NY 14624

Island Seed Co., Ltd.
P.O. Box 4278, Stn. A
Victoria, BC V8X 3X8

Japonica Seeds, Inc.
P.O. Box 727
Oakland Gardens
New York, NY 11364

Johnny's Selected Seeds
Albion, ME 04910

Jung, J.W., Seed Co.
Randolph, WI 53956

Kitizawa Seed Co.
1748 Laine Ave.
Santa Clara, CA 95051

Nichols Garden Nursery
1190 N. Pacific Hwy.
Albany, OR 97321

Park Seed Co.
Highway 254 N.
Greenwood, SC 29647

Sanctuary Seeds
2388 W. 4th
Vancouver, BC V6K 1P1

Stokes Seeds Inc.
P.O. Box 548
Buffalo, NY 14240

Stokes Seeds Ltd.
Box 10
St. Catharines, Ontario L2R 6R6

Suttons Seeds Ltd.
Reading, England RG6 1AB

Territorial Seed Co.
P.O. Box 27
Lorane, OR 97451

Thompson and Morgan Inc.
P.O. Box 1308
Jackson, NJ 08527

Tillinghast Seed Co.
P.O. Box 738
LaConner, WA 98247

Twilley Seed Co.
P.O. Box 65
Trevose, PA 19047

Vermont Bean Seed Co.
Green Lane
Bomoseen, VT 05732

Vesey's Seeds Ltd.
York
Prince Edward Island C0A 1P0

SOURCES OF HELP
Note: Master Gardener groups are scattered throughout the Northwest. They are made up of amateur gardeners who complete a course of study under the direction of university extension services and their agents. If you wish to join a Master Gardener group, call your local agency.

Governmental agencies employ professional horticulturists, food specialists and others to help farmers, gardeners, homemakers, etc., to produce and preserve food.

In the U.S., every county has an extension agent employed jointly by the county and the state university. Some of the extension service offices are large and have such amenities as a horticultural specialist and a Master Gardener coordinator; others do not. In British Columbia, government horticulturists concentrate more on the business of farming than on the hobby of gardening, but their agents can be very helpful, and there are garden clubs in most areas. Following are some agencies to contact in each region:

Region I
British Columbia:
Agriculture Canada, Sidney Research Station
Building 20
8801 E. Saanich Rd.
Victoria, BC V8L 1H3

B.C. Federation of Garden Clubs
10217-156 St.
Surrey, BC V3R 4L7
(for a list of local garden clubs and contacts)

Coordinator (Derry Walsh)
Master Gardener Program
c/o VanDusen Botanical Gardens
5251 Oak Street
Vancouver, BC V6M 4H1

District Horticulturist
4607-23rd St.
Vernon, BC V1T 4K7

Island Vegetable Coop. Assn.
2805 Quesnel St.
Victoria, BC V8T 4K2

Ministry of Agriculture
808 Douglas
Parliament Buildings
Victoria, BC V8W 2Z7

Washington:
Community Composting Education Program
710 2nd Ave.
Suite 750
Seattle, WA 98104

King/Pierce Co. Cooperative Extension
312 Smith Tower
506 Second Ave.
Seattle, WA 98104

Snohomish Co. Cooperative Extension
600 128th St. SE
Everett, WA 98204

Tilth Association
4649 Sunnyside N.
Seattle, WA 98103

Region II
Lane Co. Cooperative Extension Service
950 N. 13th
Eugene, OR 97401

Multnomah Co. Cooperative Extension
211 SE 80th
Portland, OR 97215

Region III
Douglas Co. Cooperative Extension Service
Box 1165
Roseburg, OR 97470

Jackson Co. Cooperative Extension
1301 Maple Grove Dr.
Medford, OR 97501

Region IV
Okanagan:
B.C. Ministry of Agriculture
1873 Spall Road
Kelowna, BC V1Y 4R2

B.C. Ministry of Agriculture
10-477 Martin St.
Penticton, BC V2A 5L2

Regional Vegetable Specialist
Box 940
Oliver, BC V0H 1T0

Research Scientist
Research Station
Box 198
Summerland, BC V0H 1Z0

Okanogan:
Okanogan Co. Cooperative Extension
Courthouse
Okanogan, WA 98840

Region V
E. Washington, W. Idaho:
Chelan Co. Cooperative Extension Service
400 Washington
Wenatchee, WA 98801

Douglas Co. Cooperative Extension
Courthouse, Box 550
Waterville, WA 98858

Grant Co. Cooperative Extension
Courthouse
Ephrata, WA 98823

Kittitas Co. Cooperative Extension
Courthouse, 5th and Main
Ellensburg, WA 98926

Kootenai Co. Cooperative Extension
106 Dalton Ave.
Coeur d'Alene, Idaho 83840

Spokane Co. Cooperative Extension
Agricultural Center
No. 222 Havana
Spokane, WA 99202

Yakima Co. Cooperative Extension
233 Courthouse
Yakima, WA 98901

Region VI
S.E. Washington, N.E. Oregon:
Umatilla County Cooperative Extension
13 SW Nye St.
Pendleton, OR 97801

Walla Walla Co. Cooperative Extension
314 Main St.
Walla Walla, WA 99362

Region VII
E. Oregon, W. Idaho:
Ada County/Univ. of Idaho Extension Office
5880 Glenwood Avenue
Boise, Idaho 83714

Baker Co. Cooperative Extension
Baker, OR 97814

Baker County Master Gardeners
2526 Auburn Ave.
Baker, OR 97814
(Joe and Edythe Collinson)

Canyon Co. Cooperative Extension Service
P.O. Box 1058
Caldwell, ID 83605

Region VIII
Central Oregon:
Deschutes Co. Cooperative Extension
Redmond, Oregon 97756

Region IX
N. Idaho, Montana:
Bonner County Cooperative Extension
Box 1526 or 2105 N. Boyer Ave.
Sandpoint, Idaho 83864

Flathead Co. Cooperative Extension
723 — 5th Ave. E.
Kalispell, MT 59901

Lincoln Co./MSU Extension
418 Mineral Ave.
Libby, MT 59923

Missoula Co. Cooperative Extension
126 W. Spruce
Missoula, MT 59801

State Publications Offices (for gardening publications or a list of pamphlets and bulletins available for your area):

USDA Hardiness Zone Map:
U.S. Government Printing Office
Washington, DC 20402
(ask for Miscellaneous Publication #814; send 25 cents)

Agricultural Communications Center
Ag Publications Bldg.
University of Idaho
Moscow, ID 83843

Bulletin Office, Cooperative Extension
Cooper Publications Building
Washington State University
Pullman, WA 99164-5912

Cooperative Extension Service
Montana State University
Bozeman, MT 59717

Cooperative Extension Service
Oregon State University, Extension Hall
Corvallis, OR 97331

American Horticultural Society (staff), *Vegetables.* An Illustrated Encyclopedia of Gardening: Mt. Vernon, VA, 1980.

Bailey, L.H., and Hortorium Staff, *Hortus Third:* Cornell University, Macmillan, N.Y., NY, 1976.

Ball, Jeff, *The Self-Sufficient Suburban Garden:* Rodale Press, Emmaus, PA, 1983. 236 pp.

Bartholomew, Mel, *Square Foot Gardening:* Rodale Press, Emmaus, PA, 1981.

Brady, Nyle C., *The Nature and Properties of Soils,* 8th Ed. Macmillan, N.Y., NY, 1974.

Branch, Diana S. (ed.), *Tools for Homesteaders, Gardeners, and Small-Scale Farmers: A Catalog of Hard-to-find Implements and Equipment:* Rodale Press, Emmaus, PA, 1978. 512 pp.

Carr, Anna, *Advanced Organic Gardening:* Rodale Press, Emmaus, PA, 1982.

Chan, Peter, *Better Vegetable Gardens the Chinese Way:* Garden Way Publishing, Pownal, VT, 1985.

Colebrook, Binda, *Winter Gardening in the Maritime Northwest:* Tilth Association, Arlington, WA, 1977. 128 pp.

Faust, Joan Lee, *The New York Times Book of Vegetable Gardening:* N.Y., NY, 1975.

Fell, Derek, *Vegetables — How to Select, Grow and Enjoy:* HP Books, Tucson, AZ, 1982.

Fitzgerald, Tonie J., *Gardening in the Inland Northwest* (A Guide to Growing Veg., Berries, Grapes and Fruit Trees): Arboreal Press, Spokane, WA, 1984.

Franklin, Jerry F., and C.T. Dyrness, *Natural Vegetation of Oregon and Washington:* USDA Forest Service GTR PNW-8, 1973.

Geiger, Rudolf, *The Climate Near the Ground:* Harvard University Press, Cambridge, MA, 1957.

Genders, Roy, *Simple Vegetable Growing:* Ward Lock Ltd., London, 1973.

Hansen, A.J., F.B. Seward, eds., *Gardening in the Okanagan:* Okanagan Past and Present Society, 1977.

Harrington, Geri, *Grow Your Own Chinese Vegetables:* Macmillan Publishing Co., N.Y., NY, 1978. 268 pp.

Hedla, Lenore, *Gardens for Alaskans:* Anchorage, AK, 1981. 157 pp.

Janick, Jules, Robert Schery, Frank Woods, Vernon Ruttan, *Plant Science:* W.H. Freeman & Co., San Francisco, 1969.

Kramer, Jack, *Escarole in the Bedroom — Growing Food Plants Indoors:* Little Brown and Co., Boston, 1977. 148 pp.

Lowry, William P., *Weather and Life, An Introduction to Biometeorology:* Academic Press, Orlando, FL, 1969. (Chapter 12, Artificial Control of Plant Environments.)

McNeilen, Ray A., and Ronningen, Micheline, *Pacific Northwest Guide to Home Gardening:* Timber Press, Portland, OR, 1982. (PO Box 1631, Beaverton, OR 97075)

Men's Garden Clubs of America, *Hints for the Vegetable Gardener:* Garden Way Publishing (compiled by Robt. E. Sanders, Des Moines, Iowa Chapter), 1976.

Pellegrini, Angelo M., *The Food Lover's Garden:* Madrona Publishers, Seattle, 1975.

Ruffner, James A., and Brank E. Bair, *The Weather Almanac,* Avon Books, N.Y., NY, 1977.

Severn, Jill, *Growing Vegetables in the Pacific Northwest:* Madrona Publishers, Seattle, 1978.

Solly, Cecil, *Growing Vegetables in the Pacific Northwest:* Seattle, 1944.

Solomon, Steve, *The Complete Guide to Organic Gardening West of the Cascades:* Pacific Search Press, Seattle, 1981. 171 pp.

Sunset Magazine (staff), *Western Garden Book.* Sunset Magazine, *Gardening in Containers — 1975.* Sunset Magazine, *Greenhouse Gardening — 1977.* Sunset Magazine, *Vegetable Gardening — 1976.* Menlo Park, CA.

Taylor, James, *Grow More Nutritious Vegetables Without Soil:* ParkSide Press Publishing Co., Santa Ana, CA, 1983.

University of Washington Institute of Forest Resources, *Working With Environmental Factors:* Institute of Forest Resources, Seattle, 1969.

Wallace, Dan, et al., *Getting the Most from Your Garden — Using Advanced Intensive Gardening Techniques:* Rodale, Emmaus, PA, 1980.

Willis, A.R., *The Pacific Gardener* (7th ed.): Superior Publishing Co., Seattle, 1964.

Many other fascinating books are available from
Alaska Northwest Publishing Company.
For a catalog, send your name and address to:

 Alaska Northwest Publishing Company

130 Second Avenue South
Edmonds, Washington 98020

(206) 774-4111
Or call TOLL-FREE 1-800-533-7381